Vocabulary
for Achievement

Fifth Course

Margaret Ann Ríchek

GREAT SOURCE
WILMINGTON, MA

Author

Margaret Ann Richek
Professor of Education Emerita, Northeastern Illinois University; consultant in reading and vocabulary study; author of The World of Words *(Houghton Mifflin)*

Classroom Consultants

Beth Gaby
English Chair, Carl Schurz High School, Chicago, Illinois

Chris Hausammann
Teacher of English, Central Mountain High School, Lock Haven, Pennsylvania

Malisa Cannon
Teacher of Language Arts, Desert Sky Middle School, Tucson, Arizona

Stephanie Saltikov-Izabal
Teacher of Reading and English, At-Risk Specialist, Huntington Beach High School, Huntington Beach, California

Patricia Melvin
District Secondary Reading Specialist, Duval County Public Schools, Jacksonville, Florida

Sean Rochester
Teacher of English, Parkway Central High School, St. Louis, Missouri

Acknowledgments

Editorial: Ruth Rothstein, Victoria Fortune, Dan Carsen, Amy Gilbert

Design and Production: Mazer Corporation

Text Design and Production: Mazer Creative Services

Illustrations: Susan Aiello, Barbara Samanich, of Wilkinson Studios, LLC; George Cathey, Jerry Hoare, Jeff O'Conner, Ron Zalme of Langley Creative.

Cover Design: Mazer Creative Services

Cover Photo: Creatas

Definitions for the three hundred words taught in this textbook are based on Houghton Mifflin dictionaries—in particular, *The American Heritage High School Dictionary*—but have been abbreviated and adapted for instructional purposes.

All pronunciations are reproduced by permission from *The American Heritage Dictionary of the English Language, Fourth Edition,* copyright © 2000.

International Standard Book Number -13: 978-0-669-51759-0

International Standard Book Number -10: 0-669-51759-3

17 18 19 20 21 -0304- 22 21 20 19 18
4500703103

Contents

COMPLETE WORD LIST FOR FIFTH COURSE

Words About Language

annotation	appellation	eponym	linguistics	malapropism
neologism	parlance	patois	polyglot	vulgar

Sophisticated language is one of the human developments that has made us the most powerful species on Earth. Our languages allow us to communicate across space and time: We can learn from the past, leave information for people yet to be born, or communicate with someone on the other side of the world. The words in this lesson will help you understand and discuss different aspects of language.

1. **annotation** (ăn´ō-tā´shən) *noun* from Latin *ad-*, "to" + *notare*, "to write"
   A critical or explanatory note
   • The **annotations** in my edition of Charles Dickens's *A Tale of Two Cities* explain words that are no longer used.

   annotate *verb* The food critic **annotated** her list of recommended restaurants with comments about her favorite dishes.

2. **appellation** (ăp´ə-lā´shən) *noun* from Latin *appellare*, "to entreat"
   A name, title, or designation
   • It is not clear how Indiana got the **appellation** "Hoosier State."

3. **eponym** (ĕp´ə-nĭm´) *noun* from Greek *epi-*, "on; upon" + *onoma*, "name"
   A person whose name is, or is thought to be, the source of the name of something
   • William Penn is the **eponym** of Pennsylvania.

   eponymous *adjective* Sportswriters coined the **eponymous** word *Jordanesque*, meaning "incredibly athletic, acrobatic, and graceful," after basketball star Michael Jordan.

4. **linguistics** (lĭng-gwĭs´tĭks) *noun* from Latin *lingua*, "language"
   The study of the nature, structure, and variation of language
   • Research in the field of **linguistics** can shed light on the history of human migration by tracking variations in language over time.

   linguistic *adjective* The Czech and Slovak languages are part of the same **linguistic** family.

   linguist *noun* The **linguist** studied the influence of African languages and speech patterns on American English.

appellation

The Greek word *onoma*, or "name," often appears in English words as the suffix *-nym*.

Despite the fact that it ends in *s*, *linguistics* is singular.

5. **malapropism** (măl´ə-prŏp-ĭz´əm) *noun* from French *mal,* "badly"
   + *a propos,* "to the purpose"
   Ridiculous misuse of a word, especially by confusing it with one of
   similar sound
   • I'm pretty sure it was a **malapropism,** and not a deliberate joke,
     when she said, "He's the apple of my *pie.*"

> *Malaprop* means the same
> thing as *malapropism.*

6. **neologism** (nē-ŏl´ə-jĭz´əm) *noun* from Greek *neos,* "new"
   + *logos,* "word; speech"
   A new word, expression, or usage
   • Modern technology has brought us **neologisms** including *byte,*
     software, and *download.*

7. **parlance** (pär´ləns) *noun* from French *parler,* "to speak"
   A particular manner of speaking
   • In business **parlance,** *downsizing* means laying off workers in order to
     decrease a company's size and expenses.

8. **patois** (păt´wä´) *noun*
   A regional dialect, especially a nonstandard one that has no
   written tradition
   • The Cockney **patois** of London includes colorful expressions such as
     have a butcher's (have a look) and *on your tod* (on your own).

9. **polyglot** (pŏl´ē-glŏt) from Greek *poly-,* "many" + *glotta,* "tongue;
   language"
   a. *adjective* Using several languages
   • Do many professional translators and interpreters grow up in
     polyglot neighborhoods?
   b. *noun* A person who speaks several languages
   • The linguistics professor was a true **polyglot,** fluent in five
     languages and almost a dozen dialects.

10. **vulgar** (vŭl´gər) *adjective* from Latin *vulgus,* "the common people"
    a. Of or related to the language of the common people
    • *Spider* is a **vulgar** name for a certain type of *arachnid.*
    b. Crude; indecent
    • The play's **vulgar** dialogue was effective, but offended some people.
    c. Offensively excessive in the display of one's self or one's wealth
    • The gold-plated window sills were both ugly and **vulgar.**

    vulgarity *noun* The **vulgarity** of his speech shocked listeners.

WORD ENRICHMENT

Mrs. Malaprop

The terms *malaprop* and *malapropism* come from Richard Brinsley
Sheridan's 1775 play *The Rivals.* Sheridan used French roots (see the
etymology above) to name a character—Mrs. Malaprop—who frequently
used the wrong but similar-sounding word in place of the one she intended.
Her lines included "He's the very *pineapple* of politeness" (she meant
pinnacle), and "He's as headstrong as an *allegory* on the banks of the Nile"
(she meant *alligator*).

Words About Language

WRITE THE CORRECT WORD

Write the correct word in the space next to each definition. Use each word only once.

Eponym **1.** a person whose name is the source of a word

Vulgar **2.** crude or indecent

Patois **3.** a nonstandard dialect

annotation **4.** an explanatory note

Parlance **5.** a particular manner of speaking

malapropism **6.** a humorous confusion of words

appellation **7.** a name or title

neologism **8.** a new word

Polyglot **9.** using several languages

linguistics **10.** the study of language

COMPLETE THE SENTENCE

Write the letter for the word that best completes each sentence.

__C__ **1.** The _____ form of a language is often quite different from its standard form.
   a. polyglot   **b.** eponymous   **c.** vulgar   **d.** linguistic

__C__ **2.** The children spoke only the _____ of their village.
   a. eponym   **b.** malapropism   **c.** patois   **d.** annotation

__a__ **3.** The spy had to take on a new _____ when she crossed the border.
   a. appellation   **b.** neologism   **c.** annotation   **d.** eponym

__b__ **4.** Some people frown on _____ because they dislike unfamiliar words.
   a. linguistics   **b.** neologisms   **c.** eponyms   **d.** vulgarity

__d__ **5.** The editor added _____ to the book to explain the philosophical theories the author referred to.
   a. malapropisms   **b.** polyglots   **c.** eponyms   **d.** annotations

__b__ **6.** Uncle Fred's frequent _____ were a source of laughter for the whole family.
   a. linguistics   **b.** malapropisms   **c.** parlances   **d.** eponyms

__C__ **7.** Some _____ study the slang used in different historical time periods.
   a. eponyms   **b.** neologisms   **c.** linguists   **d.** malapropisms

__a__ **8.** Children who grow up exposed to different languages often become _____ .
   a. polyglots   **b.** vulgar   **c.** eponyms   **d.** linguistics

__a__ **9.** In the _____ of microbiologists, _fastidious_ means "having complicated nutritional requirements."
   a. parlance   **b.** patois   **c.** malapropism   **d.** vulgarity

__b__ **10.** Alexander the Great is the _____ of the Egyptian city of Alexandria.
   a. patois   **b.** eponym   **c.** neologism   **d.** polyglot

Challenge: Medical _____ necessarily includes _____ because new diseases, techniques, treatments, and cures are constantly being discovered.
__C__
   a. patois...polyglots   **b.** annotation...malaprops   **c.** parlance...neologisms

Naming U.S. States

From Massachusetts to California, the names of our states sound as different as the states themselves actually are. **(1)** How did we end up with this varied collection of *appellations*?

(2) Some names are the result of the United States having always been a *polyglot* nation. The influence of French explorers and settlers shows in the names of Louisiana—named for King Louis XIV of France—and Vermont, which comes from the French words for "green mountain."

Because much of the continent was explored and conquered by Spain, many states have Spanish names. The name Florida comes from the Spanish phrase "La Florida," meaning "abounding in Flowers." Nevada means "snow-covered" or "snow-capped" in Spanish. Colorado means "red-colored." California was named for the queen of a mythical island in a Spanish novel that was written in the early 1500s.

As seems only fitting, more than half of our states' names have Native American origins. Illinois comes from an Algonquin word that roughly translates as "tribe of warriors." Here are some of the other state names with Native American roots: Alabama, Arkansas, Connecticut, the Dakotas, Iowa, Kentucky, Massachusetts, Mississippi, Minnesota, Nebraska, Ohio, Oklahoma, Tennessee, and Utah. **(3)** Some names are spoken differently from the way that Native Americans pronounced them, the result of the reshaping of native words by the *patois* used by explorers. **(4)** A few kept carefully *annotated* records of Native American languages, allowing us to trace the development of some states' names. Often, though, this information has been lost to history.

(5) One state name, Wyoming, is unique in that it reflects the *parlance* of a tribe that lived in a distant area of the country. Wyoming is a shortening of an Algonquin word roughly meaning "large prairie place." That word was taken from the name of a valley in Pennsylvania.

(6) Other English-based state names are *eponymous*. Georgia was named for King George II of England, the Carolinas for King Charles I, and Maryland for Charles's wife, Henrietta Maria. Pennsylvania, meaning "Penn's woods," was named in honor of the state's founder, William Penn. **(7)** Penn felt that this was a rather *vulgar* designation, however, so he told everyone that the new territory was actually named for his father, a famous admiral.

(8) Some state names were *neologisms*. The name Indiana was meant to pay tribute to American Indians, or Native Americans. The suffix *-ana* refers to a place or region; the state's name was intended to mean "land of Indians."

Some state names are long or difficult to pronounce. **(9)** This often leads young children to commit *malapropisms:* It is not unheard of for children to call Oregon "Oreo" or Massachusetts "Mattress."

From East to West and from North to South, the names of U.S. states reflect the country's history and culture. **(10)** They tell a *linguistic* tale that honors the people of a vast and varied nation.

Each sentence below refers to a numbered sentence in the passage. Write the letter of the choice that gives the sentence a meaning that is closest to the original sentence.

_____ **1.** How did we end up with this varied collection of _____?
  a. dialects **b.** names **c.** pronunciations **d.** regions

_____ **2.** Some names are the result of the United States having always been a _____ nation.
  a. complicated **b.** newly coined **c.** crude **d.** multiple-language

_____ **3.** Some names are the result of the reshaping of native words by a(n) _____.
  a. dialect **b.** end note **c.** name **d.** word mistake

_b_ **4.** Some explorers kept carefully _____ records of Native American languages.
  a. mistaken **b.** noted **c.** named **d.** studied

_b_ **5.** One state name, Wyoming, reflects the _____ of a tribe that lived in a distant area.
  a. language study **b.** particular language **c.** indecency **d.** new words

_C_ **6.** Other English-based state names are _____.
  a. dialectical **b.** newly coined **c.** named for people **d.** indecent

_C_ **7.** Penn felt that this was a rather _____ designation, however.
  a. mistaken **b.** critical **c.** showy **d.** insulting

_d_ **8.** Some state names were _____.
  a. word mistakes **b.** common terms **c.** end notes **d.** new words

_a_ **9.** This often leads young children to commit _____.
  a. word mistakes **b.** indecent slang **c.** new words **d.** silly behavior

_C_ **10.** They tell a(n) _____ tale that honors the people of a vast and varied nation.
  a. excessive **b.** common-dialect **c.** language-related **d.** new-word

Indicate whether the statements below are TRUE or FALSE according to the passage.

_T_ **1.** U.S. state names come from many different languages.

_F_ **2.** The exact origins of some state names are unknown.

_T_ **3.** William Penn did not want a state named after him because he was against all eponyms.

WRITING EXTENDED RESPONSES

Suppose that the United States has just admitted its fifty-first state. Based on this new state's history, population, geography, resources, or location (all of which you may invent or "borrow" from an actual state), what should this new state be called? Write a persuasive essay of at least three paragraphs in which you suggest a name and give several reasons why it is appropriate. Use three or more lesson words in your essay and underline them.

WRITE THE DERIVATIVE

Complete the sentence by writing the correct form of the word shown in parentheses. You may not need to change the form that is given.

Polyglot **1.** The fur trader needed to be a _____ in order to communicate with customers. (*polyglot*)

appellations **2.** Many _____ are of uncertain origin. (*appellation*)

parlance **3.** To nonlawyers, legal _____ may seem to be a language of its own. (*parlance*) _malaprop_   **4.** A _____ can be humorous, especially if the speaker seems pretentious. (*malapropism*)

patois   **5.** A _____ is almost always spoken, rather than written. (*patois*)

Annotations   **6.** _____ can add information to a text without disrupting its flow. (*annotation*)

Vulgarity   **7.** Luz was appalled by the _____ of the song lyrics. (*vulgar*)

Neologisms   **8.** I have always enjoyed _____ and puns. (*neologism*)

linguistics   **9.** Jakob Grimm was a folklorist and a pioneer of modern _____. (*linguistics*)

Eponymous   **10.** The Norsemen were the _____ conquerors of Normandy. (*eponym*)

FIND THE EXAMPLE

Choose the answer that best describes the action or situation.

_a_   **1.** The informal *appellation* of New York City
    a. the Big Apple   **b.** Metropolis   **c.** New York City   **d.** a state

_b_   **2.** An example of a *neologism*
    a. load   **b.** upload   **c.** reload   **d.** unload

_c_   **3.** An example of a *polyglot*
    a. a tongue twister   **b.** a novel   **c.** a translator   **d.** a parakeet

_d_   **4.** Someone most likely to use *malapropisms* intentionally
    a. reporter   **b.** politician   **c.** announcer   **d.** comedian

_b_   **5.** The opposite of *vulgar*
    a. abrupt   **b.** proper   **c.** coarse   **d.** common

_a_   **6.** Something that is NOT part of the subject of *linguistics*
    a. dining customs   **b.** word origins   **c.** grammar   **d.** slang

_d_   **7.** A familiar type of *annotation* in many textbooks
    a. introductions   **b.** pop-ups   **c.** recipes   **d.** footnotes

_c_   **8.** NOT a type of *parlance*
    a. business   **b.** legal   **c.** handwritten   **d.** scientific

_c_   **9.** A word that describes a *patois*
    a. formal   **b.** academic   **c.** nonstandard   **d.** literary

_d_   **10.** A well-known *eponym*
    a. Althea Gibson   **b.** James Bond   **c.** Harry Potter   **d.** Earl of Sandwich

Probability

contingent	eventuality	implausible	inconceivable	in vain
perchance	preposterous	proclivity	prone	theoretical

Probability, the likelihood that something will occur, is worth understanding for reasons that range from getting good math grades to good planning. What is the probability of having fun at the beach if the weather forecast projects a "90 percent chance of rain"? The words in this lesson will help you understand many aspects of probability.

1. **contingent** (kən-tǐn´jənt) from Latin *con-*, "together" + *tangere*, "to touch"
   a. *adjective* Conditional; dependent on other things
   • The house sale is **contingent** upon the results of a home inspection.
   b. *noun* A representative group forming part of a larger group
   • The small **contingent** of senators spoke on behalf of the farmers.

   contingency *noun* A possible occurrence; a possibility
   • Good defensive drivers anticipate dangerous **contingencies** and avoid potential accidents.

2. **eventuality** (ĭ-vĕn´chōō-ăl´ĭ-tē) *noun* from Latin *eventus*, "outcome"
   Something that may occur; a possibility
   • My insurance policy covers me in the case of almost any **eventuality**.

   eventual *adjective* Success is usually the **eventual** result of hard work.

3. **implausible** (ĭm-plô´zə-bəl) *adjective* from Latin *im-*, "not" + *plaudere*, "to applaud"
   Difficult to believe; not likely or credible
   • The sixty-year-old actor made an **implausible** Romeo.

   implausibility *noun* The **implausibility** of immediate success didn't prevent the scientists from trying to find a cure for the disease.

4. **inconceivable** (ĭn´kən-sē´və-bəl) *adjective* from Latin *in-*, "not" + *concipere*, "to take"
   a. Impossible to comprehend or fully grasp
   • It is almost **inconceivable** that such a capable, experienced, hard-working public servant would be voted out of office.
   b. So unlikely as to be thought impossible; unimaginable
   • At one time, space travel seemed **inconceivable**.

implausible

The opposite of *implausible* is *plausible*.

5. **in vain** (ĭn vān) *adverb* from Latin *vanus,* "empty"
   Without success; completely ineffective
   • Denise tried **in vain** to collect the papers as they blew across the street.

The phrase *in vain* is an idiom, or an expression that cannot be understood from the meanings of its elements.

6. **perchance** (pər-chăns´) *adverb* from Anglo-Norman *par chance,* "by chance"
   Perhaps; possibly
   • Instead of getting angry, he simply asked, "Might you, **perchance,** stop raising your voice at me?"

7. **preposterous** (prĭ-pŏs´tər-əs) *adjective* from Latin *pre-,* "before" + *post,* "behind"
   Absurd; contrary to nature, reason, or common sense
   • It is **preposterous** to think that an ant could carry an elephant.

8. **proclivity** (prō-klĭv´ĭ-tē) *noun* from Latin *pro-,* "forward" + *clivus,* "slope"
   A natural inclination; a tendency
   • At a very young age, Mozart had a **proclivity** for music.

9. **prone** (prōn) *adjective* from Latin *pronus,* "leaning forward"
   Having a tendency; inclined; likely to do or have something
   • Unfortunately, he was **prone** to hurting people's feelings unintentionally.

Another definition of *prone* is as an adverb, "lying with the front or face downward."

10. **theoretical** (thē´ə-rĕt´ĭ-kəl) *adjective* from Greek *theoretos,* "observable"
    Restricted to ideas; abstract or unproven
    • At this point, my hypothesis is **theoretical;** we still need to test it with experiments.

    theory *noun* There are many **theories** of how the universe came into existence.

WORD ENRICHMENT

The *"ins"* of English

In vain is just one of numerous English prepositional phrases that start with *in.* Many come from Latin and are used in the legal profession. For example, *in absentia* means "while or although not present." Fugitives or others who cannot be physically brought to trial are sometimes tried *in absentia.* Other legal language using *in* includes *in extremis,* meaning "at the point of death" or "in a grave or extreme situation"; *in loco parentis,* meaning "in the position or place of a parent"; *in situ,* "in the original position"; and *in re,* "in regard to the case of." *In re* is often used in the headings of legal briefs.

Other terms including *in* continue to be invented. *In-your-face,* which may have come from sports journalism, is an adjective meaning "marked by a bold, defiant, or aggressive manner." *In-line skates* are in some ways similar to traditional roller skates, but they have wheels arranged in a straight line.

WRITE THE CORRECT WORD

Write the correct word in the space next to each definition. Use each word only once.

Prone **1.** likely to do something

in vain **2.** without success

Preposterous **3.** absurd

Contigent **4.** conditional

theoretical **5.** restricted to ideas; unproven or abstract

Perchance **6.** perhaps

inconceivable **7.** impossible to grasp fully

eventuality **8.** a possibility

proclivity **9.** an inclination

implausible **10.** difficult to believe

COMPLETE THE SENTENCE

Write the letter for the word that best completes each sentence.

a **1.** When traveling, Lois insists on being prepared for every _____.
a. theory   b. proclivity   c. eventuality   d. inconceivability

b **2.** "_____, might he have hidden the stolen jewels in the mince pie?" asked the British detective.
a. Prone   b. Perchance   c. In vain   d. Contingently

d **3.** Though the idea is only _____ at this point, we may be able to prove it with research.
a. preposterous   b. prone   c. contingent   d. theoretical

b **4.** Bruce argued _____ that "Chubbles" was the perfect name for Ruth's new cat.
a. eventually   b. in vain   c. perchance   d. theoretically

c **5.** Going on the school field trip is _____ on parental permission.
a. prone   b. inconceivable   c. contingent   d. preposterous

a **6.** The roofer gave a _____ explanation for why the leak in our new roof wasn't his fault.
a. preposterous   b. contingent   c. perchance   d. prone

a **7.** Those cars were recalled because they were _____ to brake failure.
a. prone   b. preposterous   c. theoretical   d. contingent

d **8.** Poor Margo has a(n) _____ for saying exactly the wrong thing at any given moment.
a. contingent   b. theory   c. eventuality   d. proclivity

c **9.** Dave's parents thought his excuse for arriving home late was _____.
a. contingent   b. in vain   c. implausible   d. theoretical

b **10.** Valery trusted her brother so much that the idea of his revealing her secret was _____.
a. theoretical   b. inconceivable   c. contingent   d. in vain

Challenge: Gordon's associates grudgingly admired his _____ for making theoretical statements that at first seemed _____, but were later proved to be insightful and perceptive.
b
a. contingency…implausible   b. proclivity…preposterous   c. theory…in vain

Nature's Perfect Adhesive

(1) For years, scientists and inventors have searched *in vain* for the perfect adhesive. **(2)** As anyone who has removed an adhesive bandage strip knows, today's glues are *prone* to remaining sticky longer than you need them to. Other adhesives are wet and messy.

(3) Since great inventions—from electricity to the airplane to Velcro—have often arisen from ideas inspired by nature, researchers thought they might *perchance* discover the key to a better adhesive in the natural world. And they were right.

(4) The gecko, a small lizard, is known not only for its *proclivity* for climbing even the smoothest windows, but also for its ability to hang upside down, dangling from just one toe. **(5)** In fact, *inconceivable* as it may seem, the adhesive power of a single gecko's toes could support a 280-pound man! **(6)** This almost *preposterous* sticking power is just one of the amazing characteristics of geckos' feet. Perhaps almost as impressive, their feet seem to be self-cleaning. **(7)** However *implausibly*, given their dusty and dirty environment, gecko toes never get dirty.

Geckos have these abilities because of the structure of the bottoms of their feet, which are covered with up to two million tiny hairs, or *setae*. Each setae has more than a thousand padded tips called *spatulae*.

As a gecko walks on a wall or a ceiling, billions of spatulae come in contact with the surface, generating an attractive force, called *van der Waals force*. **(8)** Put another way, the clinging properties of a gecko's feet are *contingent* on the number of spatulae in contact with a surface, for each toe. So, to stop sticking to a surface, the gecko simply lifts one toe at a time, lessening the amount of contact. The van der Waals force weakens, and the adhesion, or sticking power, disappears.

(9) Now that researchers have a *theoretical* understanding of how the geckos' feet work, they may be able to replicate this incredible little lizard's adhesive abilities in a way that will be commercially viable. Perhaps we will soon be able to remove bandages without pain, or walk with boots that won't slip on ice or need to be cleaned. **(10)** These innovations could help us become better prepared for various weather *eventualities*. They might also give us adhesive materials that work underwater or in space.

Each sentence below refers to a numbered sentence in the passage. Write the letter of the choice that gives the sentence a meaning that is closest to the original sentence.

1. For years, scientists and inventors have searched _____ for the perfect adhesive.
  a. unsuccessfully **b.** conditionally **c.** unbelievably **d.** abstractly

2. Today's glues are _____ to remain sticky longer than you need them to.
  a. unable **b.** expected **c.** ridiculous **d.** likely

3. Researchers thought they might _____ discover a better adhesive in the natural world.
  a. probably **b.** unsuccessfully **c.** perhaps **d.** unbelievably

4. The gecko is known for its _____ for climbing even the smoothest, polished windows.
  a. inclination **b.** inability **c.** spontaneity **d.** possibility

___b___ **5.** _____ as it may seem, the adhesive power of a single gecko's toes could support a 280-pound man!

    a. Likely   **b.** Unimaginable   **c.** Obvious   **d.** Improper

___b___ **6.** This almost _____ sticking power is just one of the amazing characteristics of geckos' feet.

    a. conditional   **b.** absurd   **c.** inclined   **d.** unsuccessful

___d___ **7.** However _____, given their dusty and dirty environment, gecko toes never get dirty.

    a. abstract   **b.** inclined to fly   **c.** conditional   **d.** hard to believe

___c___ **8.** Put another way, the clinging properties of a gecko's feet are _____ the number of spatulae in contact with a surface, for each toe.

    a. required by   **b.** the same as   **c.** dependent on   **d.** unrelated to

___b___ **9.** Now that researchers have a(n) _____ understanding of how the geckos' feet work, they may be able to replicate this incredible little lizard's adhesive abilities in a way that will be commercially viable.

    a. conditional   **b.** abstract   **c.** absurd   **d.** perfect

___a___ **10.** These innovations could help us become better prepared for various weather _____.

    a. possibilities   **b.** statistics   **c.** tendencies   **d.** theories

Indicate whether the statements below are TRUE or FALSE according to the passage.

___T___ **1.** Geckos have a moist, gluelike substance on their feet.

___T___ **2.** Van der Waal's force assists geckos with climbing.

___F___ **3.** Researchers hope to make bandages out of the geckos' feet.

FINISH THE THOUGHT

Complete each sentence so that it shows the meaning of the italicized word.

1. It's *implausible* that _You arrived here at 8:00 from the airport._

2. I am *prone* to _making spelling errors._

WRITE THE DERIVATIVE

Complete the sentence by writing the correct form of the word shown in parentheses. You may not need to change the form that is given.

implausible   **1.** The jury did not believe the defendant's _____ alibi. (*implausible*)

prone   **2.** SUVs are more _____ to rolling over than sedans are. (*prone*)

eventually **3.** Will people _____ run out of clean water? *(eventuality)*

contigencies **4.** Congress, in an effort to plan for _____ such as earthquakes and hurricanes, has allocated money for emergency supplies. *(contingent)*

perchance **5.** Could you _____ spare me a moment of your time? *(perchance)*

in vain **6.** Throughout the storm, Toby waited _____ for a dial tone. *(in vain)*

inconceivably **7.** It is easy to conclude that the universe is _____ large. *(inconceivable)*

theory **8.** The professor told her student that his _____ was incomplete. *(theoretical)*

preposterous **9.** It is _____ to assume that because the moon and milk are the same color, they are made of the same substance. *(preposterous)*

proclivities **10.** The natural _____ of cats make them good pets and a good form of pest control. *(proclivity)*

FIND THE EXAMPLE

Choose the answer that best describes the action or situation.

_b_ **1.** NOT a realistic *eventuality*
  a. tides ebbing   **b.** metal corroding   **c.** the sun rising   **d.** weather never changing

_b_ **2.** Something a tired person is *prone* to do
  a. jump   **b.** yawn   **c.** holler   **d.** skip

_a_ **3.** Something *implausible*
  a. talking dog   **b.** jumping kangaroo   **c.** purring cat   **d.** singing bird

_c_ **4.** A synonym for *perchance*
  a. unlikely   **b.** always   **c.** maybe   **d.** never

_d_ **5.** A *contingency* plan
  a. A will cause B.   **b.** A can't happen.   **c.** Do nothing.   **d.** If A happens, then do B.

_d_ **6.** An emotion usually felt by a person after trying to do something *in vain*
  a. love   **b.** joy   **c.** excitement   **d.** frustration

_a_ **7.** Subject of much *theorizing*
  a. existence of aliens   **b.** sum of 1 plus 3   **c.** importance of school   **d.** correct spelling of *cat*

_d_ **8.** An *inconceivable* situation
  a. good team wins   **b.** sun rises in east   **c.** student earns an A   **d.** dog does calculus

_b_ **9.** A positive *proclivity*
  a. to sleep in class   **b.** to stay calm   **c.** to agree with everything   **d.** to shirk responsibility

_a_ **10.** Something *preposterous*
  a. tall tale   **b.** biography   **c.** world atlas   **d.** historical record

Change

WORD LIST

evolve	immutable	inveterate	malleable	metamorphosis
modulate	protean	sporadic	transmute	volatile

Perhaps the early Greek philosopher Heraclitus said it best roughly 2,500 years ago: "Change alone is unchanging." He recognized the fundamental truth that continual change is the normal state of the world. Whether it is positive or negative, we all have to deal with change. The words in this lesson will help you express ideas and understand topics related to this fact of life.

1. **evolve** (ĭ-vŏlv´) *verb* from Latin *ex-*, "out" + *volvere*, "to roll"
   To develop or achieve gradually
   • Will human society ever **evolve** to the point where violence can be eliminated?

   evolution *noun* In its six-decade **evolution,** the computer has changed from a room-sized machine to a common, portable device.

2. **immutable** (ĭ-myoō´tə-bəl) *adjective* from Latin *im-*, "not" + *mutare*, "to change"
   Unchangeable; not subject or susceptible to change
   • "The rules of ethical behavior are **immutable,** my child; they do not change with your moods or needs," said the guru.

3. **inveterate** (ĭn-vĕt´ər-ĭt) *adjective* from Latin *in-*, "in" + *vetus*, "old"
   a. Firmly established and having existed for a long time; deep-rooted
   • The idea that all people are entitled to certain basic rights is an **inveterate** American belief.
   b. Habitual; repeatedly acting according to an ingrained habit
   • Derek, an **inveterate** liar, was almost incapable of honesty.

4. **malleable** (măl´ē-ə-bəl) *adjective* from Latin *malleus*, "hammer"
   a. Capable of being shaped or formed, as by hammering or pressure
   • Many metals are more **malleable** once they are heated.
   b. Easily controlled or influenced
   • Enthroned by colonial powers who assumed he'd be **malleable,** Cambodia's prince Sihanouk proved to be strong-willed instead.

   malleability *noun* **Malleability** is essential for certain kinds of sculpting materials.

5. **metamorphosis** (mĕt´ə-môr´fə-sĭs) *noun* from Greek *meta-*, "change" + *morphe*, "form"
   A marked change in form, character, or function; a transformation
   • One well-known natural **metamorphosis** is the transformation from a caterpillar to a butterfly.

metamorphosis

The plural of *metamorphosis* is *metamorphoses.*

6. **modulate** (mŏj´ə-lāt´) *verb* from Latin *modus*, "measure"
To adjust or adapt to a certain level or proportion; to regulate
• The speaker **modulated** her voice in order to emphasize her main points.

modulation *noun* The actor's skillful **modulation** of his voice and body language effectively conveyed his character's declining health.

7. **protean** (prŏ´tē-ən) *adjective* from the Greek god *Proteus*
Readily taking on different forms, characteristics, or meanings
• The **protean** nature of modeling clay makes it a good medium for children's art classes.

Protean can also mean "exhibiting considerable variety or diversity."

8. **sporadic** (spə-răd´ĭk) *adjective* from Greek *sporadikos*, "scattered"
   a. Scattered; occurring at irregular intervals; having no regular pattern
   • Pat experienced **sporadic** hiccups throughout the day.
   b. Isolated; infrequent
   • In some parts of the world, **sporadic** outbreaks of polio still debilitate people.

9. **transmute** (trăns-myōōt´) *verb* from Latin *trans-*, "across"
+ *mutare*, "to change"
To change from one form to another; to transform
• No matter how hard they tried, alchemists were never able to **transmute** lead into gold.

transmutation *noun* It is highly unlikely that a kiss from a princess would result in the **transmutation** of a frog into a prince.

10. **volatile** (vŏl´ə-tl, vŏl´ə-tīl´) *adjective* from Latin *volare*, "to fly"
   a. Tending to vary often or widely, as in price; subject to wide variation; inconstant
   • Though mortgage rates were once relatively stable, they are now extremely **volatile.**
   b. Tending toward violence; explosive
   • Chuck's temper had become noticeably **volatile** since his pay cut.
   c. Evaporating readily at normal temperatures and pressures
   • Because their fumes spread quickly, highly **volatile** chemicals must be handled with extreme caution.

volatility *noun* The stock prices of technology companies have shown considerable **volatility** in recent years.

WORD ENRICHMENT

A *protean* god

As you read earlier, the word *protean* comes from the name of an ancient Greek god, *Proteus*. This sea god could tell the future and change shape at will. That second magic power gives rise to the modern meaning of the word *protean*, which refers to something that can assume different forms. In our world of ever-changing technology, adaptability and flexibility are highly desirable traits. Not surprisingly, the ancient Greek god *Proteus* has also lent his name to numerous modern business enterprises and products.

WRITE THE CORRECT WORD

Write the correct word in the space next to each definition. Use each word only once.

Volatile	**1.** unstable; inconstant		_evolve_	**6.** to develop gradually
immutable	**2.** unchangeable		_modulate_	**7.** to adjust; to regulate
protean	**3.** versatile; adaptable		_malleable_	**8.** easily shaped
transmute	**4.** to change form		_sporadic_	**9.** irregular; scattered
metamorphosis	**5.** a transformation		_inveterate_	**10.** firmly established

COMPLETE THE SENTENCE

Write the letter for the word that best completes each sentence.

___d___ **1.** The technician _____ the lights to indicate that the movie was about to begin.
    a. volatile   **b.** transmuted   **c.** evolved   **d.** modulated

___a___ **2.** _____ occurs when uranium decays and changes into thorium.
    a. Transmutation   **b.** Modulation   **c.** Malleability   **d.** Evolution

___a___ **3.** A(n) _____ pessimist always expects the worst to happen.
    a. inveterate   **b.** volatile   **c.** protean   **d.** sporadic

___c___ **4.** The _____ of computer technology made the Internet possible.
    a. immutability   **b.** modulation   **c.** evolution   **d.** volatility

___b___ **5.** The _____ of certain metals makes them ideal for shaping into musical instruments.
    a. volatility   **b.** malleability   **c.** modulation   **d.** metamorphosis

___a___ **6.** As supply and demand vacillates, gasoline prices can be quite _____.
    a. volatile   **b.** evolved   **c.** inveterate   **d.** protean

___c___ **7.** Versatile performers often like to display their _____ talents.
    a. modulated   **b.** transmuted   **c.** sporadic   **d.** protean

___c___ **8.** The president's speech was interrupted by _____ bursts of applause.
    a. immutable   **b.** inveterate   **c.** sporadic   **d.** malleable

___b___ **9.** During a rapid _____, the vacant lot was transformed into a well-groomed park.
    a. volatility   **b.** metamorphosis   **c.** malleability   **d.** modulation

___d___ **10.** We had assumed that the ancient cycle of seasonal migration was constant and _____.
    a. volatile   **b.** malleable   **c.** sporadic   **d.** immutable

Challenge: If left undisturbed, new ecosystems tend to _____ from a(n) _____ mix of relatively few species to a more stable, balanced community made up of a great many species.
___c___   **a.** modulate…malleable   **b.** transmute…immutable   **c.** evolve…volatile

Unsung Fasteners

As a paper holder, a bookmark, and even a symbol of resistance to fascism, the humble paper clip has served multiple purposes for more than a century. But have you ever given this little invention more than a passing thought?

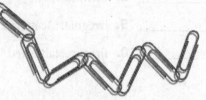

(1) Over time, ways to fasten papers together have *evolved* slowly. Before the paper clip, people used sharp straight pins or ribbons threaded through holes. **(2)** But new techniques for producing *malleable* metal wire laid the groundwork for the paper clip.

Norwegian inventor Johan Vaaler got the first patent on the paper clip in 1899. By 1907, the British company Gem Manufacturing had designed a "slide on" model with rounded edges. **(3)** Today, this seemingly *immutable* "double U" or "double oval" shape is recognizable around the world. **(4)** While many products have undergone major *metamorphoses*, the most popular paper clip design is still the one that was devised in 1907.

With the advent of the computer, many people expected the "paperless office" to drastically decrease demand for paper clips. But people seem to like recording and reading information on actual paper and paper clip sales have not declined significantly. **(5)** So manufacturers have not had to *modulate* production to accommodate a decrease in demand.

Perhaps that is partly because paper clips have served an amazing number of functions. **(6)** Though they won't *transmute* into gold, they've done just about everything else at one time or another. Their many uses—intact or unwound—include serving as bookmarks, money holders, necktie clips, suspender hooks, counters, cleaners, playthings, cuff links, and simple tools for manipulating small objects. **(7)** In one survey about this *protean* object, it was estimated that for every 100,000 paper clips in use, 17,200 hold clothing together, 14,163 are absentmindedly destroyed during phone conversations, and 15,556 are lost. Only 20,000 are actually used to clip papers together.

(8) While the paper clip isn't frequently discussed in glowing terms, *sporadic* attempts have been made to honor it. A 1973 painting of a paper clip by pop artist James Rosenquist has been displayed in major art museums. In 1999, *Fortune Magazine* named this device one of the best office products of the twentieth century. Finally, a 2004 showing at New York's Museum of Modern Art honored it as one of 120 "Humble Masterpieces."

The paper clip has also had political significance. **(9)** In the *volatile* days of World War II, Nazi Germany occupied Norway. As an act of defiance, Norwegians started attaching paper clips—a symbol of their country and their solidarity against the occupation—to their clothing. Some people wearing these clips were arrested by the Nazis.

(10) To this day, Norwegians are the most *inveterate* admirers of the paper clip. They have an official stamp that honors inventor Johan Vaaler. Famous visitors are presented with oversized paper clips to "fasten them" to Norwegians. And in Oslo, Norway, a 22–foot statue of a paper clip stands as a massive tribute to this small but amazingly useful invention.

Each sentence below refers to a numbered sentence in the passage. Write the letter of the choice that gives the sentence a meaning that is closest to the original sentence.

___ **1.** Ways to fasten papers together have _____ slowly.
     a. scattered   **b.** developed   **c.** molded   **d.** regulated

___ **2.** The production of _____ metal wire laid the groundwork for the paper clip.
     a. easily shaped   **b.** brittle   **c.** unchangeable   **d.** gradually developed

___ **3.** Today, this seemingly _____ shape is recognizable around the world.
     a. mutated   **b.** flexible   **c.** developed   **d.** unchangeable

___ **4.** While many products have undergone major _____, the most popular paper clip design is still the one that was devised in 1907.
     a. development   **b.** evaporation   **c.** changes   **d.** scatterings

_b___ **5.** Manufacturers have not had to _____ production to accommodate a decrease in demand.
    a. reformat   **b.** adjust   **c.** mold   **d.** scatter

_d___ **6.** Though they won't _____ into gold, they've done just about everything else.
    a. develop   **b.** adjust   **c.** evaporate   **d.** transform

_a___ **7.** In one survey about this _____ object, it was estimated that for every 100,000 paper clips in use, 17,200 hold clothing together.
    a. versatile   **b.** specialized   **c.** unchangeable   **d.** bendable

_d___ **8.** While the paper clip isn't frequently discussed in glowing terms, _____ attempts have been made to honor it.
    a. habitual   **b.** occasional   **c.** explosive   **d.** numerous

_d___ **9.** In the _____ days of World War II, Nazi Germany occupied Norway.
    a. peaceful, stable   **b.** unchangeable   **c.** scattered   **d.** unpredictable, violent

_a___ **10.** To this day, Norwegians are the most _____ admirers of the paper clip.
    a. steadfast   **b.** flexible   **c.** scattered   **d.** fickle

Indicate whether the statements below are TRUE or FALSE according to the passage.

_F___ **1.** The design of the paper clip has changed drastically since its early days.

_T___ **2.** According to a survey, about one paper clip out of every five is actually used to clip paper.

_F___ **3.** The Germans invented paper clips in Norway during World War II.

WRITING EXTENDED RESPONSES

You have just read about the paper clip. Choose another common object that you think deserves more appreciation than it gets, an object that people take for granted. In an expository essay of at least three paragraphs, explain how this item contributes to our lives. Your essay should describe two or more positive characteristics or important uses for this item. Use three or more lesson words in your essay and underline them.

WRITE THE DERIVATIVE

Complete the sentence by writing the correct form of the word shown in parentheses. You may not need to change the form that is given.

_Protean_____ **1.** Marissa's _____ talents as actress, soccer goalie, and class president never cease to amaze me. *(protean)*

_Volatility_____ **2.** The _____ of his temper makes him a poor choice for the job. *(volatile)*

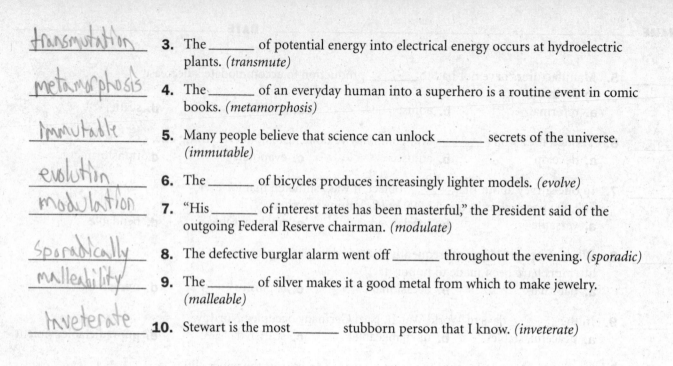

transmutation   **3.** The _____ of potential energy into electrical energy occurs at hydroelectric plants. *(transmute)*

metamorphosis   **4.** The _____ of an everyday human into a superhero is a routine event in comic books. *(metamorphosis)*

Immutable   **5.** Many people believe that science can unlock _____ secrets of the universe. *(immutable)*

evolution   **6.** The _____ of bicycles produces increasingly lighter models. *(evolve)*

modulation   **7.** "His _____ of interest rates has been masterful," the President said of the outgoing Federal Reserve chairman. *(modulate)*

Sporadically   **8.** The defective burglar alarm went off _____ throughout the evening. *(sporadic)*

malleability   **9.** The _____ of silver makes it a good metal from which to make jewelry. *(malleable)*

Inveterate   **10.** Stewart is the most _____ stubborn person that I know. *(inveterate)*

FIND THE EXAMPLE

Choose the answer that best describes the action or situation.

a   **1.** Something highly *volatile*
   a. gasoline   **b.** ice   **c.** milk   **d.** gelatin

c   **2.** Something *inveterate*
   a. a passing fancy   **b.** a head cold   **c.** an old custom   **d.** a new idea

d   **3.** The most *protean* type of writing
   a. business letter   **b.** application form   **c.** editorial   **d.** poetry

a   **4.** Something that *evolves* over a long period of time
   a. culture   **b.** water   **c.** gold   **d.** air

c   **5.** Something important to *modulate* while driving
   a. your voice   **b.** your family   **c.** your speed   **d.** your radio

b   **6.** Something *immutable*
   a. your weight   **b.** speed of light   **c.** your favorite band   **d.** tax rates

b   **7.** Something *malleable*
   a. summer breeze   **b.** aluminum foil   **c.** iron beam   **d.** concrete wall

d   **8.** A *metamorphosis*
   a. baby to baby   **b.** dog to canine   **c.** cat to feline   **d.** tadpole to frog

a   **9.** Something that occurs *sporadically* in most places
   a. rain   **b.** Thanksgiving   **c.** Wednesday   **d.** sunrise

c   **10.** A common *transmutation*
   a. adult to teen   **b.** planet to star   **c.** potato peels to compost   **d.** peasant to king

Using the Dictionary

Usage Notes

Most dictionaries contain usage notes. These notes are given within an entry or in a separate paragraph at the end of an entry. Usage notes provide information on the correct use of words. They describe the acceptable and unacceptable uses of a word, distinguish easily confused words, discuss points of grammar, and highlight issues of pronunciation. Notes are given only for words likely to cause uncertainty. Here are some examples of information provided by usage notes.

1. *Usage notes explain acceptable and unacceptable uses of a word.* Like most dictionaries, the *American Heritage Dictionary* has a Usage Panel, whose members decide whether particular usages are acceptable. Note that in the usage note below, the members of the Usage Panel do not agree about whether the usage is acceptable.

   USAGE NOTE: The phrasal verb *look to* has recently developed the meaning "expect to, hope to," as in *I'm looking to sell my car.* Probably because of its informal nature, this usage is not acceptable in writing for 52 percent of the Usage Panel.

2. *Usage notes explain the correct usage of frequently confused words.* The following note discusses the different meanings of two verbs that are often confused, *affect* and *effect.* It is found at the end of the entry for *affect.*

   USAGE NOTE: *Affect[1]* and *effect* have no senses in common. As a verb *affect[1]* is most commonly used in the sense of "to influence" *(how smoking affects health). Effect* means "to bring about or execute": *measures designed to effect savings.*

   The usage note can help you remember the differences between the two verbs. You can check whether you have used the verbs correctly in a sentence with these substitutions.

   The weather may affect *(influence) our weekend plans.*
   We will effect *(bring about) the schedule change in the fall.*

3. *Usage notes explain points of grammar.* The following usage note is given at the end of the entry for *want,* when used as a verb.

   USAGE NOTE: When *want* is followed immediately by an infinitive construction, it does not take *for: I want you to go (not want for you to go).* When *want* and the infinitive phrase are separated in the sentence, however, *for* is used: *What I want is for you to go. Want* in its meaning of "have need" normally takes *for: They'll not want for anything now that they've inherited his estate.*

4. Usage notes highlight possible difficulties in pronunciation. The following usage note presents two pronunciation options for *err.* Note that the opinion of the dictionary's usage panel is cited.

   USAGE NOTE: The pronunciation (ûr) for the word *err* is traditional, but the pronunciation (ĕr) has gained acceptability in recent years. The Usage Panel was split on the matter: 56 percent preferred (ûr), 34 percent preferred (ĕr), and 10 percent accepted both pronunciations.

Practíce

Read the dictionary entries and usage notes below. Then read the sentences in the exercise that follows. Decide whether the italicized word in each sentence is used correctly. If the word is used incorrectly, rewrite the sentence with the correct usage on the "Rewrite" line.

al•leged (ə-lĕjd´, ə-lĕj´ĭd) *adj.* Represented in a certain way without proof; supposed. —**al•leg´ed•ly** (ə-lĕj´ĭd-lē) *adv.*
USAGE NOTE: In their zeal to protect the rights of the accused, newspapers and law enforcement officials sometimes misuse *alleged*. Someone arrested for murder may be only an *alleged* murderer, for example, because no charge has been proved, but is a real, not *alleged*, suspect in that his or her status as a suspect is not in doubt. Similarly, if the money from a safe is known to have been stolen, and not merely mislaid, then we may safely speak of a theft without having to qualify our description with *alleged*.

all right *adj.* **1a.** In proper or satisfactory operational or working order . . .
USAGE NOTE: *All right*, usually pronounced as if it were a single word, probably should have followed the same orthographic development as *already* and *altogether*. But despite its use by a number of reputable authors, the spelling *alright* has never been accepted as a standard variant.

a•while (ə-hwīl´, ə-wīl´) *adv.* For a short time
USAGE NOTE: *Awhile*, an adverb, is never preceded by a preposition, such as *for*, but the two-word form *a while* may be preceded by a preposition. In writing each of the following is acceptable: *stay awhile; stay for a while; stay a while* (but not *stay for awhile*).

per•cent•age (pər-sĕn´tĭj) *n.* **1a.** A fraction or ratio with 100 understood to be the denominator . . .
USAGE NOTE: *Percentage*, when preceded by *the*, takes a singular verb: *The percentage of unskilled workers is small.* When preceded by *a*, it takes either a singular or plural verb, depending on the number of the noun in the prepositional phrase that follows: *A small percentage of the workers are unskilled. A large percentage of the crop has spoiled.*

1. The *percentage* of unsatisfied people are small.

   Correct or incorrect? _____

   Rewrite _____

2. Please practice for *a while* longer.

   Correct or incorrect? _____

   Rewrite _____

3. The *alleged* thief has been taken into custody.

   Correct or incorrect? _____

   Rewrite _____

4. It's *alright* if you want to take some time off.

   Correct or incorrect? _____

   Rewrite _____

5. A small *percentage* of students want to skip the ceremony.

   Correct or incorrect? _____

   Rewrite _____

6. After playing *awhile*, the students went home.

   Correct or incorrect? _____

   Rewrite _____

Thought and Judgment

WORD LIST

abstruse	acumen	ascertain	cerebral	faculty
obfuscate	ruminate	stymie	surmise	tenet

Thought and judgment are central to our lives. Our language reflects this in such common expressions as "to have second thoughts," "think the matter over," "sit in judgment," and "reserve judgment." This lesson presents words that deal with the human thought process.

1. **abstruse** (ăb-strōōs´) *adjective* from Latin *ab-*, "away from" + *trudere*, "to push"
   Difficult to understand
   • The undergraduate students had trouble following the philosophy professor's **abstruse** explanation of Kant's theory.

   abstruseness *noun* With less **abstruseness** than one might have guessed, the astrophysicist explained how a rocket works.

   abstruse

2. **acumen** (ăk´yə-mən) *noun* from Latin *acuere*, "to sharpen"
   Quickness and keenness of insight or judgment
   • Her fashion sense and business **acumen** enabled her to build a multimillion-dollar clothing empire.

3. **ascertain** (ăs´ər-tān´) *verb* from Latin *ad-*, "to" + *cernere*, "to determine"
   To discover or determine with certainty, especially through examination or experimentation
   • Through fingerprint analysis, the police officer was able to **ascertain** that the suspect in custody had committed the crime.

   ascertainable *adjective* Many people believe that the answers to philosophical questions such as "Why are we here?" are not **ascertainable**.

4. **cerebral** (sĕr´ə-brəl, sə-rē´brəl) *adjective* from Latin *cerebrum*, "brain"
   a. Of or relating to the brain
   • **Cerebral** swelling can result in permanent brain injury.
   b. Appealing to or requiring the use of intellect; intellectual
   • Playing chess is a **cerebral** activity requiring much strategy.

   cerebrum *noun* The human **cerebrum** is divided into the left and right hemispheres.

   > The *cerebrum* is the large, rounded part of the brain that controls motor, sensory, and higher mental functions. The plural of *cerebrum* is *cerebra*.

5. **faculty** (făk´əl-tē) *noun* from Latin *facultus*, "power; ability"
   a. A natural power or ability
   • Human beings have the **faculties** of speech and abstract reasoning.
   b. A division of a university or a group of teachers
   • The university's music **faculty** includes some famous composers.

6. obfuscate (ŏb´fə-skāt´) *verb* from Latin *ob-*, "over" + *fuscare*, "to darken"

  a. To make difficult to understand
  - The tutor's complicated explanation **obfuscated** a simple concept.

  b. To darken; to make dim or difficult to see
  - The mist **obfuscated** the nearby rowboat.

  obfuscation *noun* Having little in the way of a defense for his client, the lawyer's strategy for the trial consisted of **obfuscation** of the facts.

7. ruminate (rōō´mə-nāt´) *verb* from Latin *rumen*, "throat"

  a. To think deeply about; to turn a matter over and over in one's mind
  - I **ruminated** for hours about the meaning of the poem.

  b. To chew cud, or partially digested food
  - Animals that eat coarse grass and plants must **ruminate** in order to fully digest their food.

  rumination *noun* After much **rumination** on the behavior of the particles, the physicist formulated a new theorem.

8. stymie (stī´mē) *verb* origin unknown

  To prevent from making progress; to frustrate or thwart efforts
  - The developing country's inadequate roads have **stymied** its efforts to modernize.

> *Stymie* can also be spelled *stymy*.

9. surmise (sər-mīz´) from French *sur*, "upon" + *mettre*, "to put"

  a. *verb* To guess; to draw a conclusion without sufficient evidence
  - Looking around the half-empty conference room, the manager **surmised** that there must be a flu epidemic at the company.

  b. *noun* A guess; a conclusion drawn without sufficient evidence
  - Napoleon's **surmise** that he could conquer Russia proved disastrous, as thousands of his troops died during Russia's harsh winter.

10. tenet (tĕn´ĭt) *noun* from Latin *tenere*, "to hold"

  A principle or belief held by a person or an organization
  - The right of citizens to choose leaders is a central **tenet** of a democracy.

WORD ENRICHMENT

Ruminating

  Cows, sheep, goats, deer, and other *ruminants* are able to eat coarse grasses and plants because of the unique structure of their digestive system. Their stomachs are divided into four compartments. The first two partially digest the food. Then, any pieces that are too large or tough to continue digesting are pushed back into the mouth to be chewed again. This partially digested food is called *cud*. After chewing the cud to further break it down, the animal swallows it again, and the cud is fully digested in the third and fourth parts of the stomach.

  Similarly, if a person thinks about a problem, turning it over and over in his or her mind, we say that the person is *ruminating*. The slang phrase *chew the cud* also means "to think something over or talk about something at length."

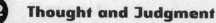

WRITE THE CORRECT WORD

Write the correct word in the space next to each definition. Use each word only once.

Stymie **1.** to thwart

acumen **2.** keenness of insight

tenet **3.** a principle or belief

cerebral **4.** relating to the brain

faculty **5.** a natural ability

surmise **6.** to guess

obfuscate **7.** to make confusing

abstruse **8.** hard to understand

ruminate **9.** to think about deeply

ascertain **10.** to determine with certainty

COMPLETE THE SENTENCE

Write the letter for the word that best completes each sentence.

c **1.** Hidden cameras allow storeowners to _____ who is stealing merchandise.
  a. obfuscate   **b.** stymie   **c.** ascertain   **d.** ruminate

a **2.** Unlike his more athletic peers, the studious boy preferred _____ activities.
  a. cerebral   **b.** ascertained   **c.** obfuscated   **d.** stymied

d **3.** Make sure you agree with the _____ of an organization before you join it.
  a. ruminations   **b.** acumen   **c.** surmise   **d.** tenets

b **4.** A raging hurricane _____ the ship's captain in his quest to reach land.
  a. surmised   **b.** stymied   **c.** obfuscated   **d.** ruminated

a **5.** General Custer incorrectly _____ the strength of the Sioux and the Cheyenne
  forces at the Battle of the Little Bighorn and suffered the worst defeat in
  American military history.
  a. surmised   **b.** obfuscated   **c.** ruminated   **d.** stymied

b **6.** Charlie found advanced trigonometry to be complex and very _____.
  a. ascertainable   **b.** abstruse   **c.** stymied   **d.** ruminated

d **7.** Mary _____ for many days over which of the two candidates she should hire.
  a. ascertained   **b.** stymied   **c.** obfuscated   **d.** ruminated

b **8.** Although his verbal skills were weak, the young boy had an amazing _____ for
  math and spatial reasoning.
  a. tenet   **b.** faculty   **c.** obfuscation   **d.** surmise

a **9.** The grand master's _____ at chess made her virtually unbeatable.
  a. acumen   **b.** obfuscation   **c.** tenet   **d.** rumination

b **10.** Some "experts" deliberately _____ the truth with irrelevant facts.
  a. ruminate   **b.** obfuscate   **c.** surmise   **d.** abstruse

Challenge: With considerable _____ and precision, the skilled cardiologist _____ the
  cause of the leaky heart valve and repaired it.
b
  a. cerebrum...surmised   **b.** acumen...ascertained   **c.** abstruseness...obfuscated

Can Gorillas Talk?

Humans and gorillas have a few things in common. Both have two arms, two legs, ten fingers, ten toes, and 32 teeth. **(1)** More surprisingly, people and apes also may share a *faculty* for learning language.

(2) Gorillas are physically incapable of speaking as humans do, but researcher Dr. Francine "Penny" Patterson *surmised* that they might be able to communicate with their hands. In 1972, Dr. Patterson tested her theory by trying to teach sign language to a one-year-old gorilla named Koko.

Within weeks, Koko learned the signs for "eat," "drink," and "more." **(3)** Dr. Patterson quickly realized, however, that sticking to the hand symbols of American Sign Language would *stymie* her work with Koko. Because apes' thumbs are shorter than the thumbs of humans, it was impossible for Koko to form certain signs. So, based on what Koko could do, Dr. Patterson developed what she calls Gorilla Sign Language.

Thirty-three years later, Koko can sign more than 1,000 words and seems to understand about 2,000. **(4)** Far from rattling off complex or *abstruse* theories, Koko uses one or two words at a time and forms simple sentences such as "I like drinks."

(5) While even Dr. Patterson agrees that Koko does not *ruminate* about philosophical matters, she does feel that Koko displays significant intelligence. Koko has scored between 80 and 90 on adapted IQ tests, somewhat lower than the human average of 100. **(6)** Dr. Patterson says that, much like a human toddler, Koko is more emotional than *cerebral*. But she points out that Koko shows clear signs of thought and imagination.

(7) For example, Koko shows *acumen* in making up logical words for things she has not yet learned to sign. When shown a ring, Koko called it a "finger bracelet." When shown a cigarette lighter, Koko called it a "bottle match." Most remarkably, Koko has attempted to teach sign language to another ape.

However, not everyone agrees that Koko is actually communicating thoughts. Skeptics suggest that Dr. Patterson and her staff simply see the hand signs that they are looking for. Some think that researchers may be so eager for Koko to communicate with humans that they innocently trick themselves into thinking that she is. **(8)** These critics hold to the common linguistic *tenet* that only humans are capable of communicating through language.

(9) A recent Internet chat session with Koko showed just how difficult it is to *ascertain* which side is correct in this debate. Depending on what observers focused on, it was possible to conclude either that Koko understood what she was saying, or that she was randomly making signs.

When asked if she felt love from the humans who raised her, Koko said, "Lips, apple give me." To skeptics, the answer made no sense. **(10)** But Dr. Patterson pointed out that not knowing Koko's code words *obfuscated* the gorilla's answer. "Lips" is what Koko calls women. "Apple" is one of her favorite foods. Koko may have been saying that she knows her caregivers love her because they give her things she likes.

While Dr. Patterson's work may seem like fun, her goals are quite serious. By showing the world that apes are gentle, thinking creatures, she hopes to build support for their protection and the conservation of habitats necessary for their survival.

Each sentence below refers to a numbered sentence in the passage. Write the letter of the choice that gives the sentence a meaning that is closest to the original sentence.

___C___ 1. People and apes also may share a(n) _____ for learning language.
   a. compulsion   **b.** judgment   **c.** ability   **d.** dedication

___a___ 2. Dr. Patterson _____ that they might be able to communicate with their hands.
   a. guessed   **b.** was certain   **c.** discovered   **d.** thought deeply

___b___ 3. Dr. Patterson quickly realized that sticking to the hand symbols of American Sign Language would _____ her work with Koko.
   a. speed up   **b.** hold back   **c.** simplify   **d.** confuse

_a_ **4.** Far from rattling off complex or _____ theories, Koko uses one or two words at a time and forms simple sentences.
  a. insightful **b.** conclusive **c.** scientific **d.** hard-to-understand

_a_ **5.** Dr. Patterson agrees that Koko does not _____ about philosophical matters.
  a. think deeply **b.** hold beliefs **c.** prevent progress **d.** draw conclusions

_c_ **6.** Koko is more emotional than _____.
  a. judgmental **b.** confused **c.** intellectual **d.** social

_d_ **7.** Koko shows _____ in making up logical words.
  a. great imagination **b.** great guessing **c.** strong principles **d.** keen judgment

_B_ **8.** These critics hold to the common linguistic _____ that only humans are capable of communicating through language.
  a. mistake **b.** principle **c.** practice **d.** conclusion

_a_ **9.** A recent Internet chat session with Koko showed just how difficult it is to _____ which side is correct in this debate.
  a. determine **b.** imagine **c.** guess **d.** disregard

_C_ **10.** Not knowing Koko's code words _____ the gorilla's answer.
  a. clarified **b.** frustrated **c.** made unclear **d.** concluded

Indicate whether the statements below are TRUE or FALSE according to the passage.

_F_ **1.** Dr. Patterson uses only American Sign Language to talk to Koko.

_F_ **2.** Koko's IQ is the same as that of a scientist.

_T_ **3.** Some skeptical scientists do not believe that Koko is actually communicating.

FINISH THE THOUGHT

Complete each sentence so that it shows the meaning of the italicized word.

1. I often _ruminate_ about ___the future___

2. I was _stymied_ by ___my inability to comprehend the book___

WRITE THE DERIVATIVE

Complete the sentence by writing the correct form of the word shown in parentheses. You may not need to change the form that is given.

___ruminating___ **1.** After much _____, Alyssa finally decided which college to attend. (_ruminate_)

___ascertainable___ **2.** Sonar has made the location of shipwrecks _____. (_ascertain_)

obfuscated   **3.** The rambling editorial ———— the argument rather than clarifying it. *(obfuscate)*

cerebrum   **4.** People used to believe that the size of one's ———— indicated the level of one's intelligence. *(cerebral)*

faculty   **5.** My principal always says that great ———— are what make great schools. *(faculty)*

stymied   **6.** The rescue team was ———— in its efforts to reach the victims. *(stymie)*

abstruseness   **7.** In order to persuade the general public, an argument should be free of jargon and ————. *(abstruse)*

tenets   **8.** Some of the basic ———— of freedom and liberty have become threatened during wartime. *(tenet)*

acumen   **9.** Joe Montana's ———— enabled him to complete amazingly accurate passes to receivers while avoiding being tackled, making him one of the best quarterbacks in history. *(acumen)*

surmise   **10.** The bumbling detective's ———— were frequently wrong, yet he still managed to catch many thieves. *(surmise)*

FIND THE EXAMPLE

Choose the answer that best describes the action or situation.

a   **1.** Members of a university *faculty*
  a. math professors   **b.** hockey players   **c.** sophomores   **d.** groundskeepers

b   **2.** Something that requires the most *cerebral* activity
  a. watching TV   **b.** taking a test   **c.** taking a nap   **d.** listening to music

a   **3.** The text most likely to be *abstruse*
  a. tax instructions   **b.** newspaper article   **c.** comic book   **d.** e-mail from a friend

b   **4.** Someone who is most likely to *obfuscate* intentionally
  a. police officer   **b.** con artist   **c.** teacher   **d.** tour guide

a   **5.** Something that contains *tenets*
  a. Bill of Rights   **b.** apartment   **c.** musical work   **d.** restaurant menu

d   **6.** A choice that one would most likely *ruminate* over
  a. lunch options   **b.** shoes to wear   **c.** show to watch   **d.** college major

b   **7.** How you would most likely feel about an answer you *ascertained*
  a. unsure   **b.** confident   **c.** indifferent   **d.** confused

a   **8.** How you would most likely feel about an answer you *surmised*
  a. unsure   **b.** confident   **c.** indifferent   **d.** confused

d   **9.** Something that does NOT *stymie* safe drivers
  a. a broken signal   **b.** a snowstorm   **c.** road construction   **d.** full gas tank

b   **10.** A profession likely to require the greatest *acumen*
  a. waiter   **b.** surgeon   **c.** usher   **d.** doorman

Avoídance

WORD LIST

abeyance	abstemious	circumvent	elude	eschew
evasion	malinger	oblique	shirk	shun

Most people attempt, at one time or another, to avoid a difficult situation. But as an old proverb says, "What the fool does in the end, the wise person does in the beginning." The words in this lesson will help you discuss various instances that involve avoidance.

1. **abeyance** (ə-bā´əns) *noun* from Latin *ad-*, "toward" + *baer*, "to gape"
   Suspension; a condition of being temporarily set aside
   • The governor held the emergency plan in **abeyance** while forecasters tried to determine whether the hurricane would hit Florida.

   > *Abeyance* is commonly used in the phrase *hold in abeyance.*

2. **abstemious** (ăb-stē´mē-əs) *adjective* from Latin *ab-*, "away" + *temum*, "liquor"
   a. Eating and drinking little or in moderation
   • After overeating throughout the holidays, Darrell resolved to be more **abstemious** in the new year.
   b. Restricted to bare necessities
   • The shortage of supplies during a long winter forced the soldiers at Valley Forge to lead an **abstemious** existence.

   an abstemious meal

3. **circumvent** (sûr´kəm-vĕnt´) *verb* from Latin *circum-*, "around" + *venire*, "to go; to come"
   a. To avoid or get around by clever maneuvering
   • Some corporations use legal loopholes to **circumvent** paying taxes.
   b. To avoid by going around; to bypass
   • We **circumvented** the traffic on the highway by taking the local roads.

   circumvention *noun* The editorial stated, "**Circumvention** of safety regulations endangers workers and is not only illegal, it is unethical."

4. **elude** (ĭ-lōōd´) *verb* from Latin *ex-*, "out of; away from" + *ludere*, "to play"
   a. To escape from, usually by daring, cleverness, or skill
   • The burglar **eluded** the police by exiting through a secret tunnel.
   b. To escape the grasp or understanding of
   • The meaning of his poem **eludes** me.

   elusive *adjective* Difficult to capture, perceive, understand, or achieve
   • Chicago Cubs fans are hopeful that their team will eventually win the **elusive** World Series championship.

5. **eschew** (ĕs-chōō´, ĕs-shōō´) *verb* from Middle English *escheuen*, "escape"

To avoid, especially on moral or practical grounds; abstain from
- Ever since she was diagnosed with high blood pressure, my aunt has **eschewed** salty foods.

6. **evasion** (ĭ-vā´zhən) *noun* from Latin *ex-*, "out of; away from" + *vadere*, "to go"

The act of escaping or avoiding by cleverness or deceit
- The reporter was disappointed by the senator's **evasion** of her question about the scandal.

   evade *verb* The soldiers **evaded** the enemy by leaving radios playing and fires burning as they retreated, giving the impression that they were still in the camp.

   evasive *adjective* The movie star was **evasive** when reporters asked if he was planning to marry his girlfriend.

7. **malinger** (mə-lĭng´gər) *verb* from French *malingre*, "sickly"

To pretend to be ill or injured in order to avoid duty or work
- When Bob was spotted at a football game after he'd called in sick, our boss accused him of **malingering.**

   malingerer *noun* The **malingerer** continued to collect disability pay long after the effects of her injury had disappeared.

8. **oblique** (ō-blēk´) *adjective* from Latin *obliquus*, "slanting"
   a. Indirect; intentionally vague or ambiguous
      - The spokesperson's comments about the company's lawsuit were so **oblique** that he might as well have said, "no comment."
   b. Misleading, devious, or dishonest
      - In a series of **oblique** statements, the candidate managed to cast doubts on the integrity of his very honorable opponent.

   obliqueness *noun* The **obliqueness** of his reference left us wondering what he meant.

> *Oblique* lines are slanted.

9. **shirk** (shûrk) *verb* from German *schurke*, "scoundrel"

To neglect, put off, or avoid a duty or responsibility
- Kai's father warned him that if he **shirked** his duties at home or at school, he would not be allowed to use the car.

10. **shun** (shŭn) *verb* from Old English *scunian*, "to abhor"

To willfully ignore; to stay away from
- Sometimes when new diseases are discovered and the causes are not understood, the victims are **shunned** by their communities.

WORD ENRICHMENT

Phrases that mean "to avoid"

In addition to individual words, English has many phrases that mean "to avoid." These include *shy away from, steer clear of, get around,* and *give a wide berth to.* One meaning of *berth* is "the amount of space sufficient for a ship to maneuver," so to *give a wide berth to* someone means "to stay a safe distance away from him or her."

WRITE THE CORRECT WORD

Write the correct word in the space next to each definition. Use each word only once.

Circumvent **1.** to go around; bypass

Shun **2.** to stay away from

oblique **3.** intentionally vague

evasion **4.** the act of cleverly avoiding

abstemious **5.** restricted to bare necessities

elude **6.** to escape from

abeyance **7.** suspension

eschew **8.** to avoid; abstain from

shirk **9.** to neglect responsibility

malinger **10.** to fake illness to avoid work

COMPLETE THE SENTENCE

Write the letter for the word that best completes each sentence.

_C_ **1.** His severance pay was held in _____ until all his assignments were completed.
   a. evasion   **b.** obliqueness   **c.** abeyance   **d.** circumvention

_d_ **2.** Somehow the mouse managed to take the cheese but _____ the trap.
   a. shirk   **b.** malinger   **c.** oblique   **d.** elude

_a_ **3.** Regular exercise and _____ eating habits are two keys to weight loss.
   a. abstemious   **b.** malingering   **c.** oblique   **d.** circumvented

_d_ **4.** The villagers _____ the young man who had violated their customs and was believed to be cursed.
   a. shirked   **b.** malingered   **c.** eluded   **d.** shunned

_b_ **5.** The corrupt businessman was convicted on federal tax _____ charges.
   a. abeyance   **b.** evasion   **c.** shunning   **d.** malingering

_d_ **6.** If you take too many sick days from work, your boss may suspect you of _____.
   a. eluding   **b.** eschewing   **c.** shunning   **d.** malingering

_a_ **7.** Jose _____ luxuries, preferring to donate his extra money to charity.
   a. eschewed   **b.** shirked   **c.** malingered   **d.** eluded

_C_ **8.** Callie's _____ description of her plans caused her parents to ask a lot of questions.
   a. malingering   **b.** shunning   **c.** oblique   **d.** abstemious

_d_ **9.** The computer hackers _____ the bank's security system and stole millions of dollars.
   a. shirked   **b.** shunned   **c.** eschewed   **d.** circumvented

_C_ **10.** The coach threatened to suspend any player who _____ her academic duties.
   a. eschewed   **b.** shunned   **c.** shirked   **d.** obliqued

Challenge: In the humorous stories about the lazy _____, his shifty ability to _____ his work responsibilities is regarded as a high art form by his friends.
_b_ **a.** abeyance…abstain   **b.** malingerer…shirk   **c.** circumvention…eschew

Maybe I'll Do It Tomorrow...

Even the most successful students sometimes put off doing homework until the last minute. Avoiding an unpleasant assignment every once in a while probably won't have long-term consequences. But procrastination can quickly become a very bad habit. **(1)** When you *shirk* school work too often, the negative effects on your academic record and your overall health can be serious.

(2) A study of 374 college freshman found that students who *shun* their textbooks until the last minute often get sick. Around exam time, procrastinators reported more colds, flu symptoms, and digestive problems than their more disciplined schoolmates did. **(3)** Part of the reason for these health effects may be that keeping tasks in *abeyance* induces stress, which can result in a loss of sleep and a lower resistance to germs. Chronic procrastination has also been found to cause low self-esteem and depression.

So, are those students who do their work promptly more intelligent or more capable than those who delay? The answer  is no. Psychologists do believe, however, that chronic procrastinators share several personality traits, including anxiety about performance, low self-control, and a tendency toward thrill-seeking. Some procrastinators may worry that they are incapable of the task and avoid it because they fear that it will prove their inadequacy. Subconsciously, they may put off the task so that they can blame their poor performance on a lack of time, not a lack of skill. Other procrastinators believe that the last-minute "rush" to get something done actually improves their performance. **(4)** They convince themselves that their best work will *elude* them if they take a more organized approach to their tasks. However, studies comparing the performance of students who procrastinate with that of nonprocrastinators have shown that procrastinators typically produce inferior work.

Students are not the only ones who avoid tasks. One study showed that 25 to 35 percent of adults procrastinate, as well. **(5)** The ways people *circumvent* their duties at work are numerous. **(6)** *Malingerers*, of course, simply call in sick. Other procrastinators are easily distracted. Computers in the office are one tempting source of diversion. **(7)** One researcher determined that 47 percent of the time office workers spent using computers was taken up with *evading* work. Employees checked e-mail, surfed the Internet, played video games, and did anything but what they were supposed to be doing.

Advice abounds on how to overcome the "I'll-do-it-tomorrow" attitude. One method is to overestimate how much time you will need to complete your task. Take your best guess at how much time you think is required, then double it to be safe. **(8)** That way, you will not find yourself offering *oblique* excuses when your teacher or boss asks to see your work.

Another pitfall is that many people assume that they will be more eager to tackle their task later, when they are in the right mood. Rarely does this "right mood" present itself. Experts suggest that you begin assignments early, regardless of your mood. Making a to-do list may help motivate you to get started. **(9)** In addition, try adopting an *abstemious* attitude while working on the task, holding out the promise of rewarding yourself after your work is done. **(10)** Knowing that pleasures await you when you're done makes it easier to *eschew* them while you work.

And, of course, experts recommend trying to stop procrastinating today, rather than waiting until tomorrow.

Each sentence below refers to a numbered sentence in the passage. Write the letter of the choice that gives the sentence a meaning that is closest to the original sentence.

___a___ **1.** When you _____ school work too often, the negative effects can be serious.
   a. neglect   **b.** complete   **c.** rush   **d.** suspend

___b___ **2.** Students who _____ their textbooks until the last minute often get sick.
   a. sit at   **b.** stay away from   **c.** morally oppose   **d.** closely study

___a___ **3.** Keeping tasks in _____ induces stress, which can result in a loss of sleep.
   a. lists   **b.** control   **c.** confusion   **d.** suspension

_b_   4. They convince themselves that their best work will _____.
    a. trick them   **b.** escape their grasp   **c.** fortify them   **d.** be set aside

_a_   5. The ways people _____ their duties at work are numerous.
    a. get around   **b.** willfully ignore   **c.** greatly minimize   **d.** think about

_a_   6. _____, of course, simply call in sick.
    a. Hard workers   **b.** Invalids   **c.** Fakers   **d.** Tricksters

_a_   7. Much of the time office workers spent using computers was taken up with _____ work.
    a. moderating   **b.** researching   **c.** completing   **d.** avoiding

_a_   8. That way, you will not find yourself offering _____ excuses when your teacher or boss asks to see your work.
    a. vague   **b.** pretend   **c.** legitimate   **d.** long-winded

_a_   9. Try adopting a(n) _____ attitude while working on your task.
    a. artful   **b.** relaxed   **c.** daring   **d.** moderate

_b_   10. Knowing that pleasures await makes it easier to _____ them while you work.
    a. maneuver   **b.** deliberately avoid   **c.** partake of   **d.** heartily enjoy

Indicate whether the statements below are TRUE or FALSE according to the passage.

_T_   1. Procrastination may lead to health problems.

_F_   2. High levels of stress heighten intelligence and performance.

_T_   3. Allowing enough time to complete tasks improves performance and relieves stress.

WRITING EXTENDED RESPONSES

All of us procrastinate from time to time. In an essay of at least three paragraphs, describe a task that you tend to avoid, why you avoid it, and how you avoid it. You may describe one task in depth, or you may describe several tasks in less detail. Then comment on whether any of the suggestions given in the article might help you complete these tasks more promptly. Use three or more lesson words in your essay and underline them.

WRITE THE DERIVATIVE

Complete the sentence by writing the correct form of the word shown in parentheses. You may not need to change the form that is given.

abeyance   1. Members of the town council agreed to hold the issue in _____ until next month's meeting. *(abeyance)*

abstemious   2. Residents of the remote island lived a very _____ lifestyle. *(abstemious)*

Shunned **3.** In India, people in the lowest caste (or social class) are known as "untouchables" and are sometimes ———— by people in higher castes. *(shun)*

shirks **4.** No one wants to work with someone who ———— responsibilities. *(shirk)*

circumvention **5.** We tipped the cab driver generously for his skillful ———— of the parade. *(circumvent)*

Obliqueness **6.** The leader's press secretary was a master of ————. *(oblique)*

elusive **7.** Many philosophers have said that true happiness in life is ————. *(elude)*

eschew **8.** Many top athletes ———— late-night parties and junk food during their playing seasons. *(eschew)*

evasive **9.** The suspect was ———— when she was asked where she was on the night of the break-in. *(evasion)*

malinger **10.** The ———— wished he had gone to work when he ran into his boss at the amusement park. *(malinger)*

FIND THE EXAMPLE

Choose the answer that best describes the action or situation.

_a_ **1.** The person LEAST likely to be *shunned*
  a. a convict   **b.** a pest   **c.** an enemy   **d.** a friend

_b_ **2.** What someone who is on an *abstemious* diet might eat for lunch
  a. two hamburgers   **b.** a celery stalk   **c.** a deep-dish pizza   **d.** a cheesecake

_a_ **3.** Something that you would try to *circumvent*
  a. a car accident   **b.** a friend's party   **c.** winning an award   **d.** meeting a celebrity

_c_ **4.** An *oblique* answer to a question
  a. Of course.   **b.** No way!   **c.** We'll see.   **d.** Absolutely.

_a_ **5.** A characteristic of a *malingerer*
  a. laziness   **b.** devotion   **c.** diligence   **d.** infirmity

_c_ **6.** A profession that requires *evasion*
  a. physician   **b.** graphic designer   **c.** spy   **d.** zookeeper

_b_ **7.** The reason a building project might be held in *abeyance*
  a. lack of housing   **b.** lack of funding   **c.** lack of red tape   **d.** lack of good food

_d_ **8.** Something that a vegetarian would *eschew*
  a. chewing gum   **b.** Brussels sprouts   **c.** black coffee   **d.** Cornish hen

_b_ **9.** Something that a person would most likely try to *shirk*
  a. playing a game   **b.** doing chores   **c.** going to a movie   **d.** spending money

_a_ **10.** Someone who would try to *elude* the police
  a. fugitive   **b.** lifeguard   **c.** scientist   **d.** private investigator

Order and Relationship

WORD LIST

converge	crux	degradation	initiate	penultimate
pivotal	sequel	supersede	tangential	terminate

In biology we study the way that the internal systems of plants and animals are ordered and how they function in relation to one another. In astronomy we learn the arrangements of stars and planets. In manufacturing we systematically design and arrange parts of a car, a washing machine, or a computer. The words in this lesson will help you better understand the orderly arrangements all around us.

1. **converge** (kən-vûrj´) *verb* from Latin *con-*, "together" + *vergere*, "to incline"
   To come together at the same point from different directions; to meet
   • Many national and regional highways **converge** in Indianapolis, making it a major trucking center.

   convergence *noun* Technological **convergence** is decreasing the distinctions between the computer, telephone, and television.

2. **crux** (krŭks) *noun* from Latin *crux*, "cross"
   The main, central, or critical point or feature
   • The **crux** of the mayor's image problem is that he has made many misleading statements to the public.

   crucial *adjective* Water is **crucial** to sustaining life.

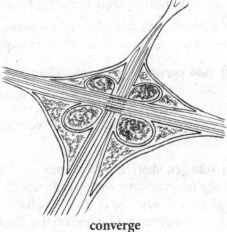

converge

3. **degradation** (dĕg´rə-dā´shən) *noun* from Latin *de-*, "reduce" + *gradus*, "step"
   A decline to a lower condition, quality, or level
   • A huge increase in construction in the area caused the **degradation** of many wildlife habitats.

   degrade *verb* While the new department store offers convenient shopping, many people feel that it **degrades** the historic downtown area.

4. **initiate** (ĭ-nĭsh´ē-āt´) *verb* from Latin *initium*, "beginning"
   a. To take the first steps in a process; to begin something
   • The city **initiated** a recycling program that used specially marked containers as recycling bins.
   b. To formally admit someone into an organization through a ritual
   • Three college students were **initiated** into the Phi Beta Kappa Society.

   initiation *noun* Peggy's **initiation** into the working world at the age of ten consisted of answering phones at her father's office.

5. **penultimate** (pĭ-nŭl´tə-mĭt) *adjective* from Latin *paene,* "almost" + *ultimus,* "last"
Second from the last; next to last
- In the word *information,* the **penultimate** syllable is stressed.

6. **pivotal** (pĭv´ə-tl) *adjective* from French *pivot,* "axis or shaft"
Being of vital importance; crucial
- The new coach was **pivotal** to the team's rise to championship status.

   pivot *noun* A short rod or shaft on which a related part rotates or swings
   - The gears were all connected and turned on a central **pivot.**

   pivot *verb* To turn as if on a pivot
   - Angry that his brother would not apologize, Mickey **pivoted** on his heels and left the room.

7. **sequel** (sē´kwəl) *noun* from Latin *sequi,* "to follow"
A continuation; something that follows; the next installment of something
- After Becky read the first mystery, she could hardly wait to buy the **sequel.**

   sequence *noun* We heard a **sequence** of bird calls from the orchard.

   sequential *adjective* Erik could only take one engineering course each term because he was required to take them in **sequential** order.

8. **supersede** (soō´pər-sēd´) *verb* from Latin *super-,* "over; above" + *sedere,* "to sit"
To replace; to take the place of
- This most recent instruction sheet **supersedes** all those that were distributed earlier.

9. **tangential** (tăn-jĕn´shəl) *adjective* from Latin *tangens,* "touching"
   a. Superficially relevant; only slightly connected
   - Although your description of the eating habits of ancient Egyptians is interesting, it is **tangential** to the assigned topic of writing development in Egypt.
   b. Merely touching; only slightly connected
   - When Farrah examined the diagram more closely, she realized that the lines were **tangential** but did not cross.

   tangent *noun* The chemistry professor's **tangent** about politics was interesting but had no clear connection to the rest of the lecture.

10. **terminate** (tûr´mə-nāt´) *verb* from Latin *terminus,* "end"
To bring to an end or halt
- The new highway will **terminate** at the entrance to the airport.

   termination *noun* To avoid any possible **termination** of his driving privileges, Frank was careful to abide by all driving and parking regulations.

   terminal *adjective* Causing death
   - Early detection and an effective course of treatment can prevent many cancers from becoming **terminal.**

One meaning of the word *ultimate* is "the last."

Supersede implies the replacement of something out-of-date or old-fashioned.

Terminal can also be used as a noun meaning an ending place; a transportation station; or a computer monitor and keyboard.

WRITE THE CORRECT WORD

Write the correct word in the space next to each definition. Use each word only once.

terminate	**1.** to end	_tangential_	**6.** slightly connected
Crux	**2.** the critical point	_degradation_	**7.** a decline
Supersede	**3.** to replace	_Converge_	**8.** to come together
Pivotal	**4.** of vital importance	_initiate_	**9.** to begin
Penultimate	**5.** next to last	_sequel_	**10.** next in a series

COMPLETE THE SENTENCE

Write the letter for the word that best completes each sentence.

d **1.** The industrial strength of the North was _____ in its winning the U.S. Civil War.
  a. superseded   **b.** penultimate   **c.** sequential   **d.** pivotal

a **2.** Fans lined up at the theater to see the _____ to the popular movie.
  a. sequel   **b.** crux   **c.** degradation   **d.** initiation

b **3.** In legal matters, the decisions made by the U.S. Supreme Court _____ all lower-court decisions.
  a. initiate   **b.** supersede   **c.** converge   **d.** degrade

c **4.** Her only consolation, after being the _____ runner to cross the finish line, was that she hadn't come in last.
  a. tangential   **b.** crucial   **c.** penultimate   **d.** pivotal

b **5.** After months of stagnation, the arbitrator was finally able to _____ talks between the management and the laborers.
  a. pivot   **b.** initiate   **c.** converge   **d.** pivot

a **6.** Air and water pollution can lead to significant _____ of the environment.
  a. degradation   **b.** initiation   **c.** crux   **d.** convergence

c **7.** I'll meet you where Lincoln and Main streets _____, right by City Hall.
  a. supersede   **b.** initiate   **c.** converge   **d.** degrade

d **8.** The _____ of the club's failure was that it didn't attract enough members.
  a. sequel   **b.** tangent   **c.** degradation   **d.** crux

d **9.** When the boosters on the shuttle malfunctioned, NASA _____ the mission.
  a. converged   **b.** initiated   **c.** superseded   **d.** terminated

b **10.** Although interesting, your discussion on waste disposal is _____ to our concerns about parking regulations.
  a. penultimate   **b.** tangential   **c.** terminated   **d.** degrading

Challenge: Carmen wasn't sure at which _____ she should get off the train, the _____ stop or the last one.
c   **a.** pivot…tangential   **b.** sequel…initiated   **c.** terminal…penultimate

Driving Green

When Rachel Burton needs to fill up her car's gas tank, she heads to the nearest restaurant. That's because Burton's car runs on cooking oil.

(1) You might think that pouring French-fry grease into a car would be the *penultimate* act before hauling it to the junkyard, but most diesel-engine cars actually run quite well on vegetable oil. The cooking oil, which would otherwise be thrown away, just needs to be mixed with a thinner fuel. Better yet, cars that are partially fueled with cooking oil produce far less pollution than gas-burning or diesel-only cars.

There is one problem, though; the exhaust smells like whatever was cooked in the oil. When Burton drives by, onlookers get a whiff of foods like donuts, egg rolls, and chicken patties.

(2) When she isn't driving, Burton spends time *initiating* discussions on better ways to power cars. By 2020, there will likely be about one billion vehicles on the world's roads. **(3)** Most scientists agree that the amount of pollution that this many vehicles would produce could seriously *degrade* the environment.

(4) Thus, scientists and engineers are trying to develop cleaner-burning technologies to *supersede* current automobile fuels and engines. **(5)** Opinions *converge* on the need for change, but there are many competing ideas as to what may be the best solution.

(6) One *pivotal* issue in the debate is whether to simply improve gas mileage (and thus reduce pollution) or to switch to entirely new fuels. Hybrid cars conserve gasoline by using both an electric motor and a gas-burning engine. The battery charges while the car is being driven, enabling the car to switch between electric and gas power. This saves a considerable amount of gas.

(7) But some people say that hybrid cars ignore the *crux* of the issue. Fossil fuels, like gasoline, are in limited supply. **(8)** Many people therefore believe that the only long-term solution is to find new fuels so we can *terminate* our dependence on, and overuse of, gasoline.

People like Burton believe that plant-based fuels—such as fuel made from corn or soybean oil—are worth pursuing. At many gas stations in Europe, where gas prices are much higher than in the United States, drivers can already buy so-called biodiesel, a fuel made partially from plants.

(9) But some critics say that biodiesel is merely a *tangential* effort in the search for new fuel technologies. To these critics, cars that run on hydrogen-fuel packs provide the most hope for the future. Hydrogen cars would emit only water and steam as exhaust. This complicated and expensive technology still faces some major hurdles, including finding a cost-efficient way to manufacture pure hydrogen. **(10)** So only time will tell what the *sequel* to our gas-guzzling car days will be.

For now, Burton and others like her will continue to stop at local diners to fill up their cars with cooking oil, in order to keep gas consumption down and produce less pollution.

Each sentence below refers to a numbered sentence in the passage. Write the letter of the choice that gives the sentence a meaning that is closest to the original sentence.

_____ **1.** You might think that pouring French-fry grease into a car would be the _____ act before hauling it to the junkyard.
   a. final   **b.** replacement   **c.** exasperating   **d.** next-to-last

_____ **2.** Burton spends time _____ discussions on better ways to power cars.
   a. replacing   **b.** explaining   **c.** beginning   **d.** continuing

_____ **3.** The amount of pollution that this many vehicles would produce could seriously _____ the environment.
   a. bring together   **b.** lower the quality of   **c.** bring to an end   **d.** improve

a **4.** Scientists and engineers are trying to develop cleaner-burning technologies to _____ current automobile fuels and engines.
   a. replace   **b.** improve   **c.** reduce   **d.** originate

c **5.** Opinions _____ on the need for change.
   a. abound   **b.** disagree   **c.** come together   **d.** differ greatly

d **6.** One _____ issue in the debate is whether to simply improve gas mileage or to switch to entirely new fuels.
   a. perplexing   **b.** next to last   **c.** emerging   **d.** important

b **7.** But some people say that hybrid cars ignore the _____ of the issue.
   a. support   **b.** main point   **c.** beginning   **d.** drawbacks

a **8.** Many people therefore believe that the only long-term solution is to find new fuels so we can _____ our dependence on, and overuse of, gasoline.
   a. end   **b.** speed up   **c.** turn   **d.** merge

b **9.** But some critics say that biodiesel is merely a _____ effort in the search for new fuel technologies.
   a. major   **b.** half-hearted   **c.** next-to-last   **d.** not very relevant

a **10.** So only time will tell what the _____ to our gas-guzzling car days will be.
   a. next installment   **b.** important moral   **c.** true story   **d.** second-to-last ending

Indicate whether the statements below are TRUE or FALSE according to the passage.

F **1.** In Europe, vegetable oil is superseding gasoline for fueling cars.

T **2.** The exhaust from cars powered with cooking oil smells like fried foods.

F **3.** Hydrogen fuel technology has no major challenges.

FINISH THE THOUGHT

Complete each sentence so that it shows the meaning of the italicized word.

1. This matter is *tangential* to our concerns because ___it's irrelevant to the task at hand___

2. The *crux* of the issue is ___that college is too expensive___

WRITE THE DERIVATIVE

Complete the sentence by writing the correct form of the word shown in parentheses. You may not need to change the form that is given.

___Converging___ **1.** The _____ of two highways caused traffic congestion. (*converge*)

___pivoted___ **2.** Justine _____ away from the player who was trying to steal the ball. (*pivotal*)

Penultimate **3.** The bandleader asked the orchestra to examine the _____ measure of the music. (*penultimate*)

initiative **4.** The club held an elaborate _____ ceremony for its new members. (*initiate*)

termination **5.** At the _____ of the difficult project, the boss rewarded his hard-working employees by giving each of them a day off. (*terminate*)

sequels **6.** When a movie is successful, filmmakers are often eager to produce several _____ . (*sequel*)

crucial **7.** When hiking in the desert, it is _____ that you bring plenty of water so that you don't become dehydrated. (*crux*)

degrade **8.** Too many special effects can _____ the quality of a Broadway show. (*degradation*)

supersedes **9.** Bad things may happen when greed _____ common sense. (*supersede*)

tangents **10.** The advisor urged the candidate to avoid _____ and focus on his message. (*tangential*)

FIND THE EXAMPLE

Choose the answer that best describes the action or situation.

_a_ **1.** The way to *terminate* a phone call
  a. hang up   **b.** dial the number   **c.** call back later   **d.** say "Hello"

_b_ **2.** Something that would most likely be found where two roads *converge*
  a. a park   **b.** a stop sign   **c.** a quiet beach   **d.** a dairy cow

_d_ **3.** The *penultimate* day of the year
  a. Jan. 1   **b.** Dec. 30   **c.** Sept. 21   **d.** Dec. 31

_c_ **4.** A product that has *superseded* audiocassettes
  a. television   **b.** radio   **c.** CDs   **d.** speakers

_d_ **5.** Something that you cannot *initiate*
  a. music lessons   **b.** friendships   **c.** conversation   **d.** a sunset

_a_ **6.** The *crux* of most traffic jams
  a. too many vehicles   **b.** too few vehicles   **c.** too many roads   **d.** too few drivers

      would likely feel if your reputation was *degraded*
  b. embarrassed   **c.** indifferent   **d.** elated

_d_ **8.** Something that is *tangential* to getting good results
  a. proper planning   **b.** working hard   **c.** paying attention   **d.** drinking tea

_c_ **9.** The most likely title of a *sequel*
  a. Wonderboy   **b.** The New King   **c.** The Journey II   **d.** The Angry Neighbor

_c_ **10.** Something that is probably NOT a *pivotal* factor in most people's choice of career
  a. needs   **b.** abilities   **c.** pets   **d.** interests

Reading and Reasoning

Three Types of Context Clues

The words, sentences, or paragraphs surrounding an unfamiliar word often provide clues to the meaning of that word. These *context clues* can help determine meaning.

Strategies

Three types of context clues are common: **definition clues, opposite clues,** and **substitution clues.**

1. *Look for definition clues.* An author might actually define the word in the text. Several methods may be used.

   - Words or phrases set off by commas, parentheses, or dashes:
     His *sanguine,* cheerfully optimistic, attitude assures that he has a healthy outlook.
     (A *sanguine* attitude is optimistic.)
     This comma construction is often called an *appositive.*

   - The use of *or* or *and:*
     A *florid,* or overly ornate, prose style sometimes makes points less clear.
     (*Florid* is overly ornate.)

   - Defining by a list of examples:
     The suborder *ophidia* includes long reptiles with scales and without arms or legs; animals in this suborder can be poisonous.
     (Since these are all characteristics of snakes, *ophidia* refers to snakes.)

   - Definition by inclusion in a list of examples:
     Options include a nurse, a physician, an accountant, and an *LMSW.*
     (Since the other items refer to occupations, it is reasonable to assume that an LMSW does as well, and in fact, it is a Licensed Medical Social Worker.)

2. *Look for opposite clues.* Sometimes an author defines a word by giving its opposite.

   - The use of *not* or *no:*
     Although many omens indicated that the time of the journey was not *propitious,* the ancient Romans set out on the trip anyway.
     (*Propitious* means favorable.)

   - Words, phrases, or prefixes signaling opposites, such as *but, nevertheless, despite, rather than, unless, despite, although, in spite of, regardless, in-, non-,* and *un-:*
     Although I found the meal *execrable,* I ate it just to be polite.
     (*Execrable* means hateful; very inferior.)
     Morissa seemed unfriendly, but her sister was most *congenial.*
     (*Congenial* means friendly.)

   - Words with negative senses, such as *barely, only, never, hardly,* and *merely:*
     I could barely breathe because of the *noisome* odor.
     (*Noisome* means disgusting, and often harmful.)

3. *Try substituting simpler words.* The meanings of some unfamiliar words can be determined by substituting simpler words in the sentence to see if they make sense.
     As the U.S. population tends to overeat and consume lots of junk food, *corpulence* has become a concern.
     (*Corpulence* means the state of being overweight.)

Practice

Read each sentence to determine the meaning of the italicized word. Write the meaning you obtain from the context clues. Then look up the word in the dictionary and write the most suitable formal definition.

1. After one sailor *fomented* discontent, the others started to talk of mutiny.

   My definition _____

   Dictionary definition _____

2. Though the times may have seemed *halcyon* to the casual observer, World War I was looming on the horizon.

   My definition _____

   Dictionary definition _____

3. He had lost his homework, missed his bus, and was walking to school in the rain when Henry realized he had reached the *nadir* of his day.

   My definition _____

   Dictionary definition _____

4. Where lies the final harbor, whence we *unmoor* no more? (from Herman Melville's *Moby Dick*)

   My definition _____

   Dictionary definition _____

5. The young are *prodigal* of life from the superabundance of it. (from William Hazlitt's *The Feeling of Immortality in Youth*)

   My definition _____

   Dictionary definition _____

6. The *parsimonious* millionaire lived in a broken-down home, wore ragged clothes, and never went on vacations.

   My definition _____

   Dictionary definition _____

7. What began as a minor disagreement has become a *protracted* argument lasting several years.

   My definition _____

   Dictionary definition _____

8. The *panegyric*, a praising composition or speech, was once an important social custom.

   My definition _____

   Dictionary definition _____

Criticism

WORD LIST

aspersions	compunction	derision	disapprobation	ostracize
rebuke	revulsion	scurrilous	spurn	vitriolic

First Lady Eleanor Roosevelt said, "Do what you feel in your heart to be right, for you'll be criticized anyway." Criticism can be spiteful or constructive. For better or worse, criticism is part of life. The words in this lesson deal with this common but often difficult facet of human interaction.

1. **aspersions** (ə-spûr´zhəns) *noun, plural* from Latin *ad-*, "at; toward" + *spargere*, "to strew"
Attacks on a person's character or honesty; damaging or unfavorable remarks
   • The magazine article cast **aspersions** on the senator's integrity.

2. **compunction** (kəm-pŭngk´shən) *noun* from Latin *com-*, "together" + *pungere*, "to prick"
A strong uneasiness caused by a sense of guilt; a sting of conscience or pang of guilt
   • The thief had few **compunctions** about lying to his partners.

3. **derision** (dĭ-rĭzh´ən) *noun* from Latin *de-*, "completely" + *ridere*, "to laugh at"
Hateful or mocking laughter; ridicule
   • Truly original thinkers may face **derision** from those who fear new ideas.

   deride *verb* Celebrities may go from being adored one moment to being **derided** the next.

   derisive *adjective* The speaker's **derisive** tone toward his audience turned the crowd against him, and loud boos soon filled the hall.

4. **disapprobation** (dĭs-ăp´rə-bā´shən) *noun* from Latin *dis-*, "not" + *ab-*, "to" + *probare*, "to test"
Moral disapproval
   • Public **disapprobation** of the candidate's role in the scandal forced her out of the congressional race.

5. **ostracize** (ŏs´trə-sīz´) *verb* from Greek *ostrakon*, "shell; potsherd"
To banish or exclude from a group; to shun
   • The man was **ostracized** by fellow club members for discussing their secret rituals with nonmembers.

   ostracism *noun* "Whistleblowers" who expose their company's wrongdoings often risk **ostracism**.

> *Cast aspersions* and *have no compunctions* are common phrases. Both are commonly used in plural forms.

> The ancient Greeks used potsherds (also called potshards), or pottery fragments, as ballots when voting for someone's *ostracism*.

6. **rebuke** (rĭ-byōōk´) from Latin *re-*, "back" + Old French *buker*,
   "to strike or chop wood"
   a. *verb* To criticize sharply
   • The lifeguard **rebuked** the swimmers for going beyond the safety
   markers.
   b. *noun* Strong criticism
   • After the robbery, security officials faced **rebukes** for their
   inadequate protection of the bank.

7. **revulsion** (rĭ-vŭl´shən) *noun* from Latin *re-*, "back" + *vellere*,
   "to tear"
   A sudden, intense feeling of disgust
   • The sight of the rotting food filled me with **revulsion.**

8. **scurrilous** (skûr´ə-ləs) *adjective* from Latin *scurra*, "buffoon"
   Vulgar, coarse, or abusive in expression; foul-mouthed
   • The presidential campaign of 1800 featured **scurrilous** attacks
   describing both Jefferson and Adams as liars and traitors.

9. **spurn** (spûrn) *verb* from Old English *spurnan*, "to kick;
   to strike against"
   To reject scornfully
   • Determined to prove her strength, Keisha **spurned** offers of help and
   carried the heavy box herself.

10. **vitriolic** (vĭt´rē-ŏl´ĭk) *adjective* from Latin *vitreolus*, "of glass"
    Intensely and bitterly harsh; stinging
    • Hal was unprepared for the **vitriolic** criticism he received after
    mumbling his lines in the play.

    vitriol *noun* **Vitriol** permeated the atmosphere in the room as the
    bitter enemies launched their verbal, personal attacks.

rebuke

> *Vitriol* is also another word
> for sulfuric acid, a highly
> corrosive chemical.

WORD ENRICHMENT

Ostracism in ancient Athens

In ancient Athens, the world's first large democracy, people who were
considered power-hungry or otherwise dangerous to the state were literally
"voted out of town."

In midwinter, the Assembly (all male citizens) held a conference to
decide whether to hold an *ostracism* vote. If they decided to do so, votes
were cast by scratching a name on a pottery shard (*ostrakon* in Greek). The
shards were divided into piles. The person named in the largest pile had to
leave the city within ten days and stay away for ten years. The system was
certainly not perfect, however. People were sometimes *ostracized* out of
jealousy or for other personal, rather than political, motives.

WRITE THE CORRECT WORD

Write the correct word in the space next to each definition. Use each word only once.

revulsion **1.** intense disgust

derision **2.** ridicule

compunction **3.** unease due to guilt

rebuke **4.** to criticize sharply

aspersions **5.** damaging or unfavorable remarks

scurrilous **6.** vulgar; abusive

disapprobation **7.** moral disapproval

spurn **8.** to reject scornfully

vitriolic **9.** very harsh; bitter

ostracize **10.** to banish, exclude, or shun

COMPLETE THE SENTENCE

Write the letter for the word that best completes each sentence.

_b_ **1.** Laughing *with* someone is friendship; laughing *at* someone is _____.
a. compunction **b.** revulsion **c.** derision **d.** ostracism

_b_ **2.** There was no need to be so _____ in your written comments, sir; the huge red F on my paper communicated your feelings quite clearly.
a. rebuked **b.** vitriolic **c.** ostracized **d.** spurned

_d_ **3.** If a shopper with a full cart is in the express line, I have no _____ about saying, "Your actions are unfair to the rest of us."
a. aspersions **b.** derision **c.** ostracism **d.** compunction

_a_ **4.** If you no longer want to be part of the group, _____ isn't much of a punishment.
a. ostracism **b.** compunction **c.** vitriol **d.** aspersion

_b_ **5.** In order to stay calm and win the argument, Manny ignored Jessie's subtle _____.
a. compunction **b.** aspersions **c.** ostracism **d.** vitriol

_c_ **6.** She _____ the offer with a snort, then added, "I don't take charity, thank you."
a. aspersions **b.** ostracized **c.** spurned **d.** rebuked

_d_ **7.** She looked at the congealed blob on her plate with _____.
a. aspersions **b.** ostracism **c.** rebuke **d.** revulsion

_a_ **8.** Some people believe that the fear of public _____ may actually affect behavior more than the law does.
a. disapprobation **b.** aspersion **c.** spurn **d.** compunction

_d_ **9.** Normally quite polite, he let loose a(n) _____ string of foul comments.
a. rebuked **b.** spurned **c.** ostracized **d.** scurrilous

_b_ **10.** A stern _____ now might keep a child out of trouble later.
a. vitriol **b.** rebuke **c.** revulsion **d.** derision

Challenge: Sherri had no _____ about casting aspersions on her coworkers, until she realized that she had been completely _____ by everyone in the office.

_c_ **a.** disapprobation…scurrilous **b.** ostracism…rebuked **c.** compunctions…ostracized

Infected by Cruelty

Imagine that you are ill and that your family abandons you instead of helping you. Your neighbors cringe and shy away at the sight of you. Your peers run you out of school or even out of town. This might sound like a nightmare, but for thousands of years, this type of treatment was typical for victims of the disease called leprosy.

If the illness is not treated, then people infected with leprosy, or "lepers," become covered with open sores and can also be disfigured in other ways. Leprosy can lead to paralysis, loss of limbs, and blindness. People who contracted the disease before the 1940s had no hope for a cure, and even today, people in remote or very poor areas face a similar predicament.

(1) Sadly, out of *revulsion* and fear, people have treated lepers cruelly. **(2)** Another factor behind this maltreatment was a general *disapprobation,* as leprosy was once believed to be a punishment for some terrible sin. **(3)** Lepers were purposefully *ostracized* from general society. Most were sent to live in closed-off communities called leper colonies. Often, these were neglected, remote institutions where the sick struggled to survive with little help. **(4)** Those who ventured out were subject to *scurrilous* verbal attacks for supposedly trying to spread the disease.

(5) With so many factors working against lepers, few people had *compunctions* about abusing them. But finally, modern science shone a light on the situation. In 1873, it was discovered that leprosy was caused not by "sin," but by bacteria.

Treatments for leprosy were developed between the 1940s and the 1970s, curing more than 13 million people. Today, doctors use even more effective medicines to treat the disease. However, leprosy—now called Hansen's disease—still exists. About 500,000 people contract it each year, with most of the cases occurring in Southeast Asia. There are about 100 cases in the United States annually.

Despite myths about lepers trying to spread their disease by venturing into the streets, leprosy is not very contagious. In fact, most people are immune to it. Those who do catch leprosy usually do so only through close, long-term contact with an infected person. And once people are cured, they can no longer spread the disease. **(6)** So casting *aspersions* on lepers who try to live among general society is not only unfair, it is a sign of ignorance.

Unfortunately, old beliefs are sometimes difficult to dispel. **(7)** Lepers in some communities are still exposed to *vitriolic* criticism, so they frequently hide their disease for as long as they can. As a result, they often seek treatment too late to prevent scars and the loss of limbs. These outward signs of leprosy have many effects on the victims, even after they are cured. **(8)** Unable to get jobs, many are forced to beg in the streets, where strangers *deride* them. **(9)** Passersby often *spurn* their desperate pleas for spare change.

Governments and volunteers are trying to help the afflicted by providing much-needed medicine. **(10)** Just as important, aid workers offer kind words and support rather than *rebukes.* Such acts of compassion are long overdue to the victims of leprosy.

Each sentence below refers to a numbered sentence in the passage. Write the letter of the choice that gives the sentence a meaning that is closest to the original sentence.

_____ **1.** Sadly, out of _____ and fear, people have treated lepers cruelly for years.
    a. ridicule   **b.** rejection   **c.** disgust   **d.** ignorance

_____ **2.** Another factor behind this maltreatment was a general _____.
    a. ugly vulgarity   **b.** unfair rejection   **c.** vicious bitterness   **d.** moral disapproval

_____ **3.** Lepers were purposefully _____ general society.
    a. banished from   **b.** ridiculed in   **c.** disgusted with   **d.** criticized with

_____ **4.** Those who ventured out were subject to _____ verbal attacks.
    a. mocking, but kind   **b.** immoral, yet fun   **c.** bitter and subtle   **d.** abusive and vulgar

44 Criticism

b   **5.** With so many factors working against lepers, few people had _____ about abusing them.
     a. harsh criticisms   **b.** guilty feelings   **c.** good reasons   **d.** harsh rejections

c   **6.** Casting _____ on lepers who try to live among general society is not only unfair, it is a sign of ignorance.
     a. compassion   **b.** disgust   **c.** insults   **d.** banishments

c   **7.** Lepers in some communities are still exposed to _____ criticism.
     a. vulgar, foul   **b.** guilty, reluctant   **c.** harsh, vicious   **d.** immoral, sinful

b   **8.** Many are forced to beg in the streets, where strangers _____ them.
     a. banish   **b.** ridicule   **c.** rob   **d.** feed

a   **9.** Passersby often _____ their desperate pleas for spare change.
     a. reject   **b.** criticize   **c.** feel   **d.** banish

d   **10.** Aid workers offer kind words and support rather than _____.
     a. foul obscenities   **b.** jail sentences   **c.** mocking laughter   **d.** sharp criticisms

Indicate whether the statements below are TRUE or FALSE according to the passage.

F   **1.** Leprosy is a highly contagious disease.

T   **2.** Leprosy is now called Hansen's disease.

F   **3.** There is no cure for leprosy.

WRITING EXTENDED RESPONSES

Victims of leprosy were once bitterly scorned and shunned. Choose a disease, condition, or action that brings negative responses from people today. In an expository essay, identify the subject you have chosen, explain why you think it evokes negative responses, and describe some of those responses. Your essay should be at least three paragraphs long. Use a minimum of three lesson words in your essay and underline them.

WRITE THE DERIVATIVE

Complete the sentence by writing the correct form of the word shown in parentheses. You may not need to change the form that is given.

Scurrilous   **1.** If you feel the need to rely on _____ language to make your point, find more suitable words in a thesaurus. *(scurrilous)*

Ostracism   **2.** She warned her friend that certain kinds of behavior could result in _____ from the club. *(ostracize)*

vitriol   **3.** The critic's contempt for the film came through in the _____ of his review. *(vitriolic)*

aspersions   **4.** Don't cast ———— on others when you are partly to blame. (*aspersions*)

rebukes   **5.** Sometimes bosses are expected to deliver ————. (*rebuke*)

disapprobation   **6.** "Governor, think of the public ———— that would result if you were caught taking illegal campaign contributions!" (*disapprobation*)

derisive   **7.** Pete's ———— laughter turned to silence when the older man scored a smooth reverse layup. (*derision*)

spurned   **8.** So far, she has ———— my efforts to win her affection. (*spurn*)

revulsions   **9.** Although some scenes will trigger ————, many of the most disturbing ones were cut from this version of the movie. (*revulsion*)

compunctions   **10.** Amoral people have few ———— about wrongdoing. (*compunctions*)

FIND THE EXAMPLE

Choose the answer that best describes the action or situation.

_d_ **1.** Something that a person who has been *ostracized* from a village would need to find
   a. new clothes   **b.** new car to drive   **c.** new enemies   **d.** new place to live

_a_ **2.** An act that would bring *disapprobation*
   a. stealing pets   **b.** helping friends   **c.** staying home   **d.** going to college

_d_ **3.** An expression of *derision*
   a. Please help me.   **b.** I'm hungry.   **c.** Nice play.   **d.** Ha ha, you fool.

_b_ **4.** Something most people have *compunctions* about
   a. buying groceries   **b.** cheating on tests   **c.** making new friends   **d.** studying for tests

_c_ **5.** An example of casting *aspersions*
   a. He's funny.   **b.** He's fast.   **c.** He's a fraud.   **d.** He's a friend.

_a_ **6.** The thing most likely to be *vitriolic*
   a. political debate   **b.** wedding vows   **c.** birthday card   **d.** love poem

_b_ **7.** How you would probably feel after being *spurned*
   a. relaxed and sleepy   **b.** hurt and angry   **c.** happy and excited   **d.** strong and quick

_d_ **8.** Symbols that are sometimes used in place of *scurrilous* language in comic strips
   a. HOO R U?   **b.** 7 × 9 = 63   **c.** A through Z   **d.** #@$%*&!

_c_ **9.** Creatures that are most likely to cause *revulsion* in humans
   a. goldfish   **b.** puppies   **c.** cockroaches   **d.** elephants

_c_ **10.** A rebuke
   a. Perfect!   **b.** Let's ski.   **c.** That was awful.   **d.** I travel.

Responsibility and Irresponsibility

WORD LIST

accountable	assiduous	default	feckless	incumbent
liability	mandatory	negligence	onerous	remiss

Responsibility is probably something you've heard a lot about. It is normal for people to take on more and more responsibility as they grow older. The words in this lesson will help you understand and describe various aspects of responsibility and irresponsibility.

1. **accountable** (ə-koun´tə-bəl) *adjective* from Latin *ad-*, "toward; to" + *computare*, "to sum up"
   a. Responsible; required to answer for one's actions
      • On field trips, teachers are usually held **accountable** for the safety and behavior of their students.
   b. Explainable
      • Shooting stars are an **accountable** phenomenon.

   account *verb* How can we **account** for the six missing chocolate bars?

   > "To hold *accountable*" is a common phrase.

2. **assiduous** (ə-sĭj´o͞o-əs) *adjective* from Latin *assidere*, "to attend to"
   Giving constant attention; hard-working; conscientious
   • Long hours of **assiduous** study are required to master the many characters used in Chinese writing.

   assiduity or **assiduousness** *noun* It takes a great deal of **assiduousness** to become an engineer.

assiduous

3. **default** (dĭ-fôlt´) from Old French *defaillir*, "to fail; to grow weak"
   a. *noun* A situation that remains in effect unless specifically set in some other way
      • The **defaults** on my word-processing program include one-inch margin settings.
   b. *noun* Failure to complete a task or meet an obligation
      • Because he's your business partner, his **default** is your responsibility.
   c. *verb* To fail to meet an obligation
      • People who **default** on numerous mortgage payments risk losing their homes.

4. feckless (fĕk´lĭs) *adjective* from Scottish *feck,* "effect" + English *-less,* "without; lacking"
  a. Ineffective; feeble; useless
   • The **feckless** referees allowed the game to get out of control.
  b. Careless and irresponsible
   • Because of Jeremy's **feckless** behavior, his unlocked bicycle was stolen from the bike rack.

> *Feckless* is almost always applied to people, not objects.

5. incumbent (ĭn-kŭm´bənt) from Latin *in-,* "on" + *-cumbere,* "to recline"
  a. *adjective* Imposed as a duty or an obligation
   • As the veterinarian's assistant, it was **incumbent** upon Harold to feed and clean up after the dogs and cats.
  b. *adjective* Currently holding an office or a position
   • The **incumbent** governor was responsible for many reforms.
  c. *noun* A person currently holding a position or an office
   • No one wanted to run against the popular **incumbent,** who had a strong track record and legendary debating skills.

> "*Incumbent* on" or "*incumbent* upon" are common phrases.

6. liability (lī´ə-bĭl´ĭ-tē) *noun* from Latin *ligare,* "to bind"
  a. A legal responsibility or obligation
   • An insurance investigator will determine the **liability** of each driver involved in the accident.
  b. Something that holds one back; a handicap
   • People who don't cooperate are a **liability** to the team, no matter how skilled they are.

  liable *adjective* Pamela knew that she was **liable** for the camera she'd borrowed and then lost.

7. mandatory (măn´də-tôr´ē) *adjective* from Latin *mandare,* "to order"
  Required or commanded by authority
   • Military service is **mandatory** in some countries.

  mandate *verb* The school board **mandated** that high-school students take at least one English course every year.

  mandate *noun* The road was closed by an emergency **mandate** because of the expected flood.

8. negligence (nĕg´lĭ-jəns) *noun* from Latin *neglegere,* "to neglect"
  Neglect; lack of proper care or attention
   • Finn's **negligence** in maintaining his car resulted in engine problems and poor resale value.

  negligent *adjective* People who are **negligent** in paying bills risk a poor credit rating.

> *Negligent* and *remiss* are synonyms.

9. onerous (ŏn´ər-əs) *adjective* from Latin *onus,* "burden"
  Difficult to bear, carry, or do; troublesome; burdensome
   • Taking care of such a big house had become an **onerous** responsibility for our grandmother.

10. remiss (rĭ-mĭs´) *adjective* from Latin *remittere,* "to remit; to slacken"
  Lax or careless in attending to duty
   • The situation was dangerous because the landlord was **remiss** in ensuring that there were functioning smoke alarms.

48 **Responsibility and Irresponsibility**

WRITE THE CORRECT WORD

Write the correct word in the space next to each definition. Use each word only once.

Onerous **1.** difficult to bear

Feckless **2.** ineffective; feeble; useless

accountable **3.** responsible

mandatory **4.** required

default **5.** the failure to complete a task

negligence **6.** neglect

assiduous **7.** conscientious

remiss **8.** lax or careless

liability **9.** a legal responsibility

incumbent **10.** holding a position

COMPLETE THE SENTENCE

Write the letter for the word that best completes each sentence.

_a_ **1.** Proof of automobile insurance is _____ to register a car in many states.
a. mandatory **b.** assiduous **c.** feckless **d.** negligent

_c_ **2.** Rick's boat was repossessed after he _____ on the loan payments.
a. accounted **b.** negligence **c.** defaulted **d.** mandated

_d_ **3.** Melanie knew that playing with a sprained ankle would be a(n) _____ to her team.
a. mandate **b.** default **c.** incumbent **d.** liability

_a_ **4.** Forgetting to lock the front door was simply _____.
a. feckless **b.** assiduous **c.** mandatory **d.** onerous

_b_ **5.** Many people consider preparing tax returns to be a(n) _____ task.
a. remiss **b.** onerous **c.** negligent **d.** feckless

_b_ **6.** I was _____ in not thanking the hosts before I left the party.
a. onerous **b.** remiss **c.** incumbent **d.** liable

_d_ **7.** Pet owners are generally held _____ for the actions of their pets.
a. feckless **b.** mandatory **c.** remiss **d.** accountable

_c_ **8.** Raul's _____ attention to detail helped him become a top-notch architect.
a. incumbent **b.** accountable **c.** assiduous **d.** default

_a_ **9.** In an election, a(n) _____ politician may have an advantage over opponents.
a. incumbent **b.** liable **c.** negligent **d.** onerous

_c_ **10.** Sal's failure to look both ways before entering traffic is an example of _____.
a. assiduity **b.** mandate **c.** negligence **d.** accountability

Challenge: Are we not _____ in our ethical duties if we continually and knowingly leave future generations—our own children and grandchildren—with economic, environmental, and national security _____?
_b_ **a.** feckless…assiduity **b.** remiss…liabilities **c.** accountable…mandates

Saving the Books of Basra

Alia Muhammad Baker was the chief librarian in the city of Basra, Iraq. The library she supervised contained more than 30,000 books, including a 700-year-old biography of the prophet Muhammad. But a good library is not made up of books alone. Under Baker's guidance, the Basra library had also become a meeting place for professionals, intellectuals, and artists. **(1)** And, although it had previously been *mandatory* that books remain in the library, she started to loan them out because she wanted to encourage reading. **(2)** She was confident that patrons would not prove *negligent* in returning them.

In 2003, when Iraq was threatened with invasion, she started to fear for the collection. **(3)** As a librarian, she felt it was *incumbent* on her to save the books. **(4)** She asked the governor of Basra, to whom she was *accountable,* for permission to move the books. He refused her request without explanation. **(5)** Feeling that the government was *defaulting* on its duty to protect the region's written heritage, she decided to take action. Every night she would fill her car with books and take them home.

When the war started, her fears increased. **(6)** Baker began to suspect that the Basra government's response to her request was worse than *feckless,* and that the government was deliberately planning to use the books as protection. Government offices were moved into the library, and an antiaircraft gun was placed on its roof. Baker and others surmised that the Iraqi regime was actually trying to ward off attacks by setting up in a place with sacred texts. At the very least, if the library was attacked, the invaders would be blamed for the destruction.

On April 6, invading coalition troops, led by the United States, entered the city of Basra. The Iraqi government quickly abandoned the library, from which valuable carpets and furniture were soon looted.

(7) Baker knew at once that she would be *remiss* if she did not hurry in her attempts to rescue the remainder of the books in the library. Next to the library, on the other side of a wall, was the Hamdam restaurant. She called the owner Anis Muhammad, who agreed to help. "What could I do?" Muhammad said, "It is the whole history of Basra." **(8)** The wall, which had once assured that the library was a quiet refuge, was now, however, a bit of a *liability.* To save the thousands of remaining books, they had to be lifted six feet up, over the wall, and into the restaurant.

Together with employees, relatives, and local shop owners, Muhammad and Baker worked through the night and into the following afternoon. **(9)** Although the work was physically demanding, people did not find it *onerous.* Even helpers who were barely able to read knew that they were rescuing something precious. Nine days later, the library was destroyed by fire.

The valiant efforts of Baker and the others saved more than 70 percent of the library's book collection. The books were soon carried from the restaurant, by truck, to safe storage places, which were, at the time of this writing, in the homes of Baker and her trusted friends.

(10) The stress of these wartime events and all of her *assiduous* efforts brought on health problems for Baker, and she now plans to retire—but only after she has seen her library rebuilt.

Each sentence below refers to a numbered sentence in the passage. Write the letter of the choice that gives the sentence a meaning that is closest to the original sentence.

_____a_____ **1.** And, although it had previously been _____ that books remain in the library, she started to loan them out because she wanted to encourage reading.
    a. required   **b.** troublesome   **c.** diligent   **d.** traditional

_____c_____ **2.** She was confident that patrons would not prove _____ in returning them.
    a. cooperative   **b.** ineffective   **c.** neglectful   **d.** burdensome

_____d_____ **3.** As a librarian, she felt it was _____ to save the books.
    a. her handicap   **b.** her failure   **c.** her burden   **d.** her duty

_C_ **4.** She asked the governor of Basra, to whom she was _____ , for permission.
  a. irresponsible   **b.** burdensome   **c.** responsible   **d.** careless

_d_ **5.** Feeling that the government was _____ its duty, she decided to take action.
  a. required to do   **b.** conscious of   **c.** troublesome with   **d.** failing in

_b_ **6.** Baker began to suspect that the Basra government's response to her request was worse than _____ .
  a. burdensome   **b.** careless   **c.** negative   **d.** duty bound

_a_ **7.** Baker knew at once that she would be _____ if she did not hurry in her attempts.
  a. lax   **b.** handicapped   **c.** in trouble   **d.** burdensome

_C_ **8.** The wall, which had once assured that the library was a quiet refuge, was now, however, a bit of a _____ .
  a. legal problem   **b.** responsibility   **c.** handicap   **d.** harsh requirement

_a_ **9.** Although the work was physically demanding, people did not find it _____ .
  a. burdensome   **b.** responsible   **c.** required   **d.** ineffective

_b_ **10.** The stress of these wartime events and all of her _____ efforts brought on health problems for Baker.
  a. burdensome   **b.** conscientious   **c.** commanded   **d.** lax

Indicate whether the statements below are TRUE or FALSE according to the passage.

_T_ **1.** Baker believed the preservation of the Basra library collection was worth great effort.

_F_ **2.** Baker believed that eventually the government would have saved the collection.

_T_ **3.** Cooperation saved most of the books.

FINISH THE THOUGHT

Complete each sentence so that it shows the meaning of the italicized word.

1. The *feckless* man _____

2. It is *incumbent* upon students _____

WRITE THE DERIVATIVE

Complete the sentence by writing the correct form of the word shown in parentheses. You may not need to change the form that is given.

fecklessly **1.** Audra _____ left for vacation without taking any money. (*feckless*)

liable **2.** The court held the owner _____ for the damage caused by his dog. (*liability*) _default_ **3.** The _____ setting on my cell phone is a simple ring, but I can change it to music. *(default)*

account **4.** Our teacher challenged the class to _____ for the low test scores. *(accountable)*

onerous **5.** Unlike some people, I don't find shoveling snow to be _____ at all; it's great exercise, and an excuse to get outside. *(onerous)*

remiss **6.** Garth apologized for being _____ in responding to the invitation. *(remiss)*

incumbent **7.** The _____ on election ballots generally benefit more from name recognition than the new candidates do. *(incumbent)*

mandate **8.** The _____ of the king cannot be ignored. *(mandatory)*

negligent **9.** The security guard was judged to be _____ for leaving his post before his shift was over. *(negligence)*

assiduity **10.** The _____ required to master a musical instrument is well worth the time and effort. *(assiduous)*

FIND THE EXAMPLE

Choose the answer that best describes the action or situation.

_C_ **1.** A likely result of being *remiss* in your duties at work
    a. achieving success   **b.** getting an award   **c.** getting fired   **d.** getting promoted

_b_ **2.** Something that you would likely be held *accountable* for
    a. your height   **b.** your behavior   **c.** your parents   **d.** your eye color

_d_ **3.** A duty NOT *incumbent* on most parents
    a. feeding children   **b.** housing children   **c.** protecting children   **d.** joking with children

_a_ **4.** An example of a *liability*
    a. injury   **b.** skill   **c.** knack   **d.** strength

_b_ **5.** The way that a *feckless* person would often behave
    a. sensitively   **b.** irresponsibly   **c.** carefully   **d.** effectively

_a_ **6.** Something that is *mandatory*
    a. obeying laws   **b.** eating well   **c.** getting sleep   **d.** saving money

_C_ **7.** How something *onerous* feels
    a. rather easy   **b.** quite humorous   **c.** very difficult   **d.** feather-light

_d_ **8.** A word that describes an *assiduous* person
    a. lazy   **b.** lucky   **c.** irresponsible   **d.** hard-working

_b_ **9.** The *default* language used for most cash machines in the United States
    a. Armenian   **b.** English   **c.** French   **d.** Latin

_a_ **10.** A likely result of *negligence*
    a. punishment   **b.** reward   **c.** popularity   **d.** raise

Willingness and Unwillingness

WORD LIST

acquiesce	adamant	balk	camaraderie	cantankerous
compliance	presumptuous	propitiate	tractable	volition

It is no secret that having a good attitude can make unpleasant tasks less arduous. An ancient proverb states that whatever is borne willingly is borne easily. This lesson deals with the states of willingness and unwillingness.

1. acquiesce (ăk´wē-ĕs´) *verb* from Latin *ad-*, "to" + *quiescere*, "to rest"
To agree or accept passively or without protest
• I was sure that my idea for the science project would work, if only I could convince my partner to **acquiesce** to my plan.

acquiescent *adjective* When it came to following his parents' rules, the teenager was sometimes rebellious and other times **acquiescent.**

acquiescence *noun* With a slight nod of her head, our boss signaled her **acquiescence** to our plans.

2. adamant (ăd´ə-mənt) *adjective* from Latin *adamas*, "diamond; hard steel"
Stubbornly determined; not swayed by pleas, appeals, or reason
• Nicole was **adamant** that her mother drive her to the mall, even though there was a blizzard raging outside.

3. balk (bôk) *verb*
a. To stubbornly or suddenly refuse to do something
   • The teachers **balked** when the administration tried to make them work longer hours for the same salary.
b. To stop short and refuse to go on
   • Just as we entered the riding ring, the horse **balked** when it heard the loud rumble of thunder.

4. camaraderie (kä´mə-rä´də-rē) *noun* from Old French *camarade*, "roommate"
Comradeship; lighthearted good will and friendliness among companions
• Obviously enjoying their **camaraderie**, the musicians laughed, joked, and teased one another on stage.

5. cantankerous (kăn-tăng´kər-əs) *adjective*
Disagreeable; bad-tempered; likely to quarrel
• No matter how quiet we tried to be, our **cantankerous** neighbor always complained that we made too much noise.

> The noun *adamant* means "an extremely hard substance." The adjective *adamantine*, like *adamant*, can mean "inflexible" or "diamondlike."

balk

6. compliance (kəm-plī´əns) *noun* from Latin *complere*, "to complete"
The act of going along with a request, demand, or rule; obedience
- Carefully driving below the speed limit and coming to a full halt at stop signs, Paulo made sure he was in **compliance** with traffic rules.

compliant *adjective* When the principal instituted the new rule, almost everyone was **compliant.**

comply *verb* Arlen was reprimanded after refusing to **comply** with the dress code at work.

7. presumptuous (prĭ-zŭmp´chōo-əs) *adjective* from Latin *pre-*, "before" + *sumere*, "to take"
Excessively bold or forward; going beyond what is proper or right
- I thought it was **presumptuous** of him to give me advice on how to save money when I hadn't asked for it.

presume *verb* She **presumed** that she was the guest of honor, so she sat down at the head of the table.

presumption *noun* The actor was offended by the **presumption** that he couldn't handle the role.

> *Presume* is also used to mean "assume," and *presumption* can be used to mean "assumption."

8. propitiate (prō-pĭsh´ē-āt´) *verb* from Latin *propitius*, "favorable"
To soothe bad feelings; to appease; to regain friendship or good will
- No amount of apologizing could **propitiate** Walter, who was furious at being left in the parking lot while everyone else got a ride home.

propitiatory *adjective* Ancient peoples who believed that suffering was a result of having offended the gods often presented **propitiatory** offerings to regain the favor of the gods.

9. tractable (trăk´tə-bəl) *adjective* from Latin *tractare*, "to manage"
Easily managed or controlled
- The trainer was pleased that the new dog proved **tractable** and quickly learned her commands.

10. volition (və-lĭsh´ən) *noun* from Latin *velle*, "to be willing"
The power of choosing or deciding; free will
- Andrew left the company of his own **volition** because he wanted to attend school full time.

> The phrase *of one's own volition* is common.

WORD ENRICHMENT

As hard as . . . adamant

According to ancient legend, *adamant* was a rock or mineral of surpassing hardness and brilliance, and supposedly impenetrable. The mythical substance was said to have qualities of both a diamond and a lodestone (a mineral with magnetic properties).

As science advanced, people realized that this element did not exist, and *adamant* came to be a synonym for a diamond or other extremely hard substance. (*Adamantine* describes minerals with a shiny, diamondlike luster.) Eventually, *adamant* came to mean *stubborn.*

Although *adamant* is not a real mineral, *adamantine spar* refers to a brown-colored variety of the mineral *corundum.* The best-known varieties of corundum include rubies (red) and sapphires (blue).

WRITE THE CORRECT WORD

Write the correct word in the space next to each definition. Use each word only once.

balk **1.** to stubbornly refuse

tractible **2.** manageable

Compliance **3.** obedience

Presumptuous **4.** excessively bold

adamant **5.** stubbornly determined

Propitiate **6.** to appease

Camaraderie **7.** comradeship

Volition **8.** one's own free will

Cantankerous **9.** disagreeable

acquiesce **10.** to agree without protest

COMPLETE THE SENTENCE

Write the letter for the word that best completes each sentence.

_b_ **1.** You know, Alex, people might enjoy talking with you more if you weren't so _____.
 a. tractable **b.** cantankerous **c.** compliant **d.** acquiescent

_a_ **2.** The company was fined for failing to _____ with health and safety regulations.
 a. comply **b.** balk **c.** presume **d.** propitiate

_c_ **3.** When standing up to pressure to do wrong, it's good to be _____.
 a. acquiescent **b.** tractable **c.** adamant **d.** compliant

_a_ **4.** One negative person can spoil the _____ of the whole team.
 a. camaraderie **b.** volition **c.** presumption **d.** cantankerousness

_c_ **5.** It is _____ to believe that you know exactly what another person is feeling.
 a. compliant **b.** acquiescent **c.** presumptuous **d.** tractable

_c_ **6.** The sheep _____ and refused to enter their pen.
 a. presumed **b.** complied **c.** balked **d.** propitiated

_a_ **7.** Did she do that of her own _____, or was she forced to do it?
 a. volition **b.** camaraderie **c.** acquiescence **d.** presumption

_c_ **8.** You can't always _____ to her demands; sometimes you have to stand up for yourself.
 a. acquiesce **b.** presume **c.** propitiate **d.** balk

_c_ **9.** The complexity of climate change is one reason why it is not a(n) _____ problem.
 a. adamant **b.** cantankerous **c.** tractable **d.** presumptuous

_b_ **10.** People who have been offended can often be _____ by a sincere apology.
 a. presumed **b.** tractable **c.** balked **d.** propitiated

Challenge: To work well in a group, you must walk a fine line between _____ to the ideas of others and _____ putting forth your own ideas.
_b_ **a.** complying…tractably **b.** acquiescing…adamantly **c.** balking…presumptuously

The *Endurance*

On October 26, 1914, twenty-eight men, sixty-nine sled dogs, and one cat, named Mrs. Chippy, set sail from Argentina en route to the South Pole. The name of their ship was the *Endurance*, and the crew's goal was to sail to the Antarctic and make the first crossing of the Antarctic continent on foot. Instead, their journey would become one of the greatest survival stories in modern history.

(1) Conditions were harsh near the South Pole, but the crew did not *balk* at the prospect of a dangerous journey. After stopping at a remote island for supplies, they battled through 1,000 miles of ice-covered water.

Then, on January 18, 1915, when they were just one day's sail from their destination, the ice closed in around them, trapping the *Endurance*. January is midsummer in the Southern Hemisphere. The ship's captain, Ernest Shackleton, knew that the ice would likely not break until early the next summer, some nine months away. The crew would have to endure the long, dark Antarctic winter on the ship.

They had enough food, but would the men remain peaceful? **(2)** While sailing, a good-natured *camaraderie* had developed among them. **(3)** But Shackleton worried that stress would make his crew *cantankerous*, and that minor conflicts could grow into dangerous fights.

(4) As part of his plan to help keep the peace, Shackleton was *adamant* that the men keep to a strict daily routine of work. **(5)** Officers who *presumptuously* thought that they would escape their duties were wrong. **(6)** Every man was treated equally and had to *acquiesce* to the plan. To ensure that the men remained occupied after their work was done, Shackleton insisted on regular entertainment. The men played soccer, raced the dogs, and performed music.

Things went well until October 23, 1915. On that day, the ice shifted and closed in with a terrible force. On October 27, the crew had to abandon the ship and watch helplessly from the ice as the *Endurance* slowly cracked and snapped under the pressure, and finally sank.

There was nothing left to do but trudge to open water. Hauling tents, supplies, and three wooden lifeboats, they began the difficult trek across the ice. **(7)** Most of the crew remained *tractable*. However, the ship's carpenter, McNish, rebelled. Perhaps it was partly from heartbreak: To save food and reduce their load, Shackleton had ordered that the carpenter's cat, Mrs. Chippy, and some of the dogs be shot.

Shackleton knew that any hope of survival depended on keeping the men united. **(8)** Rather than trying to *propitiate* the rebel, Shackleton declared that all crew members must accept the captain's authority. Secretly, he was prepared to shoot the carpenter, if necessary. **(9)** Luckily, McNish *complied* with Shackleton's demand. Later, the carpenter's skills would help save the rest of the crew's lives.

Surviving on penguin and seal meat, and after months of walking, the men finally reached water. Sadly, once there, they had to kill the rest of the dogs because the boats were too small to include them. Then, they traveled by boat for seven days to a deserted, wind-raked island. At that point, Shackleton decided that one boat would sail from there to South Georgia Island—800 bitter cold miles—to find help.

(10) Of his own *volition*, McNish reinforced one of the lifeboats with planks from the other two boats, using seal's blood as glue. Against unimaginable odds, six men managed to navigate that twenty-two-foot boat through storms and colossal waves and reached South Georgia Island, a tiny speck of land surrounded by the roughest seas on Earth. It took them months to get a rescue boat back to the stranded men. When the rescue crew got there, what they found was equally unimaginable: All the men were still alive.

The expedition never achieved the goal of walking across Antarctica. Instead, the crew of the *Endurance* performed the even more astounding feat of surviving twenty-two months stranded at the end of the earth.

Each sentence below refers to a numbered sentence in the passage. Write the letter of the choice that gives the sentence a meaning that is closest to the original sentence.

___a___ **1.** The crew did not _____ the prospect of a dangerous journey.
     a. stop short at   **b.** accept   **c.** assume   **d.** ignore

___b___ **2.** While sailing, a good-natured _____ had developed among them.
     a. competition   **b.** comradeship   **c.** good humor   **d.** boldness

a   **3.** But Shackleton worried that stress would make his crew _____.
    a. bad-tempered   **b.** homesick   **c.** insane   **d.** resistant

C   **4.** Shackleton was _____ that the men keep to a strict daily routine of work.
    a. accepting   **b.** hopeful   **c.** determined   **d.** annoyed

d   **5.** Officers who _____ thought that they would escape their duties were wrong.
    a. passively   **b.** obediently   **c.** lightheartedly   **d.** boldly

d   **6.** Every man was treated equally and had to _____ the plan.
    a. be swayed by   **b.** defend against   **c.** argue for   **d.** agree to

b   **7.** Most of the crew remained _____.
    a. healthy   **b.** controllable   **c.** relaxed   **d.** stubborn

C   **8.** Rather than trying to _____ the rebel, Schackleton declared that all crew members must accept the captain's authority.
    a. punish   **b.** argue with   **c.** appease   **d.** manage

b   **9.** Luckily, McNish _____ Shackleton's demand.
    a. understood   **b.** obeyed   **c.** rebelled against   **d.** stood up for

a   **10.** Of his own _____, McNish reinforced one of the lifeboats with planks.
    a. free will   **b.** expense   **c.** kindness   **d.** imagination

Indicate whether the statements below are TRUE or FALSE according to the passage.

F   **1.** The Shackleton expedition to the South Pole went largely according to plan.

T   **2.** Shackleton believed that keeping his men occupied was important to their mental health.

T   **3.** Shackleton's leadership was critical to the crew's survival.

WRITING EXTENDED RESPONSES

You have just read about a situation in which working as a team was critical to a group's survival. Think of another endeavor that requires teamwork. Then, in an expository essay of at least three paragraphs, explain why teamwork is essential for that endeavor. Include at least two reasons and provide support for each. Use a minimum of three lesson words in your essay and underline them.

WRITE THE DERIVATIVE

Complete the sentence by writing the correct form of the word shown in parentheses. You may not need to change the form that is given.

tractable   **1.** Colin was _____ as a one-year-old, but became stubborn around the age of two. *(tractable)*

volition   **2.** Tim did not quit the team of his own _____, but was pressured to do so by his friends. *(volition)*

acquiescence   **3.** The mayor's ———— surprised the board members, for he rarely agreed to their proposals. *(acquiesce)*

comply   **4.** Mom suggested that it would be in our best interest to ———— with Dad's request for a little peace and quiet. *(compliance)*

propitiatory   **5.** The ———— language of the negotiators helped them reach an agreement acceptable to both sides. *(propitiate)*

adamantly   **6.** Both debaters held to their positions ————. *(adamant)*

presumed   **7.** Everyone ———— that the dessert was homemade, but, in fact, it had been purchased at a local bakery. *(presumptuous)*

balked   **8.** Uncle Ned ———— when Aunt Edna tried to get him to wear a tie to the party he didn't even want to attend. *(balk)*

camaraderie   **9.** The staff's ———— made the project proceed smoothly. *(camaraderie)*

cantankerous   **10.** Mrs. Barbosa was tired of dealing with ———— customers. *(cantankerous)*

FIND THE EXAMPLE

Choose the answer that best describes the action or situation.

_a_   **1.** A living thing that has the most *volition*
    a. a leader   **b.** a servant   **c.** a pet   **d.** a plant

_d_   **2.** Something that is important for people to *acquiesce* to
    a. sarcastic threats   **b.** insane requests   **c.** spam e-mails   **d.** traffic laws

_b_   **3.** An animal with a reputation for *balking*
    a. a dog   **b.** a mule   **c.** a parrot   **d.** a frog

_a_   **4.** Something with which you must *comply*
    a. court summons   **b.** insults   **c.** sarcasm   **d.** suggestions

_b_   **5.** Something about which many people are *adamant*
    a. favorite colors   **b.** political beliefs   **c.** price of milk   **d.** puzzling dreams

_c_   **6.** The most *tractable*
    a. herd of cats   **b.** gaggle of geese   **c.** guide dog   **d.** angry elephant

_a_   **7.** Something that a *cantankerous* person is likely to do
    a. scowl   **b.** smile   **c.** sing   **d.** wave

_d_   **8.** Something that suggests *camaraderie*
    a. silence   **b.** weeping   **c.** angry voices   **d.** laughter

_d_   **9.** The most likely beginning of a *presumptuous* comment
    a. Can I help . . .   **b.** May I see . . .   **c.** If you'd like . . .   **d.** In my opinion . . .

_b_   **10.** An example of a *propitiatory* comment
    a. Get lost!   **b.** I'm sorry.   **c.** Why not?   **d.** You're wrong.

Reading and Reasoning

Context Clues in Reading Primary Sources

As your history courses become more advanced, you will read more primary sources, or works written during the period you are studying. You have already studied some techniques for determining the meaning of unfamiliar words by using context clues. These additional strategies will help you read and understand primary sources.

Strategies

1. *Consider the date of the work.* This will alert you to the fact that some words may be used in unfamiliar ways. In the eighteenth century, for example, *enthusiasm* meant something closer to *fanaticism.*

2. *Consider the type of writing and the subject.* A personal letter will have a different level of vocabulary than a formal speech. Scientific writing and political tracts often use specific vocabulary. Keeping in mind the literary form and subject will help you make more accurate determinations of the meanings of unfamiliar words.

3. *Find out what you can about the author.* Knowing who wrote a work might provide additional clues to word meanings.

4. *Allow for unusual spellings, grammatical constructions, and punctuation.* Spelling was not standardized in the United States until the twentieth century. Remember also that universal access to education is a relatively modern phenomenon.

5. *Consult a dictionary.* If you can't figure out the meaning of a critical word, use a reference source. In some cases, a rare or obsolete word can only be found in an unabridged dictionary.

Practice

The following passage is from a journal kept by Meriwether Lewis and William Clark during their heralded exploration of the American West. The passage is written by Lewis and dated April 7, 1805. Read the entire passage once to get a general idea of what it is about. Then slowly reread the passage, writing your own definition for each italicized word. Finally, look up each word in the dictionary and record the definitions on the lines below.

Our vessels consisted of six small canoes, and two large (1) *pirogues.* This little fleet altho' not quite so respectable as those of Columbus or Capt. Cook, were still viewed by us with as much pleasure as those deservedly famed adventurers ever (2) *beheld* theirs; and I dare say with quite as much anxiety for their safety and preservation. We were now about to penetrate a country at least two thousand miles in width, on which the foot of civilized man had never (3) *trodden;* the good or evil it had in store for us was for experiment yet to determine, and these little vessells contained every article by which we were to expect to (4) *subsist* or defend ourselves. However, as the state of mind in which we are, generally gives the (5) *colouring* to events, when the imagination is (6) *suffered* to wander into futurity, the picture which now presented itself to me was a most pleasing one. Enterta[in]ing as I do, the most confident hope of succeeding in a voyage which had formed a (7) *da[r]ling* project of mine for the

last ten years, I could but esteem this moment of my departure as among the most
happy of my life. The party are in excellent health and sperits, zealously attached to
the enterprise, and anxious to proceed; not a whisper or murmur or discontent to be
heard among them, but all act in unison, and with the most perfect harmony. Capt.
Clark myself the two Interpretters and the woman [Sacajewea] and the child sleep in a
tent of dressed skins. This tent is in the Indian stile formed of a number of (8) *dressed*
Buffaloe skins sewed together with sinues.

1. pirogues

My definition _____

Dictionary definition _____

2. beheld

My definition _____

Dictionary definition _____

3. trodden

My definition _____

Dictionary definition _____

4. subsist

My definition _____

Dictionary definition _____

5. colouring

My definition _____

Dictionary definition _____

6. suffered

My definition _____

Dictionary definition _____

7. da[r]ling

My definition _____

Dictionary definition _____

8. dressed

My definition _____

Dictionary definition _____

Ability and Inability

WORD LIST

acuity	consummate	cunning	deft	endowment
facile	inept	prescient	proficient	prowess

The grace of a dancer or an athlete seems effortless, but such ability is usually the result of hard work and lots of practice. As Isaac Newton said, "If I have made any valuable discoveries, it has been owing more to patient attention than to any other talent." The words in this lesson are related to ability or to inability.

1. acuity (ə-kyōō′ĭ-tē) *noun* from Latin *acutus,* "sharp"
Sharpness of vision or perception
- Incredible **acuity** enables hawks and other raptors to spot their prey from great distances.

acute *adjective* His **acute** intelligence allowed him to quickly understand the problem.

2. consummate from Latin *com-,* "together" + *summa,* "sum"
a. *adjective* (kŏn′sə-mət′) Supremely accomplished or skilled; superior or perfect in every respect
- The **consummate** actor played Shakespearean tragedy, modern drama, and farce all with equal skill.
b. *verb* (kŏn′sə-māt′) To bring to completion or fulfillment
- To **consummate** the deal, Mr. Lopez agreed to remain as the company's CEO for one more year.

consummation *noun* Ernest's college degree was the **consummation** of much hard work.

3. cunning (kŭn′ĭng) from Middle English *connen,* "to know"
a. *adjective* Marked by or tending to use sly deception; crafty
- The thief used several **cunning** strategies to shift attention away from what he was doing.
b. *adjective* Executed with or exhibiting ingenuity
- Coyotes are extremely **cunning** when it comes to finding food.
c. *noun* Skill in deception
- With considerable **cunning,** the thief convinced the security guard that his father owned the building.
d. *noun* Skill or cleverness in execution or performance
- First to cross the finish line, the seasoned skipper had relied on all his **cunning** to outmaneuver, and finally overtake, the faster, newer boats.

cunning scavenger

4. deft (dĕft) *adjective*
Quick and skillful
* It takes **deft** weavers to produce the intricate designs on those beautiful carpets.

deftness *noun* The concert pianist's fingers moved over the keyboard with great **deftness.**

5. endowment (ĕn-dou´mənt) *noun* from Old French *douer,* "to provide with a dowry"
a. A natural gift, ability, or quality
* Test pilots need great **endowments** of courage, confidence, and calmness to do their job.
b. Funds or property donated to an institution, individual, or group that provide income for the recipient
* Harvard University has one of the biggest **endowments** of any institution in the world.

endow *verb* Florence's parents **endowed** her with a passion for learning.

> A *dowry* is money or property brought by a bride to her husband at marriage.

6. facile (făs´əl) *adjective* from Latin *facere,* "to do; to make"
a. Easy; done or achieved with little effort or difficulty
* "Slam-dunking is **facile** for me," said the seven-foot-tall player.
b. Working, acting, or speaking with effortless ease and fluency
* Bettina wanted to become a **facile** public speaker, so she joined the speech and debate club.
c. Arrived at without sufficient care or effort; superficial
* Beware of people who give **facile** answers to complex problems.

facility *noun* Liz learned foreign languages with great **facility.**

> A *facility* is also something created to serve a particular function, as in a "health-care *facility.*"

7. inept (ĭn-ĕpt´) *adjective* from Latin *in-,* "not" + *aptus,* "suitable"
Lacking skill or judgment; incompetent; clumsy
* The **inept** cook splattered the walls of the kitchen with sauce.

ineptness or **ineptitude** *noun* Due to his **ineptness,** the financial manager lost much of his clients' money.

8. prescient (prĕsh´ənt, prĕsh´ē ənt) *adjective* from Latin *pre-,* "before" + *scire,* "to know"
Having foresight; having knowledge of events before they occur
* The **prescient** fisherman had already sensed that a storm was coming.

prescience *noun* No one has the **prescience** to predict with certainty how the stock market will behave next year.

9. proficient (prə-fĭsh´ənt) *adjective* from Latin *pro-,* "forward" + *facere,* "to do; to make"
Able to do something very well; highly skilled; expert
* The **proficient** programmer knew all the latest computer languages.

proficiency *noun* Angela was required to pass an examination to demonstrate her **proficiency** in the subject that she would be teaching.

10. prowess (prou´ĭs) *noun* from Old French *prou,* "brave"
Superior strength, skill, courage, or daring
* It takes tremendous physical **prowess** to win a triathalon.

WRITE THE CORRECT WORD

Write the correct word in the space next to each definition. Use each word only once.

facile **1.** easy

deft **2.** quick and skillful

proficient **3.** highly skilled; expert

cunning **4.** cleverness; craftiness

acuity **5.** sharpness of vision

consumate **6.** to complete or fulfill

inept **7.** incompetent

prescient **8.** having foresight

prowess **9.** great strength

endowment **10.** a natural ability

COMPLETE THE SENTENCE

Write the letter for the word that best completes each sentence.

_b_ **1.** Animals seem to be _____ about natural events such as storms and earthquakes.
a. facile **b.** prescient **c.** endowed **d.** proficient

_c_ **2.** A generous _____ would enable the library to update its reference section.
a. cunning **b.** prowess **c.** endowment **d.** acuity

_a_ **3.** The mayor's _____ explanation of the complicated budget failed to persuade the voters to support him at the town meeting.
a. facile **b.** acuity **c.** endowed **d.** prescient

_a_ **4.** The doctor will test your visual _____ to determine whether you need glasses.
a. acuity **b.** cunning **c.** prescience **d.** consummation

_d_ **5.** The surgeon's _____ hands successfully completed the procedure without making a mistake.
a. inept **b.** prescient **c.** acute **d.** deft

_d_ **6.** Young Mike's weight lifting _____ attracted the attention of the football coaches.
a. prescience **b.** acuity **c.** ineptness **d.** prowess

_c_ **7.** Most people feel _____ when first learning to play a musical instrument.
a. deft **b.** acute **c.** inept **d.** prescient

_b_ **8.** She's a(n) _____ professional; you never have to worry about the quality of her work.
a. inept **b.** consummate **c.** prescient **d.** acute

_d_ **9.** As soon as the farmer looked away, the _____ fox slipped into the hen house.
a. inept **b.** endowed **c.** consummate **d.** cunning

_a_ **10.** Interpreters who work at the United Nations must be _____ in two or more languages.
a. proficient **b.** inept **c.** prescient **d.** consummate

Challenge: Since juggling one tennis ball at a time isn't much of a challenge, we asked him to demonstrate his _____ by performing a less _____ task.
_b_ **a.** ineptness…deft **b.** prowess…facile **c.** prescience…cunning

Not Doubtful About Horse Jumping

(1) Jumping up, over, and down, Doubtful, the horse, *deftly* clears the red and white pole. **(2)** The horse and rider make it look *facile*, but each jump is actually the result of hours and hours of practice.

Helen Schatzberger trains and sometimes rides horses in the British Show Jumping Association's competitions. To be successful, Schatzberger must choose the right horses. **(3)** She often starts by looking at animals that have never been ridden, so this requires some *prescience*. **(4)** First, she looks for physical *endowments* that make for a good jumper—well-balanced legs and shoulders, for example. But Schatzberger also must judge whether a horse has the right temperament: a special mix of calmness and the will to compete. **(5)** Without that competitive desire, a horse may become a *proficient* jumper, but will never become a champion.

(6) Schatzberger's *acuity* helps her assess each horse's personality. "Hot," nervous horses need calm riders. "Cold," lazy horses need more aggressive handling. **(7)** Schatzberger thinks that a trainer who treats all horses as though they were the same is *inept*.

(8) Schatzberger knows that the horses' training is crucial, for even *consummate* riders can perform no better than their mounts. **(9)** The training process requires some *cunning;* horses have to be convinced that, despite their great physical strength, the trainer is in command. To accomplish this, Schatzberger never permits a horse to become willful. If a horse starts to resist her, she reins it in and sets it straight immediately.

Schatzberger spends hours training horses to walk, trot, and canter precisely according to her demands.

Schatzberger must teach horses to respond to her commands to either shorten or lengthen their steps. The horses must also learn to start a jump exactly when their rider wants them to.

Good trainers also help animals overcome their fears. One of Schatzberger's horses, Siris, once became trapped between two other horses in a crowded practice ring. In a natural panic reaction, Siris began to kick the other horses. The next time Siris was in the ring, she started to kick at every horse that came near her. Schatzberger had to retrain Siris gradually, first putting her in a ring with one other horse, then with two, three, and so on.

Doubtful is perhaps Schatzberger's favorite horse. In 2003, they competed together in a British Show Jumping Association event. Of the 2,500 entries, only forty pairs made it to the final round. Schatzberger and Doubtful were the only amateur pair to qualify. **(10)** Doubtful demonstrated her *prowess* by clearing all of the poles and racing to the finish. The amateur rider and her horse finished in eighth place, triggering tremendous cheers and applause from the crowd. Schatzberger feels that, from the crowd's reaction, Doubtful knew how well she had performed. Getting her favorite treat—a horse mint —didn't hurt, either.

Each sentence below refers to a numbered sentence in the passage. Write the letter of the choice that gives the sentence a meaning that is closest to the original sentence.

_____ **1.** Jumping up, over, and down, Doubtful, the horse, _____ clears the red and white pole.
   a. skillfully   **b.** clumsily   **c.** acrobatically   **d.** sharply

_____ **2.** The horse and rider make it look _____, but each jump is actually the result of hours and hours of practice.
   a. clumsy   **b.** clever   **c.** easy   **d.** skilled

_____ **3.** She often starts by looking at animals that have never been ridden, so this requires some _____.
   a. skill   **b.** perception   **c.** strength   **d.** foresight

_____ **4.** First, she looks for physical _____ that make for a good jumper.
   a. flaws   **b.** lacks   **c.** gifts   **d.** skills

___b___ **5.** Without that competitive desire, a horse may become a _____ jumper, but
          may never become a champion.
          a. natural   **b.** competent   **c.** crafty   **d.** clumsy

___a___ **6.** Schatzberger's _____ helps her assess each horse's personality.
          a. perceptiveness   **b.** craftiness   **c.** strength   **d.** skill

___d___ **7.** Schatzberger thinks that a trainer who treats all horses as though they were the
          same is _____.
          a. sly   **b.** superior   **c.** gifted   **d.** incompetent

___c___ **8.** Even _____ riders can perform no better than their mounts.
          a. clumsy   **b.** clever   **c.** excellent   **d.** natural

___d___ **9.** The training process requires some _____.
          a. perception   **b.** ease   **c.** strength   **d.** craftiness

___c___ **10.** Doubtful demonstrated her _____ by clearing all of the poles and racing to
          the finish.
          a. incompetent feet   **b.** good breeding   **c.** strength and skill   **d.** light touch

Indicate whether the statements below are TRUE or FALSE according to the passage.

___F___ **1.** In a way, deceiving the horse is part of the training process.

___F___ **2.** Retraining former racehorses occupies most of Schatzberger's time.

___T___ **3.** Schatzberger thinks training should be tailored to each horse's personality.

FINISH THE THOUGHT

Complete each sentence so that it shows the meaning of the italicized word.

1. It took *cunning* to _____

2. It was *prescient* of her to _____

WRITE THE DERIVATIVE

Complete the sentence by writing the correct form of the word shown in
parentheses. You may not need to change the form that is given.

___cunning___ **1.** Some people try to achieve their goals through _____ and shortcuts, while
          others rely on hard work. *(cunning)*

___deftness___ **2.** The chef's _____ was obvious as she sliced and diced the ingredients. *(deft)*

Prowess **3.** Our team showed its _____ on the football field by winning the state championship. (*prowess*)

acute **4.** Most people know that cats have terrific vision, even at night, but cats' hearing is highly _____, too. (*acuity*)

facility **5.** Mia's _____ with language was well known among her teachers. (*facile*)

consummation **6.** The international conference was the _____ of five years of planning. (*consummate*)

Prescience **7.** The investor's _____ enabled him to make a great deal of money without much effort. (*prescient*)

endowed **8.** Your genes have _____ you with the traits that make you a unique human being. (*endowment*)

Ineptness **9.** The _____ of the technician resulted in an unreadable X-ray. (*inept*)

Proficiency **10.** Many colleges waive course requirements for students who can demonstrate _____ in a specific subject. (*proficient*)

FIND THE EXAMPLE

Choose the answer that best describes the action or situation.

_d_ **1.** An opportunity to demonstrate one's physical _prowess_
   a. math test   **b.** spelling bee   **c.** friendly gathering   **d.** track meet

_b_ **2.** A creature known for visual _acuity_
   a. mole   **b.** eagle   **c.** bat   **d.** earthworm

_a_ **3.** A natural _endowment_ that helps on the basketball court
   a. height   **b.** experience   **c.** skill   **d.** discipline

_c_ **4.** A task that would be _facile_ for most auto mechanics
   a. lung surgery   **b.** 300-foot ski jump   **c.** oil change   **d.** interstellar navigation

_b_ **5.** Someone most likely to have _deft_ moves
   a. famous novelist   **b.** karate expert   **c.** statistician   **d.** infant

_a_ **6.** An example of _ineptness_
   a. stumbling dancer   **b.** soaring bird   **c.** hunting lion   **d.** shooting star

_c_ **7.** The person with the most _proficiency_
   a. teenage laborer   **b.** chef's apprentice   **c.** concert pianist   **d.** kindergarten student

_d_ **8.** Something a _consummate_ chef would most likely do
   a. perform in stadium   **b.** prefer fast food   **c.** throw away food   **d.** prepare great food

_d_ **9.** Someone who most often relies on _prescience_
   a. young archaeologist   **b.** lazy freeloader   **c.** local historian   **d.** fortune teller

_b_ **10.** A person expected to be _cunning_
   a. trolley driver   **b.** undercover detective   **c.** guidance counselor   **d.** librarian

Requests and Demands

WORD LIST

beseech	cajole	elicit	enjoin	exigency
imperious	injunction	mendicant	query	servile

Most of us have to deal with other people's requests or demands all the time. The words in this lesson relate to different modes and styles of requests or demands.

1. beseech (bǐ-sēch´) *verb* from Old English *be-*, "completely; thoroughly" + *secan*, "to seek"
To request earnestly; to implore or beg
• I **beseech** you to see a doctor before your illness gets worse.

2. cajole (kə-jōl´) *verb* from Old French *cageoler*, "to chatter like a jay" and *gaioler*, "to lure into a cage"
To urge with gentle, repeated appeals, teasing, or flattery; to wheedle
• Pointing out the trip's educational value, Molly managed to **cajole** her grandparents into paying for her journey through France.

cajolery *noun* Arthur resorted to **cajolery** to convince his supervisor to give him an office with a view.

3. elicit (ǐ-lǐs´ǐt) *verb* from Latin *ex-*, "out" + *lacere*, "to entice"
To bring out or call forth
• The play's tragic ending **elicited** tears from the audience.

> Don't confuse *elicit* with *illicit*, which means "unlawful," or with *solicit*, which refers to attempts to persuade.

4. enjoin (ĕn-join´) *verb* from Latin *in-*, "cause to be" + *iungere*, "to join"
a. To direct or order with authority
• The judge **enjoined** members of the jury to keep their deliberations secret until after the trial.
b. To prohibit or forbid
• Regulations **enjoined** the soldiers from leaving the base without permission.

5. exigency (ĕk´sə-jən-sē) *noun* from Latin *exigere*, "to demand"
a. The state or quality of requiring much effort or immediate action
• The fire was spreading rapidly, and given the **exigency** of the situation, firefighters from neighboring towns were called in to help.
b. An urgent crisis or situation
• The coming hurricane is an **exigency** for residents on this island.

exigent *adjective* When a larger leak opened up in the bottom of the boat, the situation became much more **exigent**.

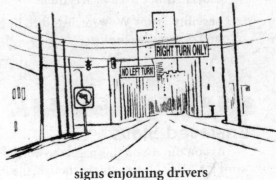

signs enjoining drivers

6. **imperious** (ĭm-pîr´ē-əs) *adjective* from Latin *imperare*, "to command"
Arrogantly bossy; domineering; overbearing
- The **imperious** president ordered her spokesperson to usher the reporters out of the press room.

7. **injunction** (ĭn-jŭngk´shən) *noun* from Latin *in-*, "in" + *iungere*, "to join"
A command, a directive, or an order
- While the lawsuit is pending, attorneys are seeking a court-ordered **injunction** to stop sales of the allegedly unsafe toy.

8. **mendicant** (mĕn´dĭ-kənt) from Latin *mendicare*, "to beg"
   a. *adjective* Dependent on begging for a living
   - In order to eat, many of the city's **mendicant** people must rely on the help of charitable organizations.
   b. *noun* A beggar
   - A veritable army of **mendicants** ply the streets of Calcutta.

9. **query** (kwîr´ē) *noun* from Latin *quest*, "ask"
   a. *noun* A question; an inquiry
   - In response to a **query** about the Middle Ages, the librarian directed the student to an authoritative Web site.
   b. *verb* To question, often with doubt
   - The teacher **queried** Toby again about whether his homework was really destroyed in a bizarre plumbing accident.

10. **servile** (sûr´vəl, sûr´vīl´) *adjective* from Latin *servus*, "slave"
    a. Slavish; behaving like a servant; excessively submissive
    - When asked to wash his boss's car, the **servile** employee replied as usual: "Yes, sir. Right away, sir."
    b. Like that of a slave or servant
    - Mario refused to take out the trash, considering it a **servile** task that was beneath his dignity.

    servitude *noun* Completely bound to their masters' lands, serfs in feudal Europe lived in **servitude.**

    servility *noun* We were disturbed by her **servility** toward her spoiled and demanding brother.

> *Servileness* is a less-common synonym of *servility*.

WORD ENRICHMENT

Enslaved Slavs

As you can see on this page, the word *servile* comes from the Latin word for "slave." Interestingly, though, the English word *slave* comes from a different source entirely. In medieval Eastern Europe, so many Slavic-speaking people—or "Slavs"—were enslaved that the word *slav* became synonymous with their position.

Of course, in the Slavic language, the way people referred to themselves did not mean *slave*. Slavic-speakers referred to themselves as *Slovenci,* which comes from an Indo-European root meaning "to hear," but translates roughly into "fame" or "renown." Thus, the Slavs are "the famous people." Slavic names that end in *-slav* incorporate the same concept. For example, the name *Stanislaw* means "famous for withstanding (enemies)."

WRITE THE CORRECT WORD

Write the correct word in the space next to each definition. Use each word only once.

exigency	**1.** an urgent crisis
query	**2.** a question
elicit	**3.** to bring out
injunction	**4.** a command or directive
beseech	**5.** to beg or plead

servile	**6.** slavish or submissive
enjoin	**7.** to prohibit or forbid
mendicant	**8.** a beggar
cajole	**9.** to urge with gentle methods
imperious	**10.** arrogantly bossy

COMPLETE THE SENTENCE

Write the letter for the word that best completes each sentence.

_C_ 1. The ability to subtly _____ people is important in many sales jobs.
   a. exigency   **b.** beseech   **c.** cajole   **d.** enjoin

_d_ 2. Mom gave us a new _____: absolutely no eating in the living room.
   a. exigency   **b.** query   **c.** mendicant   **d.** injunction

_d_ 3. Please, I _____ you: Do not go down that path alone!
   a. query   **b.** elicit   **c.** cajole   **d.** beseech

_a_ 4. Roy's coworkers were amused by his _____ manner, considering that his title was "Alternate Assistant Night Manager."
   a. imperious   **b.** exigent   **c.** queried   **d.** elicited

_b_ 5. Often, people who become _____ have tragic life stories.
   a. exigent   **b.** mendicant   **c.** queried   **d.** enjoined

_b_ 6. Catnip _____ frisky behavior in most cats.
   a. queries   **b.** elicits   **c.** enjoins   **d.** beseeches

_C_ 7. Terry put in a(n) _____ to the computer specialists about when the terminal would be operational.
   a. injunction   **b.** mendicant   **c.** query   **d.** exigency

_a_ 8. By the power of this court, I _____ Foulwater Incorporated to cease operations.
   a. enjoin   **b.** cajole   **c.** elicit   **d.** beseech

_b_ 9. Which is more _____, a tornado warning or a tornado watch?
   a. beseeching   **b.** exigent   **c.** imperious   **d.** mendicant

_a_ 10. Some bosses appreciate _____ in their employees, while others foster independent thinking.
   a. servility   **b.** exigency   **c.** injunction   **d.** queries

Challenge: The prospect of a big sale, bonus, or payoff is often enough to _____ all sorts of _____ from enthusiastic salespeople.
_C_   **a.** cajole…injunctions   **b.** beseech…mendicants   **c.** elicit…cajolery

Psyche and Eros

According to Greek mythology, Psyche, the daughter of a king, was considered by some to be more beautiful than Aphrodite, the goddess of love and beauty. **(1)** But goddesses were an *imperious* lot who did not wish to be outdone by mere mortals. **(2)** Infuriated by her lovely rival, Aphrodite issued an *injunction* to her son, Eros, the god of love (whom the Romans called Cupid). She ordered him to punish Psyche for her beauty by making her fall in love with someone unsuitable. **(3)** A deformed old man, or perhaps a *mendicant*, would do.

(4) As Eros approached Psyche, however, her beauty *elicited* an unexpected response. He fell deeply in love with her. It was as though he had been struck by one of his own arrows. Disregarding his mother's orders, he began plotting to make Psyche his wife.

Time passed on Earth. Psyche's two sisters got married. But curiously, despite her beauty, no one asked for Psyche's hand. **(5)** Finally, her parents decided to *query* the Oracle of Apollo. The Oracle answered that Psyche was not destined for a mortal man, and that her future husband—a monster whom no one could resist —awaited her on a mountaintop.

Her parents were filled with grief as Psyche prepared herself for her destiny. Standing alone on a mountaintop, dressed as a bride, she waited in fear. But gentle Zephyrus—god of the west wind—lifted her up and carried her to a flowery meadow. There, she entered an elegant palace and was treated like a queen. Finally, when night came, her husband visited her in the dark. **(6)** He treated her with love and respect, but *enjoined* her never to look at him. By the time daylight came, he had vanished. This routine was repeated each night.

Passing the days alone, Psyche began to long for company. **(7)** She *beseeched* her reluctant husband to allow her sisters to visit. Finally, he gave in. It was a move they would both regret.

Seeing Psyche's good fortune, the sisters grew jealous. They asked Psyche many questions about what her husband was like, but she could not answer them. Finally, she had to admit that she had never seen her husband. Her sisters then filled her with suspicion: How did she know he was not a monster? Could she trust him? Would he harm her? **(8)** They *cajoled* her into trying to discover who (or what) he was. So, one night, Psyche took an oil lamp into the bedchamber of her sleeping husband. There, she saw not some frightening monster, but the handsome god Eros. Unfortunately, as she leaned over for a better look, two drops of oil fell on him, and he awoke. He took one look at her and vanished through the window.

Psyche was heartbroken! **(9)** She went to Aphrodite and pleaded for her assistance, asking the goddess to recognize the *exigency* of her situation. Her former enemy reacted sternly. Hadn't Psyche humiliated her and then disobeyed her son? Yet, Aphrodite's heart held some pity. **(10)** The goddess said that if Psyche performed three *servile* tasks, she would be reunited with her husband. And so it was that Psyche, with the help of several divine forces, sorted enormous piles of grain, gathered wool from fierce sheep, and descended to the underworld to gather beauty in a box. At the end of her labors, Zeus, father of all the gods, rewarded Psyche with immortality, and she and Eros were reunited forever in love.

Each sentence below refers to a numbered sentence in the passage. Write the letter of the choice that gives the sentence a meaning that is closest to the original sentence.

_____ **1.** But goddesses were a(n) _____ lot who did not wish to be outdone by mere mortals.

    a. domineering   **b.** urgent   **c.** poor   **d.** slavish

_____ **2.** Aphrodite issued a _____ to her son, Eros.

    a. gentle request   **b.** servant   **c.** command   **d.** tough question

_____ **3.** A deformed old man, or perhaps a _____, would do.

    a. command   **b.** beggar   **c.** slave   **d.** thief

___d___ **4.** As Eros approached Psyche, however, her beauty _____ an unexpected response.
      a. begged   **b.** demanded   **c.** ordered   **d.** brought out

___d___ **5.** Finally, her parents decided to _____ the Oracle of Apollo.
      a. urge with flattery   **b.** ask favors from   **c.** beg money from   **d.** put a question to

___b___ **6.** He treated her with love and respect, but _____ her never to look at him.
      a. wheedled   **b.** ordered   **c.** tricked   **d.** asked

___c___ **7.** She _____ her reluctant husband to allow her sisters to visit.
      a. ordered   **b.** directed   **c.** begged   **d.** asked

___a___ **8.** They _____ her into trying to discover who (or what) he was.
      a. wheedled   **b.** ordered   **c.** pleaded   **d.** questioned

___d___ **9.** She went to Aphrodite and pleaded for her assistance, asking the goddess to recognize the _____ of her situation.
      a. slavishness   **b.** impoverishment   **c.** commands   **d.** urgency

___c___ **10.** The goddess said that if Psyche performed three _____ tasks, she would be reunited with her husband.
      a. arrogant   **b.** urgent   **c.** slavish   **d.** prohibited

Indicate whether the statements below are TRUE or FALSE according to the passage.

___F___ **1.** Eros and Cupid were two gods who never got along with each other.

___T___ **2.** According to Greek mythology, an oracle was someone who could predict the future.

___T___ **3.** Psyche was eventually reunited with her husband, the god Eros.

WRITING EXTENDED RESPONSES

The story of Psyche includes many requests and demands. Think of a real-life situation in which requests or demands played an important part. Write a narrative essay, at least three paragraphs long, that describes what happened. You may write about something that happened to you or to someone else. Use a minimum of three lesson words in your essay and underline them.

WRITE THE DERIVATIVE

Complete the sentence by writing the correct form of the word shown in parentheses. You may not need to change the form that is given.

___beseeched___ **1.** I _____ her, but it had little effect: She would not agree to let me go with her.
      (beseech)

___servitude___ **2.** Sadly, degrading forms of human _____ still exist in many parts of the world.
      (servile)

elicited   **3.** Hearing that song yesterday _____ all sorts of bittersweet memories. *(elicit)*

imperiously   **4.** "Bring me my dinner, you witless oaf!" thundered the queen _____. *(imperious)*

exigent   **5.** Running out of water in the middle of a desert could be considered an _____ situation. *(exigency)*

enjoined   **6.** Ever since his outburst in Judge Stern's courtroom, Mr. Smith has been _____ from observing any more trials there. *(enjoin)*

queried   **7.** On a hunch, the detective _____ Lola about her whereabouts on the night of the theft. *(query)*

cajolery   **8.** Your _____ is amusing, but it is transparent and will not change my mind. *(cajole)*

injunction   **9.** The court issued an emergency _____ to stop the sale of the potentially lethal medication. *(injunction)*

mendicants   **10.** Every night, Mr. Palozza delivers sandwiches and hot chocolate to _____ around town. *(mendicant)*

FIND THE EXAMPLE

Choose the answer that best describes the action or situation.

_C_   **1.** Something a *mendicant* would most likely have
    a. car   **b.** mutual funds   **c.** clothes   **d.** high-paying job

_b_   **2.** Most likely to *elicit* a response from a sleeping person
    a. waving   **b.** shaking the bed   **c.** thinking   **d.** making faces

_a_   **3.** A word or phrase most likely to be used in the act of *beseeching*
    a. please   **b.** cheese   **c.** okay   **d.** or else

_d_   **4.** The person most likely to be *imperious*
    a. slave   **b.** assistant   **c.** vendor   **d.** boss

_d_   **5.** The person who LEAST depends on *cajolery* to do his or her job
    a. teacher   **b.** salesperson   **c.** trial lawyer   **d.** football player

_d_   **6.** An example of an *injunction*
    a. That tastes good.   **b.** Please, Mom.   **c.** Ten dollars off.   **d.** Fishing prohibited.

    with a high degree of *exigency*
    a. burst appendix   **b.** blizzard last year   **c.** itch on finger   **d.** hiccups

_b_   **8.** A role that does NOT require occasional *servility*
    a. butler   **b.** dictator   **c.** guide dog   **d.** assistant

_c_   **9.** The punctuation that usually follows a *query*
    a. :   **b.** ;   **c.** ?   **d.** !

_b_   **10.** Something that a parent would probably *enjoin* a child to do
    a. play on the road   **b.** stay off thin ice   **c.** drive very fast   **d.** swim alone at night

Sizes and Amounts

WORD LIST

abound	amplitude	augment	behemoth	brevity
diminish	infinitesimal	modicum	prodigious	quotidian

In order to help describe sizes and amounts, human beings have created systems of numbers, units of measurement, and mathematics. The importance of quantity is also reflected in the many words that relate to it. The words in this lesson all deal with some aspect of size or amount.

1. **abound** (ə-bound´) *verb* from Latin *ab-*, "away" + *undare*, "to flow"
   To be great in number or amount
   • Caribou **abound** in some arctic regions of the world.

   abundant *adjective* There was an **abundant** supply of fruits and vegetables at the farmers' market.

2. **amplitude** (ăm´plĭ-tood´) *noun* from Latin *amplus*, "large"
   Greatness of size or range; magnitude
   • The **amplitude** of the soprano's voice made it easy to hear, even in the last row of the enormous opera house.

   ample *adjective* Miriam thought that the five-room apartment would provide **ample** space for her family.

> *Amplitude* has specific, technical definitions in the fields of astronomy, physics, mathematics, and electronics.

3. **augment** (ôg-mĕnt´) *verb* from Latin *augere*, "to increase"
   To add to; to increase the size, extent, or quantity of
   • Mario took on a second job to **augment** his income.

   augmentation *noun* The recent **augmentation** of police patrols in city neighborhoods shows the police chief's determination to prevent street crime.

4. **behemoth** (bĭ-hē´məth, bē´ə-məth)
   noun from Hebrew *behema*, "beast"
   Something enormous in size or power
   • The proposed multimillion-dollar merger would create a **behemoth** in the communications industry.

behemoth

> The word *Behemoth*, when capitalized, describes a large animal referred to in the Bible.

5. **brevity** (brĕv´ĭ-tē) *noun* from Latin *brevis*, "short"
   a. The quality of being short in duration; briefness
   • Students appreciated the **brevity** of the graduation speech.
   b. Brief or concise expression; terseness
   • **Brevity** is not only "the soul of wit" but the backbone of most good writing.

   brief *adjective* Please be **brief** because I'm in a rush.

6. **diminish** (dĭ-mĭn´ĭsh) *verb* from Latin *de-*, "reduce; degrade" + *minutus*, "small"
   a. To make or become smaller or less
   - Decreasing the seating capacity of the stadium **diminished** the city's chances of hosting a Super Bowl.
   b. To lessen the authority, reputation, or prestige of
   - Her repeated errors **diminished** her reputation among her coworkers.

   diminishment *noun* A **diminishment** in retail sales led economists to forecast an economic recession.

   undiminished *adjective* Despite the actor's unflattering photos in the tabloids, his reputation remained **undiminished.**

7. **infinitesimal** (ĭn´fĭn-ĭ-tĕs´ə-məl) *adjective* from Latin *in-*, "not" + *finire*, "to limit"
   Too small to measure or calculate
   - The chances of winning the lottery are almost **infinitesimal.**

8. **modicum** (mŏd´ĭ-kəm) *noun* from Latin *modus*, "measure"
   A small or token amount
   - Even a **modicum** of that hot pepper sauce will add a strong "kick" to your chili.

9. **prodigious** (prə-dĭj´əs) *adjective* from Latin *prodigium*, "omen"
   a. Impressively great in size, force, or extent
   - By the time she entered college, Molly had done a **prodigious** amount of reading.
   b. Extraordinary; marvelous
   - Tyrik's **prodigious** talent allowed him to perform with a professional symphony orchestra at the age of twelve.

   prodigy *noun* A person with exceptional talents or powers
   - Clarisse is a **prodigy** in math, just as Mozart was in music.

10. **quotidian** (kwō-tĭd´ē-ən) *adjective* from Latin *quot*, "as many as" + *dies*, "day"
    Everyday; commonplace
    - With *Death of a Salesman*, playwright Arthur Miller crafted a tragedy from the **quotidian** experience of work and family life.

WORD ENRICHMENT

Wavy words

As you saw on the previous page, the word *abound* comes from the Latin verb *undare*, "to flow." *Undare* comes from *unda*, the Latin word for "wave." *Unda* is also the root of *undulate*, which means "to move in waves or in a smooth, wavelike motion." Another wavy word is *inundate*, meaning "to cover with water, especially floodwaters" or "to overwhelm as if with a flood; to swamp."

74 **Sizes and Amounts**

WRITE THE CORRECT WORD

Write the correct word in the space next to each definition. Use each word only once.

modicum **1.** a small amount

augment **2.** to add to; to increase

prodigious **3.** extensive or extraordinary

behemoth **4.** something enormous in size

diminish **5.** to lessen the authority of something

brevity **6.** shortness of duration

abound **7.** to be great in number

quotidian **8.** everyday; common

Amplitude **9.** greatness of size or range

Infinitesimal **10.** too small to measure

COMPLETE THE SENTENCE

Write the letter for the word that best completes each sentence.

C **1.** That big _____ of a truck costs a lot of money to run.
    a. modicum   **b.** brevity   **c.** behemoth   **d.** augmentation

a **2.** The _____ of the tragedy was clear once we'd heard the bad news.
    a. amplitude   **b.** prodigy   **c.** brevity   **d.** modicum

d **3.** Unless you're getting paid by the word, _____ and simplicity are good goals to have in mind while writing a news story.
    a. amplitude   **b.** behemoth   **c.** diminishment   **d.** brevity

b **4.** The teacher cautioned that a _____ of self-control now would spare us lots of trouble later.
    a. behemoth   **b.** modicum   **c.** diminishment   **d.** brevity

d **5.** The chances of finding a message in a floating bottle while you are at sea are basically _____.
    a. prodigious   **b.** quotidian   **c.** ample   **d.** infinitesimal

a **6.** The researcher explained that the results of the study show that video games have become a(n) _____ distraction.
    a. quotidian   **b.** brief   **c.** diminished   **d.** augmented

C **7.** Your right to free speech _____ my chances of getting some peace and quiet!
    a. abounds   **b.** amplifies   **c.** diminishes   **d.** augments

b **8.** If we don't _____ the support structure soon, the bridge could crumble.
    a. brevity   **b.** augment   **c.** abound   **d.** diminish

d **9.** Some bird species are known for their _____ ability to mimic sounds.
    a. infinitesimal   **b.** augmented   **c.** brief   **d.** prodigious

a **10.** Trouble _____ in that dangerous part of town.
    a. abounds   **b.** diminishes   **c.** augments   **d.** quotidian

Challenge: With just a _____ of _____, your storm shelter will be able to house your family for a month.
b
    a. behemoth…brevity   **b.** modicum…augmentation   **c.** diminishment…prodigy

The First African-American Holiday

(1) Books that describe the tragic details of slavery in America *abound*. Besides harsh working conditions, brutal punishments, and other kinds of abuse, African slaves were also purposely separated from their families and from other slaves who spoke the same language and shared the same culture. **(2)** For obvious reasons, most of the history written about African-American slaves addresses the *quotidian* suffering they endured.

(3) But despite this *prodigious* maltreatment, some slaves held on to their traditions. One example is a little-known holiday called Johnkankus, which slaves celebrated on Christmas Day because that was the one day of the year they were permitted to rest. Historian and author Irene Smalls hopes that more people will learn about Johnkankus, the first African-American celebration.

Smalls first learned of the holiday when she read Harriet Jacobs's book *Incidents in the Life of a Slave Girl, Written by Herself.* **(4)** Jacobs's *brief* reference to Johnkankus provided little information, but it made Smalls curious.

From her extensive research, Smalls learned that Johnkankus likely originated in what is now known as Ghana, on the west coast of Africa. The holiday probably began as a communal tribute to respected chiefs.

Just as their relatives in Africa did, slaves in America celebrated the day by donning costumes and masks, and by dancing and singing in parades. **(5)** They moved along in unison, like a graceful, brightly colored *behemoth*, with a Johnkankus, or parade master, at the head.

(6) In the United States, slaves *augmented* the range of costumes and the purposes of the holiday. Having no possessions of their own, they made costumes from rags, garbage, plants—whatever they could find. Their songs sometimes made fun of their masters. More important, the parades allowed slaves to secretly spread word of planned uprisings or escapes.

(7) Johnkankus also provided what must have seemed like *ample* pleasures. There was music and food to enjoy, and opportunities to see family members who were enslaved on other plantations. **(8)** On this one day, slaves were allowed a *modicum* of freedom and joy. **(9)** No matter how *infinitesimally* short this period of happiness may have seemed, it at least gave the slaves something to look forward to.

When slavery was declared illegal in the United States, Johnkankus was no longer celebrated by African Americans. **(10)** But to Smalls, the value of Johnkankus remains *undiminished* with the passage of time, for it connects African Americans to their African history. Smalls also believes that celebrating Johnkankus once again would honor the men, women, and children who managed to hold on to their culture despite the cruel realities they endured as slaves.

Each sentence below refers to a numbered sentence in the passage. Write the letter of the choice that gives the sentence a meaning that is closest to the original sentence.

___b___ **1.** Books that describe the tragic details of slavery in America _____.
    a. add to history   **b.** are common   **c.** lessen burdens   **d.** increase knowledge

___C___ **2.** Most of the history written about African-American slaves addresses the _____ suffering they faced.
    a. large   **b.** immeasurable   **c.** everyday   **d.** bountiful

___A___ **3.** Despite this _____ maltreatment, some slaves held on to their traditions.
    a. extensive   **b.** commonplace   **c.** short-lived   **d.** increased

___C___ **4.** Jacobs's _____ reference to Johnkankus provided little information.
    a. powerful   **b.** lessened   **c.** short   **d.** extraordinary

_____d____ **5.** They moved along in unison, like a graceful, brightly colored _____.
  a. moderate amount   **b.** daily event   **c.** loud serpent   **d.** huge object

_____d____ **6.** In the United States, slaves _____ the range of costumes and the purposes of the holiday.
  a. added to   **b.** tamed down   **c.** learned every day   **d.** lowered the value of

_____b____ **7.** Johnkankus also provided what must have seemed like _____ pleasures.
  a. tiny   **b.** plentiful   **c.** almost daily   **d.** not large

_____d____ **8.** On this one day, slaves were allowed a _____ of freedom and joy.
  a. huge amount   **b.** large beast   **c.** short song   **d.** little bit

_____d____ **9.** No matter how _____ short this period of happiness may have seemed, it at least gave slaves something to look forward to.
  a. plentifully   **b.** obviously   **c.** immeasurably   **d.** concisely

_____a____ **10.** To Smalls, the value of Johnkankus has _____ with the passage of time.
  a. stayed the same   **b.** grown a lot   **c.** been added to   **d.** become immeasurable

Indicate whether the statements below are TRUE or FALSE according to the passage.

_____F____ **1.** The word *Johnkankus* refers both to a holiday and to a specific role played in the celebration of that holiday.

_____F____ **2.** Before Irene Smalls did her research, the mistreatment of African-American slaves had never been documented.

_____T____ **3.** American celebrations of Johnkankus served, in part, as a way to pass secret messages.

FINISH THE THOUGHT

Complete each sentence so that it shows the meaning of the italicized word.

1. With only an *infinitesimal* _____

_____

2. One of my *quotidian* pastimes is _____

_____

WRITE THE DERIVATIVE

Complete the sentence by writing the correct form of the word shown in parentheses. You may not need to change the form that is given.

___Prodigious___ **1.** The expert surfer rode the _____ wave. (*prodigious*)

___modicum___ **2.** After being in the loud stadium, we were relieved to have a _____ of silence. (*modicum*)

quotidian   **3.** Even a list of her most _____ accomplishments reads like an adventure novel. _(quotidian)_

undiminished   **4.** Coach was proud of the way Jamie chased down every loose ball with _____ intensity, even in the fourth quarter. _(diminish)_

infinitesimal   **5.** She was so hungry that the reasonable dinner portions seemed _____. _(infinitesimal)_

abounding   **6.** The blossoms were _____ after the unexpected rain. _(abound)_

brevity   **7.** We were relieved by the _____ of the speech because we were anxious for the lecture to be over. _(brevity)_

augment   **8.** If Chief Allen doesn't _____ our highway patrol unit, we'll be overrun by speeders and other reckless drivers. _(augment)_

behemoth   **9.** The intelligent _____ used its trunk to pick up a tree and then lay it across the stream so we could cross to the other side. _(behemoth)_

amplitude   **10.** The small pack was hardly sufficient to carry the _____ supplies for the two-week camping trip. _(amplitude)_

FIND THE EXAMPLE

Choose the answer that best describes the action or situation.

_d_   **1.** An _infinitesimal_ amount
     a. 1 times 4   **b.** a dozen   **c.** everything   **d.** almost nothing

_c_   **2.** A place where food is _abundant_
     a. high desert   **b.** outer space   **c.** grocery store   **d.** operating room

_a_   **3.** Something that you would NOT want to _augment_
     a. your problems   **b.** your knowledge   **c.** your strength   **d.** your bank account

_b_   **4.** Something that is designed to move a _prodigious_ amount of cargo
     a. a house cat   **b.** a freight train   **c.** a knapsack   **d.** a spoon

_d_   **5.** A type of writing in which _brevity_ is necessary
     a. campaign speech   **b.** wedding vow   **c.** funeral eulogy   **d.** classified ad

_a_   **6.** The one most likely to be a _quotidian_ activity among seafaring people
     a. fishing for food   **b.** planting crops   **c.** playing football   **d.** mountain climbing

_c_   **7.** An example of a _behemoth_
     a. peregrine falcon   **b.** salamander   **c.** rhinoceros   **d.** mouse

_b_   **8.** Someone highly unlikely to eat just a _modicum_ of food
     a. a writer   **b.** a glutton   **c.** a senior citizen   **d.** a small child

_d_   **9.** A sound of great _amplitude_
     a. whisper   **b.** whistle   **c.** humming   **d.** shout

_c_   **10.** Something that could rapidly _diminish_ the financial value of a house
     a. a cleaning   **b.** a good neighbor   **c.** a fire   **d.** a blue sky

Taking Tests

SAT Writing Tests

The new SAT, first administered in 2005, has a Writing section that includes an essay question and a set of multiple-choice questions on grammar, usage, and composition. There are three different kinds of multiple-choice questions. Each kind is described below.

Strategies

1. The **identification of sentence error** questions require you to look at four underlined parts of a sentence and determine whether one of them is faulty. First, read the entire sentence. Then reread the sentence and choose the part that has an error in grammar, usage, or syntax. (No more than one part can be incorrect.) If you find no errors, choose E.

2. **Sentence correction** items also present a sentence with underlined words. Here, your task is to choose the correct version of the underlined part in order to improve the sentence. Note that choice A is the same as the underlined version.

3. **Paragraph improvement** items present a paragraph with several sentences. Each item asks how a specific sentence or part of the paragraph can be improved. Your task is to choose the correct change needed to improve the paragraph. To answer these kinds of questions, read through the paragraph and all of the answer choices first. The key is to choose the answer that improves the paragraph without changing its meaning. Decide what the sentences mean, and then choose the answer that is best written and retains the same meaning.

Practice

In questions 1–3, choose the underlined part of the sentence that contains an error in grammar, usage, or word choice. If there is no error, choose answer E.

_____ **1.** Damarcus <u>thinks</u> <u>that</u> he is older and <u>more experienced</u> than <u>me</u>.
                      A   B   C   D
    <u>No error</u>
     E

_____ **2.** Mr. Welles <u>contacted</u> the people <u>whom</u> <u>had lived</u> in the house
                           A   B   C
    previously. <u>No error</u>
       D   E

_____ **3.** Rosalind <u>was convinced</u> that the <u>lack of sunlight</u> <u>effected</u> the results
                     A   B   C
    of the experiment. <u>No error</u>
       D   E

In questions 4–6, the underlined part of the sentence may need to be corrected.
Choice A is the same as the original underlined part; the other choices are different.
Choose the answer that best expresses the meaning of the original sentence.

_____ **4.** Having lived in town for years, <u>the roads were familiar to him.</u>
   a. the roads were familiar to him.
   b. the roads became familiar to him.
   c. him and the roads were familiar.
   d. the roads to him were familiar.
   e. he was familiar with the roads.

_____ **5.** These two movies, <u>which are very entertaining</u>, were directed by the same woman.
   a. which are very entertaining
   b. which was very entertaining
   c. who are very entertaining
   d. which is very entertaining
   e. that are being very entertaining

_____ **6.** <u>The computer was invented, and</u> many new words have been added to our language.
   a. The computer was invented, and
   b. Then the computer was invented, and
   c. Since the computer was invented,
   d. Although the computer was invented,
   e. Having invented the computer,

For questions 7–8, read the paragraph. Some parts of it need to be improved.
Choose the best answer to each question about the way the paragraph is written.

(1) Some of the names given to U.S. states have fascinating origins. (2) The name California, for example, came from the name of an imaginary island in a Spanish romance novel written in 1510. (3) Maryland was named after a queen of England. (4) Virginia was also named after an English queen. (5) Georgia and Louisiana both derived from the names of kings—one English and one French. (7) Idaho, one of the most interesting names, which was supposedly invented by an early explorer. (8) It means "gem of the mountains."

_____ **7.** Which is the best way to combine sentences 3 and 4?
   a. Maryland was named after a queen of England, and so was Virginia.
   b. Maryland was named after a queen of England, but Virginia wasn't.
   c. While Maryland was named after a queen of England, Virginia was, too.
   d. Both Maryland and Virginia were named after queens of England.
   e. Since Maryland was named after a queen of England, Virginia was, too.

_____ **8.** Which is the best version of sentence 7?
   a. Idaho, one of the most interesting names, which was supposedly invented by an early explorer.
   b. One of the most interesting names is Idaho, which was supposedly invented by an early explorer.
   c. Idaho, which was supposedly invented by an early explorer, one of the most interesting names.
   d. Idaho is one of the most interesting names invented by an explorer.
   e. Supposedly one of the most interesting names, Idaho was invented by an early explorer.

Copying and Repeating

WORD LIST

banal	camouflage	emulate	mimicry	platitude
prototype	redundant	rendition	sham	simulation

The acts of copying and repeating are central to learning. As young children, we learn to speak by imitating sounds. When we go to school, copying helps us learn how to write. Not all copying or repeating is good, however. This lesson will further your knowledge of words related to copying and repeating.

1. **banal** (bə-năl´) *adjective* from Old French *ban,* "summons to military service"
   Unoriginal and commonplace; trite
   • The phrase "no pain, no gain" has been used so many times that it has become **banal.**

   banality *noun* The **banality** of the last few movies I have seen has prompted me to start reading movie reviews before I choose the next one.

2. **camouflage** (kăm´ə-fläzh´) from French *camoufler,* "to disguise"
   a. *noun* Concealment by disguise or by coloring that matches the surrounding environment
   • In the desert, shades of tan and gray are often used as **camouflage** for military equipment.
   b. *verb* To hide by disguising or by blending in with the surroundings
   • During her job interview, she **camouflaged** her nervousness beneath an outward show of confidence.

3. **emulate** (ĕm´yə-lāt´) *verb* from Latin *aemulus,* "rival"
   a. To strive to equal or excel, especially through imitation
   • Many young writers **emulate** the literary styles of their favorite authors.
   b. To approach or achieve equality with; to compete with successfully
   • "I think that it's fair to say that young LeBron James is **emulating** Michael Jordan," said the commentator.

   emulation *noun* Enlightened and effective government policies make the African country of Botswana worthy of **emulation.**

4. **mimicry** (mĭm´ĭ-krē) *noun* from Greek *mimos,* "imitator; mime"
   Imitation or copying, especially of expression and gesture
   • The impersonator's **mimicry** of Frank Sinatra delighted the crowd.

   mimic *noun* The **mimic** did a near-perfect job of reproducing the actor's voice and mannerisms.

   mimic *verb* Sticklike insects **mimic** the appearance of twigs as a means of protection against natural predators.

> *Banal* can also be pronounced bā´nəl or bə-näl´.

chameleon camouflage

> The past tense of the verb *mimic* is *mimicked* and the gerund is *mimicking.* Note that both forms require a *k.*

5. platitude (plăt´ĭ-tōōd´) *noun* from French *plat*, "flat"
An overused, dull, and unoriginal remark or statement, especially one delivered as if it were original or significant
  • The reporter said, "Sir, we would like legitimate answers to our questions, not long strings of slogans and empty **platitudes.**"

6. prototype (prō´tə-tīp´) *noun* from Greek *proto-*, "original" + *tupos*, "model"
  a. An original type, form, or instance that serves as a basis or standard for those that follow; a test or trial model
    • The editors developed a **prototype** for the magazine's style section.
  b. An early typical example
    • In many people's minds, German shepherds are the **prototype** of police dogs.

  prototypical *adjective* Henry Ford's assembly lines were **prototypical** of an innovative, large-scale industrial system called mass production.

7. redundant (rĭ-dŭn´dənt) *adjective* from Latin *re-*, "again" + *undare*, "to surge"
  a. Extra; exceeding what is necessary
    • When the couple moved into the city, they decided that having two cars was **redundant,** so they sold one.
  b. Repetitive or needlessly wordy in expression
    • "Red in color" is an example of a **redundant** expression.

  redundancy *noun* **Redundancy** is something to avoid in your writing, especially when you have space limitations.

8. rendition (rĕn-dĭsh´ən) *noun* from Latin *re-*, "back" + *dare*, "to give"
An interpretation or a performance of a musical or dramatic piece
  • The local theater group's **rendition** of *Romeo and Juliet* is set in a modern high school.

  render *verb* To represent in verbal form or in a drawing or painting
    • I think the painter was trying to **render** the bittersweet joy that one feels at the end of a perfect, late-summer day.

9. sham (shăm)
  a. *noun* Something false or empty that is presented as genuine; a fake
    • The television game show was a **sham,** for some contestants were given the answers beforehand.
  b. *adjective* Not genuine; fake
    • The unfortunate man realized that he had paid thousands of dollars for a **sham** diamond necklace.
  c. *verb* To put on the false appearance of; to feign
    • Jacques **shammed** illness to avoid competing in the race.

10. simulation (sĭm´yə-lā´shən) *noun* from Latin *similis*, "like"
An imitation, a representation, or a reproduction of a situation or an experience
  • The roller-coaster ride was a **simulation** of a trip through space.

  simulate *verb* Mock trials **simulate** actual courtroom conditions.

WRITE THE CORRECT WORD

Write the correct word in the space next to each definition. Use each word only once.

emulate   **1.** to strive to equal

redundant   **2.** needlessly repetitive

rendition   **3.** an artistic interpretation

banal   **4.** unoriginal and commonplace; trite

Camouflage   **5.** a disguise or concealment

mimicry   **6.** imitation; copying

Platitude   **7.** an overused, dull remark

Sham   **8.** a fake

Prototype   **9.** a test model or a typical example

Simulation   **10.** a reproduction of a situation

COMPLETE THE SENTENCE

Write the letter for the word that best completes each sentence.

_C_   **1.** Flight _____ allow young pilots to train without the danger and expense of flying in an actual aircraft.
  a. platitudes   **b.** prototypes   **c.** simulations   **d.** camouflages

_a_   **2.** Green and brown materials provide _____ in the forest.
  a. camouflage   **b.** rendition   **c.** banality   **d.** platitudes

_b_   **3.** The tenor performed an operatic _____ of "Pop Goes the Weasel."
  a. simulation   **b.** rendition   **c.** prototype   **d.** platitude

_d_   **4.** Test drivers pushed the hydracar _____ to its limits.
  a. platitude   **b.** sham   **c.** emulation   **d.** prototype

_a_   **5.** Mockingbirds are known for their _____ of other birds' songs.
  a. mimicry   **b.** sham   **c.** platitude   **d.** camouflage

_c_   **6.** The politician's speech was so _____ that it seemed as if he simply repeated the same three phrases for an hour.
  a. emulated   **b.** mimicked   **c.** redundant   **d.** prototypical

_b_   **7.** She urged the Ph.D. candidates to _____ the work of history's great thinkers.
  a. camouflage   **b.** emulate   **c.** sham   **d.** simulate

_d_   **8.** The snores in the audience hinted that the play was tedious and _____.
  a. camouflaged   **b.** rendered   **c.** simulated   **d.** banal

_a_   **9.** The _____ "to err is human" is a poor defense against a major felony charge.
  a. platitude   **b.** mimicry   **c.** simulation   **d.** emulation

_C_   **10.** The investment opportunity was merely a _____ designed to swindle wealthy widows.
  a. simulation   **b.** camouflage   **c.** sham   **d.** platitude

Challenge: The comedians who planned to remake a Three Stooges film tested a _____ of a scene before a live audience to determine whether their _____ of the classic appealed to the crowd.

_C_   **a.** rendition…banality   **b.** simulation…camouflage   **c.** prototype…rendition

Does Polly Really Want a Cracker?

(1) No matter how simple the word or *banal* the phrase, when a parrot says something, people listen. The spectacle of a talking animal never ceases to hold our attention.

Interestingly, parrots do not have a larynx or vocal chords, which humans use to make sounds. **(2)** Instead, parrots *simulate* the sounds of human speech by using the muscles and special membranes in their throats. By directing the airflow in just the right way, parrots can form words and phrases that are recognizable to us. But do our feathered friends have any idea what they are really saying when they are chatting away in human language?

The answer to that question may depend on the bird and its training. **(3)** While a number of parrot species seem as though they have learned to "speak," many of these sounds are simple *mimicry*. Parrots are often taught to speak by their owners, who reward their pets with treats whenever the birds say something. Researchers believe that these parrots probably don't understand the words that they are saying; instead, they have simply learned that making the word sounds brings rewards. Nevertheless, these birds can learn to say very complicated phrases. **(4)** Some parrots even do their own *renditions* of opera lyrics.

Recent research has shown that parrots are smarter than was originally thought. Dr. Irene Pepperberg works with African gray parrots at Brandeis University and at the Massachusetts Institute of Technology. **(5)** Alex, the oldest parrot in the group, does far more than repeat simple words or *platitudes*. Alex can count. He can also recognize colors, shapes, and the names of forty objects, including bananas, popcorn, and green beans. He makes requests and demands. He even bosses the laboratory staff around, telling them to give him snacks, toys, or showers. If a staff member gives him the wrong item, Alex says, "No," and then he asks again. Dr. Pepperberg believes Alex's reactions suggest that he understands what he says and sees. According to Dr. Pepperberg, what makes Alex special is the fact that scientists have spent twelve years teaching him language skills in the same way that many children are taught.

(6) Some people who haven't met Alex have suspected that his supposed communication is a *sham*. They say that Alex may simply be making the sounds he has been trained to repeat. **(7)** But Dr. Pepperberg has made no attempt to *camouflage* her research methods. On the contrary, she has described her work with this talkative bird in detail in the articles she has published in many respected scientific journals. **(8)** Those who observe her training techniques think that she *emulates* the careful, conscientious standards and methods expected of all disciplined scientists. **(9)** In fact, the methods Dr. Pepperberg developed for teaching Alex to speak have served as a basic *prototype* for teaching some children who have problems in language development.

Dr. Pepperberg's experiments with parrots require great effort. **(10)** After all, the number of repetitions needed to teach a parrot a word would be *redundant* for a child. But Dr. Pepperberg loves her work. She hopes that her research may lead to legislation for protection of parrots in the wild. In addition, Dr. Pepperberg's work provides insight, not only into the mind of another species, but into how language is acquired in general. Plus, she thinks Alex is pretty cute, especially when he asks to be tickled.

Each sentence below refers to a numbered sentence in the passage. Write the letter of the choice that gives the sentence a meaning that is closest to the original sentence.

___a___ **1.** No matter how simple the word or _____ the phrase, when a parrot says something, people listen.
    a. original   **b.** fake   **c.** unoriginal   **d.** short

___b___ **2.** Instead, parrots _____ the sounds of human speech by using the muscles and special membranes in their throats.
    a. test   **b.** reproduce   **c.** disguise   **d.** conceal

___a___ **3.** Many of these sounds are simple _____.
    a. imitation   **b.** experimentation   **c.** concealment   **d.** representation

_a_ **4.** Some parrots can even do their own _____ of opera lyrics.
    a. disguises   **b.** originals   **c.** sayings   **d.** performances

_c_ **5.** Alex, the oldest parrot in the group, does far more than repeat simple words or _____.
    a. disguised insults   **b.** art performances   **c.** unoriginal remarks   **d.** extra phrases

_a_ **6.** Some people suspect that his supposed communication is a _____.
    a. fake   **b.** test model   **c.** disguise   **d.** great performance

_b_ **7.** But Dr. Pepperberg has made no attempt to _____ her research methods.
    a. fake or forge   **b.** conceal or hide   **c.** imitate or copy   **d.** repeat or reproduce

_c_ **8.** She _____ the careful, conscientious standards expected of all disciplined scientists.
    a. tests   **b.** feigns   **c.** achieves   **d.** disguises

_d_ **9.** The methods Dr. Pepperberg developed for teaching Alex to speak have served as a basic _____ for teaching some children who have problems in language development.
    a. repetition   **b.** disguise   **c.** saying   **d.** model

_a_ **10.** The number of repetitions needed to teach a parrot a word would be _____ for a child.
    a. obscure   **b.** feigned   **c.** excessive   **d.** reproduced

Indicate whether the statements below are TRUE or FALSE according to the passage.

_F_ **1.** Parrots use their vocal chords in the same way as humans do.

_F_ **2.** There is universal agreement that Alex understands what he says.

_T_ **3.** Dr. Pepperberg's teaching methods may be adapted to help teach children with language-acquisition problems.

WRITING EXTENDED RESPONSES

You have just read about talking parrots. In an essay at least three paragraphs long, describe how people and animals usually communicate with one another. You may choose a type of animal—such as dogs, cats, horses, or birds—or you may choose an individual animal, like your dog, cat, or other pet. Use a minimum of three lesson words in your essay and underline them.

WRITE THE DERIVATIVE

Complete the sentence by writing the correct form of the word shown in parentheses. You may not need to change the form that is given.

banality **1.** The _____ of the speaker's remarks almost put me to sleep. *(banal)*

simulate **2.** Some computer games _____ extraordinary situations that you would never want to face in real life. *(simulation)*

Prototype   **3.** The genius of Louis Armstrong's _____ trumpet solos has set the standard for generations of horn players who have followed. (*prototype*)

Mimicing   **4.** Comical impersonators have an exceptional ability for _____ the subtle nuances of people's expressions. (*mimicry*)

emulating   **5.** Basketball player Charles Barkley cautioned the public about _____ athletes when he said, "I am *not* a role model." (*emulate*)

   6. The thieves _____ the stolen jewelry by covering it up with brush. (*camouflage*)

Camouflaged

Sham   **7.** Some people use the Internet unlawfully for _____ enterprises. (*sham*)

renders   **8.** The way the actor _____ the part of the villain made the character seem far too mild and harmless. (*rendition*)

redundancy   **9.** The _____ of the warning over the loudspeaker made travelers in the airport tune it out. (*redundant*)

platitudes   **10.** Audiences are not inspired by _____ . (*platitude*)

FIND THE EXAMPLE

Choose the answer that best describes the action or situation.

_a_   **1.** How you would likely feel if someone said your writing was *banal*
     a. insulted   **b.** proud   **c.** admired   **d.** elated

_b_   **2.** The *prototypical* percussion instrument
     a. sleigh bell   **b.** drum   **c.** flute   **d.** tenor sax

_c_   **3.** Someone most people would like to *emulate*
     a. prisoner   **b.** toddler   **c.** hero   **d.** victim

_b_   **4.** Person who most likely engages in *mimicry* on the job
     a. accountant   **b.** actor   **c.** lawyer   **d.** scientist

_d_   **5.** Something LEAST likely to be *camouflaged*
     a. army scout   **b.** motionless prey   **c.** stalking predator   **d.** businessman

_a_   **6.** Something you would be LEAST likely to do a *rendition* of
     a. a smell   **b.** a song   **c.** a sketch   **d.** a scene

_c_   **7.** A type of *sham*
     a. a pass   **b.** a friend   **c.** a lie   **d.** a pen

_d_   **8.** A phrase that has become a *platitude* in U.S. politics
     a. the Kenyan way   **b.** Work hard.   **c.** I am lying.   **d.** the American way

_c_   **9.** A description of *redundant* writing
     a. short and snappy   **b.** sharp and clever   **c.** wordy and repetitive   **d.** clear and concise

_b_   **10.** NOT a *simulation*
     a. a war movie   **b.** a family reunion   **c.** a video game   **d.** a battle reenactment

Frequently Confused Words

WORD LIST

adverse	averse	ingenious	ingenuous	persecute
prosecute	quorum	quota	respectfully	respectively

The word pairs in this lesson are often confused. The words in each pair are similar in their spelling and sound, and may have similar meanings as well. Try to remember the differences that give each word its distinctive meaning.

1. **adverse** (ăd-vûrs´) *adjective* from Latin *ad-*, "toward" + *vertere*, "to turn"
   Opposing; contrary to one's interests; harmful or unfavorable
   • High interest rates are **adverse** to those borrowing money.

   adversity *noun* Orphaned and without money, the hero of the Dickens novel was used to **adversity**.

2. **averse** (ə-vûrs´) *adjective* from Latin *ab-*, "away from" + *vertere*, "to turn"
   Referring to a feeling of avoidance and dislike
   • The intensely private businessman was **averse** to any type of publicity.

   aversion or **averseness** *noun* Through the years, the investor developed an **aversion** to high-risk stocks.

adversity

3. **ingenious** (ĭn-jēn´yəs) *adjective* from Latin *ingenium*, "inborn talent"
   Marked by inventive skill and imagination; extremely clever
   • The idea of using solar cells to capture sunlight and convert it to other forms of energy is **ingenious.**

   ingenuity *noun* The **ingenuity** of the advertising campaign greatly increased the sale of raisins.

> Both *ingenuity* and *ingeniousness* can be noun forms of *ingenious.*

4. **ingenuous** (ĭn-jēn´yoo-əs) *adjective* from Latin *ingenuus*, "honest; freeborn"
   Unable to deceive; openly straightforward
   • The **ingenuous** five-year-old had an unfortunate habit of revealing family secrets to the neighbors.

   ingenuousness *noun* Assuming an attitude of **ingenuousness**, the young assistant hid her ambitions.

5. **persecute** (pûr´sĭ-kyoot´) *verb* from Latin *per-*, "completely" + *sequi*, "to follow"
   To continuously mistreat or be cruel to someone; to annoy persistently
   • People who are **persecuted** for their political beliefs may flee from their homelands.

   persecution *noun* The novel *Les Miserables* deals with police chief Javert's **persecution** of a man whose crime was stealing a loaf of bread.

6. **prosecute** (prŏs´ĭ-kyōōt´) *verb* from Latin *pro-*, "forward" + *sequi*, "to follow"
   a. To bring action against, in a court of law
      • The attorney general's office **prosecuted** company executives for deceiving stockholders.
   b. To continue an activity until it is completed
      • Until their goal was achieved, the group **prosecuted** their campaign to bring wolves back to Yellowstone Park.

   prosecution *noun* The **prosecution** of the neglectful landlord was not a lengthy court case.

   prosecutor *noun* The **prosecutor** didn't seem to have enough evidence to establish the guilt of the defendant.

In a trial, the *prosecution* tries to establish guilt; the *defense* tries to establish innocence.

7. **quorum** (kwôr´əm) *noun* from Latin *qui*, "who"
   The minimum number of people who must be present to make a decision
      • The bylaws of the organization state that a **quorum** is the majority of the membership.

A *quorum* can also mean a select group of people.

8. **quota** (kwō´tə) *noun* from Latin *quotus*, "of what number"
   a. The amount of goods assigned to a person; an allotment
      • During World War II, federal **quotas** limited the amount of gasoline that an individual could purchase.
   b. A number or percentage, especially of people, that represents an upper limit or a required minimum
      • Many countries are lowering their **quotas** on immigration.

9. **respectfully** (rĭ-spĕkt´fə-lē) *adverb* from Latin *respectus*, "regard"
   With regard and esteem; politely
      • The members of the international-affairs seminar stood up **respectfully** when the African leader arrived for her lecture.

   respect *noun* Show some **respect** for your elders.

   respect *verb* Please **respect** our privacy.

10. **respectively** (rĭ-spĕk´tĭv-lē) *adverb* from Latin *respectus*, "regard"
    Referring to things or people in the order given
      • Morgan and Alyssa are, **respectively**, the captains of the soccer and softball teams.

   respective *adjective* Particular; each to each
      • After the assembly, students should return to their **respective** classrooms.

WORD ENRICHMENT

Ingenious and ingenuous

Ingenious and *ingenuous* are formed from the same root, *gen*, and the same suffix, *-ous*, yet they have different meanings. *Ingenious* means "gifted with genius," or "having natural talent." In Roman mythology, a *genius* was a guiding spirit assigned to watch over a person from birth. Gradually the idea of "spirit" came to mean "talent." So, today, *genius* means "a person born with a natural talent."

Ingenuous refers to someone who is innocently straightforward and honest. The word originally meant that someone had the virtues of "freeborn people"—people who were not born into slavery.

WRITE THE CORRECT WORD

Write the correct word in the space next to each definition. Use each word only once.

respectfully **1.** with esteem

quorum **2.** a minimum needed

ingenious **3.** very clever

averse **4.** feeling dislike

Prosecute **5.** to bring action against in a court of law

Persecute **6.** to mistreat

adverse **7.** unfavorable

ingenuous **8.** unable to deceive

quota **9.** an amount assigned

respectively **10.** in the order given

COMPLETE THE SENTENCE

Write the letter for the word that best completes each sentence.

___b___ **1.** The Coast Guard battled _____ weather conditions during the rescue mission.
    a. averse   **b.** adverse   **c.** ingenious   **d.** respective

___a___ **2.** The negotiator's solution to the conflict was so _____ that both parties felt like they had won.
    a. ingenious   **b.** respective   **c.** ingenuous   **d.** averse

___a___ **3.** Maria met her _____ by getting 25 people to sponsor her in the walk for charity.
    a. quorum   **b.** prosecution   **c.** quota   **d.** persecution

___d___ **4.** It is important to treat your elders _____.
    a. aversely   **b.** adversely   **c.** respectively   **d.** respectfully

___a___ **5.** Andy and Heather ran in second and third place, _____.
    a. respectively   **b.** ingenuously   **c.** ingeniously   **d.** respectfully

___b___ **6.** Although she isn't a fan of country music, Lauren is not _____ to going to the bluegrass concert.
    a. ingenious   **b.** averse   **c.** ingenuous   **d.** adverse

___c___ **7.** A prominent sign read: "This store will _____ shoplifters."
    a. persecute   **b.** adverse   **c.** prosecute   **d.** averse

___c___ **8.** Once Josh arrived, the student council had the necessary _____ to vote.
    a. quorum   **b.** ingenuousness   **c.** quota   **d.** ingenuity

___d___ **9.** Intolerant people may _____ those with different ideas or lifestyles.
    a. ingenuous   **b.** prosecute   **c.** ingenious   **d.** persecute

___b___ **10.** With an _____ disregard for danger, the kitten jumped on the sleeping dog.
    a. adverse   **b.** ingenuous   **c.** averse   **d.** ingenious

Challenge: Our city needs an _____ plan that will maintain economic prosperity while simultaneously addressing the _____ effects of poverty.

___a___   **a.** ingenious…adverse   **b.** ingenuous…averse   **c.** ingenuous…quorum

Azerbaijan's New ABCs

(1) Although an *ingenuous* kindergartner might admit to finding the ABC's difficult to learn, the alphabet is second nature to most literate people—except in a place like Azerbaijan. **(2)** In this small country, the alphabet and the script used to write it have been changed three times in the last 100 years, surely more than its *quota*! For twelve centuries, the Persian script was used. Then in the twentieth century, the Latin and Cyrillic alphabets came into use under the influence of Russia, and in the last twenty years, the script has changed again.

The changes were caused by fast-moving political situations. **(3)** The various alphabets were instituted by the *respective* regimes that ruled the country. Azerbaijan is a small country surrounded by Iran, Turkey, and Russia. Because it is rich in oil, it has often been a tempting target for conquest. After being part of the Russian empire, it enjoyed a brief independence from Russia from 1918 to 1920. But in 1920, the country was conquered by Soviet Russia. **(4)** The Soviets made many moves to modernize the country, and *persecution* of those who still followed traditional Azeri customs was not uncommon. **(5)** Some of the people who resisted Russian edicts were *prosecuted* by the new government.

(6) The Soviets believed that changing the alphabet was an *ingenious* way to further modernization. After all, most library books would become unreadable to children who were educated in another script. So in 1929, a committee chose to replace Persian script with the Latin alphabet for use throughout the Turkish Muslim area of the Soviet Union.

But in 1939, Soviet dictator Joseph Stalin suddenly announced that the alphabet would change again. **(7)** As in any dictatorship, there was no need for a *quorum* of citizens to vote on the decision. Overnight, Azerbaijan was forced to use the Cyrillic, or Russian, script. By changing the script, Stalin could force the countries he'd conquered to leave their past behind.

Latin: **Azerbaijan**

Persian: **آذربایجان,**

Cyrillic: **Азәрбајчан**

In 1991, after the collapse of the Soviet empire, Azerbaijan regained its independence. In a third change of alphabets, it reestablished the Latin script. Because the Azeri language contains some unique sounds, four letters were added to its alphabet.

(8) Some Azeris *respectfully* disagreed with their government's decision. **(9)** They were *averse* to implementing yet another alphabetic change. Now, however, all official documents, books, and newspapers are printed in Latin script. **(10)** But this latest change in alphabets has had some *adverse* effects on literacy.

Leyla Gafurova, director of the National Library in Baku, pointed out that most of the library's 4.5 million books are written in the Persian or Cyrillic alphabets. She worried that people would not be able to enjoy the work of their famous national poets. Parents who had not been taught the Latin alphabet complained that they couldn't help their children learn to read and write.

Despite the challenges, Azeris have adjusted to their situation. Today, stalls carrying Latin-alphabet newspapers can be found alongside old stone buildings and monuments carved with Persian script and bearing Cyrillic inscriptions.

Each sentence below refers to a numbered sentence in the passage. Write the letter of the choice that gives the sentence a meaning that is closest to the original sentence.

_____ **1.** A(n) _____ kindergartner might admit to finding the ABC's difficult to learn.
    a. clever   **b.** admiring   **c.** unruly   **d.** straightforward

_____ **2.** The alphabet has been changed three times in the last 100 years, surely more than its _____ !
    a. allotted amount   **b.** number of voters   **c.** given order   **d.** inventive cleverness

_____ **3.** The various alphabets were instituted by the _____ regimes that ruled the country.
    a. opposing   **b.** particular   **c.** honorable   **d.** peculiar

_C_   **4.** _____ of those who still followed Azeri customs was not uncommon.
    a. Certain percentages   **b.** The kindness   **c.** Mistreatment   **d.** The completion

_a_   **5.** People who resisted Russian edicts were _____ by the new government.
    a. brought to court   **b.** warmly welcomed   **c.** cruelly mistreated   **d.** deliberately ignored

_d_   **6.** The Soviets believed that changing the alphabet was a(n) _____ way to further modernization.
    a. orderly   **b.** admirable   **c.** deceptive   **d.** clever

_b_   **7.** There was no need for a(n) _____ of citizens to vote on the decision.
    a. accusation   **b.** minimum number   **c.** ballot   **d.** harmful event

_b_   **8.** Some Azeris _____ disagreed with their government's decision.
    a. happily   **b.** politely   **c.** loudly   **d.** needlessly

_C_   **9.** They _____ implementing yet another alphabetic change.
    a. favored   **b.** feared   **c.** disliked   **d.** ignored

_a_   **10.** But this latest change in alphabets has had some _____ effects on literacy.
    a. harmful   **b.** positive   **c.** helpful   **d.** dramatic

Indicate whether the statements below are TRUE or FALSE according to the passage.

_F_   **1.** Azerbaijan is a large country situated near India, Turkey, and Russia.

_T_   **2.** The Soviets believed that changing the alphabet was one way that they could make the Azeris modernize and forget their past.

_F_   **3.** The three alphabets of Azerbaijan are very similar.

FINISH THE THOUGHT

Complete each sentence so that it shows the meaning of the italicized word.

1. An *ingenious* machine might _____

2. Because of *adverse* conditions _____

WRITE THE DERIVATIVE

Complete the sentence by writing the correct form of the word shown in parentheses. You may not need to change the form that is given.

adversity   **1.** She overcame hardship and _____ to become a chief justice. (*adverse*) _prosecutor's_ **2.** The _____ excellent case led to the defendant's conviction. (*prosecute*)

quotas **3.** Some administrators would like to put strict _____ on the amount of newly hired people. (*quota*)

persecution **4.** Mass hysteria caused the _____ of innocent women in Salem, Massachusetts, during the witch trials in the 1600s. (*persecute*)

aversity **5.** It seems like he has an _____ to eating any kind of vegetable. (*averse*)

quorum **6.** Chris raced to the meeting so there would be a _____ for the important vote. (*quorum*)

ingenuity **7.** Technological _____ has enabled us to carry phones and computers wherever we go. (*ingenious*)

respective **8.** After the international summit, each leader returned to his or her _____ country. (*respectively*)

respect **9.** I have a tremendous amount of _____ for my science teacher. (*respectfully*)

ingenuity **10.** The child actor was skilled at portraying _____. (*ingenuous*)

FIND THE EXAMPLE

Choose the answer that best describes the action or situation.

_a_ **1.** Something to which you are NOT likely to be *averse*
  a. getting a reward **b.** enduring pain **c.** being criticized **d.** getting a failing grade

_c_ **2.** Something that is *adverse* to safety on the road
  a. wearing glasses **b.** braking **c.** speeding **d.** turning

_a_ **3.** The number of a majority *quorum* in a group of 100
  a. 51 **b.** 100 **c.** 50 **d.** 37

_d_ **4.** Something you should do if you had to meet a *quota* for buying music CDs
  a. listen to them **b.** sell one **c.** keep some at home **d.** buy more

_b_ **5.** Someone unlikely to be *ingenuous*
  a. first grader **b.** con man **c.** puppy **d.** newborn

_b_ **6.** Most likely to require *ingenuity*
  a. reading a book **b.** solving a puzzle **c.** watching a movie **d.** washing a car

_a_ **7.** A way to behave *respectfully*
  a. saying "please" **b.** loud insults **c.** stylish dress **d.** quiet scorn

_b_ **8.** If a skunk, deer, raccoon, and possum were to walk by, the first, *respectively*.
  a. raccoon **b.** skunk **c.** possum **d.** deer

_b_ **9.** How you would be most likely to feel if you were *persecuted*
  a. indifferent **b.** victimized **c.** amused **d.** appreciated

_a_ **10.** Where you would likely be if you were *prosecuted*
  a. in court **b.** on vacation **c.** in your room **d.** at work

Releasing and Taking Back

WORD LIST

abdicate	absolve	catharsis	countermand	impunity
recant	recoup	renounce	rescind	waive

The actions of releasing and taking back are found in everything from warfare to children's games. Kings and queens *abdicate* the throne. Generals *countermand* orders. Teachers *waive* homework assignments. The words in this lesson deal with variations on these themes.

1. **abdicate** (ăb´dĭ-kāt´) *verb* from Latin *ab-*, "away" + *dicare*, "to proclaim"
   To formally give up control, authority, or a high office
   • When King Edward VIII **abdicated** the throne of England in 1936, his new title became Duke of Windsor.

   abdication *noun* Critics claim that the CEO's hands-off management style was an **abdication** of his responsibility to stockholders.

2. **absolve** (əb-zŏlv´) *verb* from Latin *ab-*, "away" + *solvere*, "to loosen"
   a. To clear of guilt or blame
   • When another employee confessed to the theft, Mike was **absolved.**
   b. To relieve from a requirement or obligation
   • Just saying you are sorry doesn't **absolve** you of the responsibility for correcting the problem.

3. **catharsis** (kə-thär´sĭs) *noun* from Greek *katharos*, "pure"
   A purifying or refreshing release of emotional tension
   • Crying as he listened to the tragic opera was a **catharsis** for Julio after his stressful day.

   cathartic *adjective* Leticia finds that writing about her feelings in her journal has a **cathartic** effect.

4. **countermand** (koun´tər-mănd´) *verb* from Latin *contra*, "against" + *mandare*, "to order"
   To cancel or reverse an order or a policy
   • The general **countermanded** the lieutenant's order.

5. **impunity** (ĭm-pyōō´nĭ-tē) *noun* from Latin *in-*, "not" + *poena*, "penalty"
   Exemption from punishment or injury
   • Our justice system was designed to ensure that people cannot commit crimes with **impunity.**

abdicate

> Aristotle, a Greek philosopher, felt that tragic drama had a *cathartic* effect on viewers.

6. recant (rĭ-kănt´) *verb* from Latin *re-*, "back" + *cantare*, "to sing"

To formally take back or reject a statement or belief

- Despite the prosecutor's tenacious approach, the witness refused to **recant** her testimony.

7. recoup (rĭ-kōōp´) *verb* from Latin *re-*, "back" + Old French *couper*, "to cut"

To regain; to make up for

- In an attempt to **recoup** his lost income, the traveling salesman sued the dealership that sold him the defective car.

8. renounce (rĭ-nouns´) *verb* from Latin *re-*, "back" + *nuntiare*, "to announce"

a. To give up, especially by formal announcement

- As the story goes, the prince **renounced** his claim to the throne and married his true love.

b. To reject; to disown

- She decided to **renounce** any further involvement in the organization because she was upset with its leadership.

renunciation *noun* The king's announcement that landowners' taxes would be increased resulted in the nobles' **renunciation** of their oaths of loyalty to their sovereign.

9. rescind (rĭ-sĭnd´) *verb* from Latin *re-*, "back" + *scindere*, "to split"

To take back; to make void; to repeal

- When the rioting died down and the city became more peaceful, the mayor **rescinded** the order for a curfew at sundown.

10. waive (wāv) *verb* from Anglo-Norman *waif,* "ownerless property"

a. To give up voluntarily; to relinquish

- By signing the treaty with England, France **waived** all its rights to Canada and the Northwest Territory.

b. To refrain from insisting on or enforcing

- Kiko was such a talented violinist that Mrs. Vamos **waived** the requirement that students must be at least twelve years old to study with her.

waiver *noun* Although there was an ordinance against building additions on to existing structures, the city planners issued a **waiver** that allowed the family to add on to their home.

WORD ENRICHMENT

Penalizing words

The word *impunity* comes from the Latin word *poena*, which means "pain" or "penalty." The prefix *im-*, however, changes the meaning of *impunity* to "lack of penalty or punishment." Several other common English words are formed from *poena*, including *pain* and *painful.*

Many words that have to do with crime come from *poena*, as well, such as *penalty* and *penal.* You have probably heard of a *penal institution*, or a jail. A *subpoena* is a document that is given to a person who is then required to appear at court to give testimony. Because the prefix *sub-* means "under" and *poena* means "penalty," that person will be under penalty, or *penalized*, for not appearing at court.

WRITE THE CORRECT WORD

Write the correct word in the space next to each definition. Use each word only once.

recoup   **1.** to regain

abdicate   **2.** to formally give up a high office

catharsis   **3.** a release of emotional tension

recant   **4.** to take back a statement

countermand   **5.** to cancel or reverse an order or a policy

renounce   **6.** to reject or disown

waive   **7.** to refrain from insisting or enforcing

absolve   **8.** to clear of guilt or blame

rescind   **9.** to make void or to repeal

impunity   **10.** exemption from punishment or injury

COMPLETE THE SENTENCE

Write the letter for the word that best completes each sentence.

_b_   **1.** Many of the citizens were unhappy with the queen's edict and demanded that she _____ her throne.
    a. absolve   **b.** abdicate   **c.** recoup   **d.** rescind

_a_   **2.** When he sold his idea to the company, he _____ his right to a personal patent.
    a. waived   **b.** recanted   **c.** absolved   **d.** recouped

_c_   **3.** After the stock market crashed, many investors scrambled to _____ their losses.
    a. recant   **b.** absolve   **c.** recoup   **d.** rescind

_d_   **4.** The politician's career was ruined when she _____ her entire campaign platform.
    a. absolved   **b.** recouped   **c.** abdicated   **d.** recanted

_a_   **5.** The heiress _____ her father's money after they had a serious disagreement.
    a. abdicated   **b.** renounced   **c.** recanted   **d.** countermanded

_a_   **6.** After 86 years of disappointment, Red Sox fans had a(n) _____ when the team finally won a World Series in 2004.
    a. catharsis   **b.** renunciation   **c.** impunity   **d.** waiver

_b_   **7.** The spoiled, willful child misbehaved with complete _____.
    a. renunciation   **b.** impunity   **c.** abdication   **d.** catharsis

_c_   **8.** After years of not speaking to each other, Kristos apologized to his sister, finally _____ himself of his guilt.
    a. recanting   **b.** recouping   **c.** rescinding   **d.** absolving

_b_   **9.** The owner of the company _____ her offer, so the workers decided to strike.
    a. recouped   **b.** rescinded   **c.** absolved   **d.** abdicated

_b_   **10.** The sergeant risked a court-martial when he _____ the general's direct order.
    a. abdicated   **b.** countermanded   **c.** recouped   **d.** renounced

Challenge: Although the mayor was _____ of any involvement in the corruption scandal, he decided to _____ his position in order to spare the city embarrassment.
_a_   **a.** absolved…abdicate   **b.** recouped…rescind   **c.** countermanded…renounce

The Magna Carta

A document that has had a great impact on basic political and legal rights was drawn up and signed in England in 1215. This document was the Magna Carta, which means "Great Charter." It has been credited as the basis for civil liberties in both England and the United States.

Like many great political advancements, the Magna Carta arose out of a conflict. When King Richard I died in 1199, his brother John became king. Because Richard had spent all but six months of his ten-year reign outside of England, fighting in the Crusades, his barons had had free reign to control England.

The barons were unprepared for a tyrant like John. **(1)** King Richard had been revered, and the emotional and political *catharsis* that resulted from his death had hardly subsided when the barons felt the heavy hand of the new king. **(2)** John increased old taxes and imposed new ones with apparent *impunity*. **(3)** He *rescinded* freedoms and showed little respect for the law. **(4)** The barons, angered and alienated, would have wholeheartedly welcomed John's *abdication* of the throne.

During this time, King John had two strong adversaries—King Philip II of France, who wanted to attack England in order to gain more power, and Pope Innocent III who wanted his favorite bishop appointed archbishop of Canterbury. But King John refused to grant the pope's request. Therefore, with the pope's blessing, King Philip prepared to attack England. **(5)** Realizing that the clergy would not support his decision, King John *recanted* his previous statements, making peace with the pope, and accepting the pope's choice for archbishop of Canterbury.

(6) Knowing it was unlikely that King John would *countermand* the decisions that had affected the nobility, and seeing that his power had weakened, the barons rebelled. **(7)** By 1215, at least one-third of the barons had *renounced* their oaths of loyalty to John and prepared for war against him. **(8)** They were determined to *recoup* the privileges that they had lost. The king was not willing to give up any more of his authority; yet, without assistance, he could not oppose the barons. Finally, he was forced into meeting with the rebellious nobility at Runnymede, on the River Thames, and he agreed to sign the document that they had drawn up.

While a few of its sixty-three clauses dealt with the rights of the middle class, the Magna Carta primarily benefited the nobility. Nonetheless, this document has had an extraordinary effect on the evolution of constitutional government. **(9)** Certain clauses, including one in which King John *waived* his power to buy or sell justice, resulted in what we now know as the due process of law. **(10)** Another key clause, which *absolved* the barons from paying taxes that were not approved by a council of their own choosing, has come to be known as "no taxation without representation." Thus, the efforts of the barons in the early thirteenth century have helped to guarantee "liberty and justice for all" who live in the United States today.

Each sentence below refers to a numbered sentence in the passage. Write the letter of the choice that gives the sentence a meaning that is closest to the original sentence.

_____ **1.** The emotional and political _____ that resulted from his death had hardly subsided.
  a. release of tension   **b.** agreement   **c.** revolt   **d.** gain in support

_____ **2.** John increased old taxes and imposed new ones with apparent _____.
  a. limitless cruelty   **b.** freedom from punishment   **c.** loss of money   **d.** good sense

_____ **3.** He _____ freedoms and showed little respect for the law.
  a. strengthened   **b.** described   **c.** repealed   **d.** limited

_b_ **4.** The barons would have wholeheartedly welcomed John's _____ of the throne.
   a. alienation   **b.** resignation   **c.** triumph   **d.** release

_d_ **5.** Realizing that the clergy would not support his decision, King John _____ his previous statements.
   a. reaffirmed   **b.** grew to accept   **c.** ceased to blame   **d.** took back

_a_ **6.** Knowing it was unlikely that King John would _____ the decisions that had affected the nobility, and seeing that his power had weakened, the barons rebelled.
   a. reverse   **b.** free from injury   **c.** clear of blame   **d.** renew

_c_ **7.** By 1215, at least one-third of the barons had _____ their oaths of loyalty to John.
   a. regained   **b.** sworn   **c.** given up   **d.** admired

_d_ **8.** They were determined to _____ the privileges that they had lost.
   a. destroy   **b.** disrupt   **c.** give up   **d.** regain

_b_ **9.** Certain clauses, including one in which King John _____ his power to buy or sell justice, resulted in what we now know as the due process of law.
   a. raised   **b.** gave up   **c.** voiced   **d.** enforced

_a_ **10.** Another key clause _____ the barons from paying taxes that were not approved by a council of their own choosing.
   a. cleared   **b.** reversed   **c.** persecuted   **d.** accused

Indicate whether the statements below are TRUE or FALSE according to the passage.

_F_ **1.** King John was a peacemaker who ruled with understanding and compassion.

_F_ **2.** The barons believed that heavy taxes would make England stronger.

_T_ **3.** King John signed the Magna Carta to avoid war.

WRITING EXTENDED RESPONSES

Imagine what it would have been like to be an angry baron in the time of King John's reign. Then write a letter to a close friend describing the reasons for your anger. Your letter should be at least three paragraphs long and should address your friend personally. Detail two reasons that support or justify your feelings. Use a minimum of three lesson words in your letter and underline them.

WRITE THE DERIVATIVE

Complete the sentence by writing the correct form of the word shown in parentheses. You may not need to change the form that is given.

rescinded **1.** When a general issues an order, it is rarely _____. (rescind)

renunciation **2.** His _____ of the unjust laws of the old regime made the new leader very popular. (renounce) _abdication_ **3.** The princess's aides wondered what would become of them after her _____. (*abdicate*)

waiver **4.** Before she went on the class trip, Lila's parents signed a _____ that released the school from responsibility for any accidents she may have. (*waive*)

recanted **5.** The district attorney's office _____ its earlier statements to the press. (*recant*)

cathartic **6.** Some dramatic performances have a _____ effect on audiences. (*catharsis*)

absolved **7.** The court _____ Luke of responsibility for his actions. (*absolve*)

recouped **8.** Thanks to my insurance policy, I _____ all the financial losses that I had incurred from my injury. (*recoup*)

countermanded **9.** The vice-chancellor has _____ the trade embargo called for by the prime minister. (*countermand*)

impunity **10.** Because he was the prince, he was allowed by the royal family to behave with _____. (*impunity*)

FIND THE EXAMPLE

Choose the answer that best describes the action or situation.

_d_ **1.** Something most likely to cause a *catharsis*
    a. going shopping   **b.** waiting for a bus   **c.** doing homework   **d.** an unexpected victory

_a_ **2.** A likely action for which you would want to be *absolved*
    a. hurting a friend   **b.** taking a test   **c.** taking a nap   **d.** getting a tan

_b_ **3.** Something one would *abdicate*
    a. an employee   **b.** a position   **c.** a meal   **d.** a sporting event

_c_ **4.** Something you would most want to *recoup*
    a. blame   **b.** guilt   **c.** stolen jewelry   **d.** lost paper clip

_d_ **5.** Something you would be LEAST likely to want *waived*
    a. bill payments   **b.** math quiz   **c.** homework   **d.** rights as a citizen

_d_ **6.** An order you would NOT want to be *countermanded*
    a. detention   **b.** pay reduction   **c.** extra work   **d.** promotion

_b_ **7.** The most likely thing that people would want *rescinded*
    a. lottery winnings   **b.** unjust laws   **c.** good memories   **d.** high-school graduation

_a_ **8.** Something a person with *impunity* would never be
    a. punished   **b.** happy   **c.** free   **d.** regretful

_c_ **9.** Something you would NOT want *recanted*
    a. harsh criticism   **b.** false accusation   **c.** good references   **d.** unfair taxation

_a_ **10.** Something heroes would quickly *renounce*
    a. forces of evil   **b.** their families   **c.** loyal companions   **d.** their country

Taking Tests

Sentence Completion with Two Blanks

Standardized tests may contain sentence-completion items with either one or two blanks. You practice answering two-blank items in this book when you do the Challenge that is found in each lesson. You can apply what you have already learned about context clues to sentence-completion test items. Following these steps will help you to choose the correct answers.

Strategies

1. *Read the directions carefully.* You can lose credit if you don't follow the directions.

2. *Read the sentence completely.* Because "two-blank" items involve different parts of the sentence, it is wise to get an overview by carefully reading the entire sentence. Substitute the word *blank* for the empty spaces as you read.

3. *Look for words that fit the first blank.* To start, try to narrow your choices down to words that fit the first empty space. Make sure the word is the correct part of speech and fits in the context. Eliminate the other choices. Here is an example:

   Although some of the man's most admirable traits were not addressed in the _____, why _____ with an address that was so generally excellent?

a. laudable . . . simmer	**d.** eulogy . . . quibble
b. critique . . . eradicate	**e.** homage . . . dissuade
c. myopia . . . accolade	

   By focusing on the first blank, you can eliminate choices (a) and (c); neither *laudable* nor *myopia* will fit.

4. *From the remaining choices, look for words that fit into the second blank.* Eliminate any remaining choices in which the second word doesn't fit in the second blank. In the example above, try the second word for choices (b), (d), and (e) in the second blank. You can eliminate choices (b) and (e), for the critique cannot be *eradicated*, nor can the *homage* be *dissuaded*. Only *quibble* fits. The answer is (d).

5. *Reread the sentence with your choices inserted.* Two-item tests are difficult. Make certain to check your choices. At times, a few choices may fit, and you must choose the one that fits best.

Notice that in the following example, the two missing words (which have been filled in for you) are related.

Although just about everyone was <u>amenable</u> to the agreement, one political party remained <u>defiant</u> and refused to cooperate.

The word *although* signals that the first blank and the second blank are opposites in some way. So you can check your answer by making sure that the two words you've chosen are opposing. Some other key words that might indicate a relationship include:

- *not, but, never, hardly,* and *in spite of* (signaling opposites)
- *and, as well as,* or *in addition to* (signaling agreement)

Practice

Each sentence below has two blanks, each blank indicating that something has been omitted. Beneath the sentence are five lettered sets of words labeled a through e. Choose the word or set of words that, when inserted in the sentence, *best* fits the meaning of the sentence as a whole.

_____ 1. As he once again prepared to meet his _____ in the debate, he devised arguments that he hoped would _____ his opponent's points.
   a. detractor . . . extract
   b. official . . . detract
   c. raconteur . . . cease
   d. nemesis . . . refute
   e. epicure . . . mar

_____ 2. When the student asked for his coach's _____ opinion of his performance in the game, the coach admitted that it was only _____.
   a. candid . . . mediocre
   b. outspoken . . . retracted
   c. disinterested . . . laudable
   d. judicious . . . gloat
   e. humble . . . obstructed

_____ 3. The tentative statements of the _____ first-year students contrasted with the _____ pronouncements of their overconfident leader.
   a. swaggering . . . efficacious
   b. diffident . . . pompous
   c. intricate . . . infirm
   d. convoluted . . . egocentric
   e. modest . . . oblivious

_____ 4. Once feared for its _____, tuberculosis is now considered a(n) _____ that can be controlled through the appropriate use of antibiotics.
   a. pallor . . . munificence
   b. notoriety . . . infirmity
   c. prognosis . . . reverie
   d. susceptibility . . . deterrence
   e. virulence . . . malady

_____ 5. Jerome's reading of the seventeenth-century journal entries was _____ by the _____ language.
   a. obstructed . . . error
   b. hampered . . . archaic
   c. commenced . . . semantic
   d. scuttled . . . prototype
   e. obstructed . . . standard

_____ 6. The child was _____ enough to believe the most fantastic story that was _____ by those who sought to have fun at her expense.
   a. hypocritical . . . masqueraded
   b. guileless . . . verified
   c. gullible . . . generated
   d. duplicitous . . . envisioned
   e. astute . . . broached

_____ 7. Frankly, our hunger _____ from our politeness, so with barely a word, we rushed to _____ the savory morsels that were awaiting us.
   a. detracted . . . devour
   b. retracted . . . quaff
   c. extracted . . . simmer
   d. dissuaded . . . obliterate
   e. procrastinated . . . deliberations

_____ 8. Apprehensive and _____ by thoughts of the upcoming test, she simply wasn't _____ to the prospect of attending the play, no matter how entertaining it promised to be.
   a. refuted . . . pulverized
   b. preoccupied . . . receptive
   c. reproached . . . overt
   d. baffled . . . discerning
   e. eradicated . . . heedless

Negotiation and Diplomacy

WORD LIST

arbitration	attaché	consul	covenant	discretion
entente	insular	Machiavellian	protocol	status quo

Diplomats are officials who represent a government in its relations with other governments. Their jobs require great *diplomacy,* or "tact and skill in dealing with people"—something that can benefit most everyone. Learning how to negotiate and be diplomatic is the key to success in many aspects of life. The words in this lesson will help you understand and discuss matters of negotiation and diplomacy.

1. **arbitration (är´bǐ-trā´shən)** *noun* from Latin *arbitrari,* "to give judgment"
   The process in which parties involved in a dispute allow an impartial party to settle their differences
   • Because the ballplayers and the team owners could not come to an agreement on their own, they had to settle their contract dispute through **arbitration.**

   arbitrate *verb* The legal scholar often **arbitrated** trade disputes between companies from different countries.

   arbitrator *noun* As the recess monitor, Mr. Munck became the **arbitrator** for arguments on the playground.

an arbitrator

2. **attaché (ăt´ə-shā´)** *noun* from French *attacher,* "to attach"
   A person assigned to serve in a specific capacity on a diplomatic mission
   • An **attaché** accompanied the diplomat to the summit meeting to advise him about legal matters related to the issues on the agenda.

3. **consul (kŏn´səl)** *noun* from Latin *consulere,* "to take counsel"
   A diplomatic official who represents his or her own government's economic interests in a foreign country and assists fellow citizens living or traveling there
   • The French **consul** met with administration officials at the White House to discuss France's position on the new U.S. trade policy.

   consulate *noun* The residence or official premises of a consul; collective term for consuls of a given country
   • Many countries have **consulates** in both Washington, D.C., and New York City.

   consular *adjective* Her **consular** duties provided the opportunity to live abroad.

4. **covenant (kŭv´ə-nənt)** *noun* from Latin *com-,* "together" + *venire,* "to come"
   A binding agreement; a legal contract
   • The Geneva Convention is an international **covenant** that calls for humane treatment of soldiers and civilians during wartime.

5. discretion (dĭ-skrĕsh´ən) *noun* from Latin *dis-*,"apart" + *cernere*, "to perceive"
   a. The quality of using good judgment and self-restraint; the quality of acting wisely based on awareness of the potential consequences of one's actions
   • The personal assistant had enough **discretion** not to discuss the movie star's personal business with anyone.
   b. The ability or power to decide responsibly
   • Decisions about the reading curriculum were left to the **discretion** of the reading supervisor.

discreet *adjective* Editors are generally **discreet** about the text they are working on before it gets published.

discretionary *adjective* The school district granted the principal a small **discretionary** fund to use for anything he felt the school needed.

> Don't confuse *discreet* with *discrete*, which means "separate."

6. entente (ŏn-tŏnt´) *noun* from Old French *entendre*, "to understand" An understanding or agreement between two or more political powers, providing for a common course of action or policy
   • The United States and Canada reached an **entente** about immigration policies.

> The pronunciation of *entente* reflects its French origin.

7. insular (ĭn´sə-lər) *adjective* from Latin *insula*, "island"
   a. Suggestive of the isolated life on an island
   • The residents of the tiny mountain town lived an **insular** existence, disturbed only by a weekly newspaper and mail delivery.
   b. Having a narrow viewpoint
   • He was brought up in an **insular** suburban setting, so he is fascinated by the big, diverse city.

insularity *noun* The CEO's **insularity** became apparent when he asked for only the managers' opinions, ignoring the workers' viewpoints altogether.

insulate *verb* To live in harmony with nature, Henry David Thoreau **insulated** himself from the rest of society by living in a rough cabin in the woods at Walden Pond.

8. Machiavellian (măk´ē-ə-vĕl´ē-ən) *adjective* from Italian philosopher Niccolò Machiavelli's 1513 work, *The Prince*
Cunning, deceitful, and underhanded in business or politics; aiming to maintain power by whatever means necessary
   • In a **Machiavellian** maneuver, the company's vice president secretly secured enough votes from board members to have himself appointed the new president.

9. protocol (prō´tə-kôl´) *noun* from Greek *protokollon*, "table of contents"
A code of correct conduct
   • **Protocol** dictates that women curtsy and that men bow when presented to a queen.

> *Protocol* also means a code of conduct for diplomats, a plan for giving medical treatment, a first draft of an official document, or a way for computers to transmit data.

10. status quo (stăt´əs kwō) *noun* from Latin *status*, "state" + *quo*, "in which"
The existing condition or state of affairs
   • The new president plans to maintain the **status quo** for the time being before unveiling her new agenda.

WRITE THE CORRECT WORD

Write the correct word in the space next to each definition. Use each word only once.

Status Quo **1.** the existing state of affairs

Machiavellian **2.** cunning; deceitful

insular **3.** isolated

Protocol **4.** correct conduct

arbitration **5.** submission of a dispute to an impartial party

entente **6.** an agreement among nations

discretion **7.** good judgment

Covenant **8.** a contract

attaché **9.** a special staff on a diplomatic mission

consul **10.** a diplomat working in a foreign country

COMPLETE THE SENTENCE

Write the letter for the word that best completes each sentence.

_b_ **1.** The neighboring nations agreed to a(n) _____, promising they would work together to reduce air pollution.
a. discretion **b.** entente **c.** status quo **d.** attaché

_d_ **2.** People on that remote island chain must live a(n) _____ existence.
a. consular **b.** discretionary **c.** Machiavellian **d.** insular

_a_ **3.** The company and the labor union agreed to let a(n) _____ settle their dispute.
a. arbitrator **b.** attaché **c.** status quo **d.** covenant

_a_ **4.** In keeping with the proper _____, the two leaders exchanged gifts.
a. protocol **b.** covenant **c.** entente **d.** consulate

_c_ **5.** Mary's artwork is bold and original, and doesn't just go along with the _____.
a. arbitration **b.** insulation **c.** status quo **d.** attaché

_b_ **6.** Recently, Paul's father was named to serve as the economic _____ to Brazil.
a. protocol **b.** attaché **c.** entente **d.** discretion

_c_ **7.** In keeping the surprise party a secret, we all showed great _____.
a. consul **b.** status quo **c.** discretion **d.** covenant

_d_ **8.** We were shocked to hear of the _____ plan to rig the results of today's contest.
a. consular **b.** discretionary **c.** insular **d.** Machiavellian

_a_ **9.** Today at the wedding, the couple made a solemn _____ to be husband and wife.
a. covenant **b.** attaché **c.** arbitration **d.** status quo

_b_ **10.** In New York City, the Haitian _____ is located on Madison Avenue.
a. protocol **b.** consulate **c.** entente **d.** discretion

Challenge: It is amazingly easy for _____ voters, who have little awareness of the issues, to be deceived by _____ candidates who are only looking out for their own interests.
a. status quo…attaché **b.** discreet…consulate **c.** insular…Machiavellian

_c_

Diplomacy—Avoiding War

Diplomacy, the art of conducting international relations, is a crucial part of global politics. **(1)** There are two main ways that serious disputes between nations can be settled—by *covenants* or by war. It has been said that war is the failure of diplomacy.

Diplomacy has existed ever since the first disagreement was settled. **(2)** The first diplomats most likely were prominent people who were asked to *arbitrate* disputes among neighbors or neighboring peoples. Records of treaties between Mesopotamian city-states date back to about 2850 B.C. **(3)** Around that time, *insular* civilizations began to trade goods with one another. The rise in contact among people of different cultures led to an increase in conflicts and a need for diplomacy.

In places where many governments operated within a small area, as in the ancient Greek city-states of about 500 B.C., diplomacy was particularly important. Official representatives traveled between city-states to deliver messages. **(4)** These ambassadors were required to observe specific *protocol* and carry special documents.

During the Renaissance Era, Italy also had separate states ruled by powerful groups, such as the Medici family of Florence. Italian states sent permanent representatives to critical locations throughout Europe to protect the interests of their home governments. In this environment, diplomacy took on an even greater importance.

Considering the focus on politics, it is not surprising that Italy produced an important political theorist. Niccolo Machiavelli's (1469–1527) work, *The Prince*, written primarily for the Medici family, provided an analysis of effective leadership. In it, Machiavelli argued that a leader must set aside morals and use cunning, deceit, and any means necessary to maintain power and control. **(5)** The work remains controversial almost 500 years after its original publication, perhaps partly because some *Machiavellian* rulers have used the book's arguments to justify ruthless cruelty and deception.

The diplomatic system has continued to evolve along with civilization. **(6)** Today, embassies around the world protect their countries' interests in foreign lands and work to maintain the *status quo* with allies. **(7)** An embassy's staff is made up of *attachés,* advisors, and administrators, who are overseen by an ambassador. An embassy is usually considered to be part of the country it represents. This means that the United States' embassies located in other countries are actually considered to be on U.S. soil.

(8) *Consuls,* another part of the diplomatic system, are less involved in political affairs. Consulates perform such functions as regulating commerce, protecting foreign visitors, and granting visas.

Modern technology has changed the nature of diplomacy so that it moves at a much more rapid pace than it once did. **(9)** Government officials, such as prime ministers, presidents, and secretaries of state, can travel from place to place to negotiate *ententes* with allies. **(10)** Whatever form it takes, diplomacy requires tact and *discretion.* When practiced well, it has helped countless nations keep the peace.

Each sentence below refers to a numbered sentence in the passage. Write the letter of the choice that gives the sentence a meaning that is closest to the original sentence.

_b_ **1.** Serious disputes between nations can be settled by _____ or by war.
    a. ceremonies   **b.** agreements   **c.** arguments   **d.** money

_a_ **2.** The first diplomats most likely were prominent people who were asked to _____ disputes.
    a. settle   **b.** retreat from   **c.** strengthen   **d.** conduct

_d_ **3.** _____ civilizations began to trade goods with one another.
    a. Desperate   **b.** Informal   **c.** Official   **d.** Isolated

_C_ **4.** These ambassadors were required to observe specific _____.
    a. advice   **b.** footpaths   **c.** conduct   **d.** contracts

_B_ **5.** Some _____ rulers have used the book's arguments to justify ruthless cruelty.
    a. isolated   **b.** underhanded   **c.** grassroots   **d.** judgmental

_d_ **6.** Today, embassies work to maintain the _____ with allies.
    a. informal treaty   **b.** special ceremony   **c.** good cheer   **d.** current condition

_C_ **7.** An embassy's staff is made up of _____, advisors, and administrators.
    a. CEOs   **b.** principals   **c.** special staff   **d.** judges

_d_ **8.** _____ are less involved in political affairs.
    a. Cunning leaders   **b.** City halls   **c.** Financial leaders   **d.** Nonpolitical diplomats

_a_ **9.** Government officials can travel from place to place to negotiate _____ with allies.
    a. agreements   **b.** judgments   **c.** binding contracts   **d.** payment arrangements

_a_ **10.** Whatever form it takes, diplomacy requires tact and _____.
    a. good judgment   **b.** special staff   **c.** cunning   **d.** isolation

Indicate whether the statements below are TRUE or FALSE according to the passage.

_F_ **1.** The world's first treaties were created and recorded about 500 years ago.

_T_ **2.** Machiavelli's groundbreaking work, *The Prince*, is still a controversial book.

_T_ **3.** Consulates are less involved with political affairs than embassies are.

FINISH THE THOUGHT

Complete each sentence so that it shows the meaning of the italicized word.

1. Her *insular* views _____

2. After they reached an *entente* _____

WRITE THE DERIVATIVE

Complete the sentence by writing the correct form of the word shown in parentheses. You may not need to change the form that is given.

insulated **1.** I _____ myself from TV, video games, and other distractions so I could concentrate on my homework. *(insular)*

entente **2.** Several Asian nations reached an _____ about studying coastal erosion. *(entente)*

discreetly **3.** Keith _____ let his friend Tom know that he had a piece of food stuck to his tooth. (_discretion_)

machiavellian **4.** The steps you took to become the club president were downright _____. (_Machiavellian_)

arbitrator **5.** The two brothers couldn't agree about whose turn it was to use the skateboard, so they asked their older sister to serve as an _____. (_arbitration_)

covenant **6.** This _____ will assure that our two nations can continue to trade with one another. (_covenant_)

attaché **7.** The agricultural _____ confirmed that Argentina would export more wheat this year. (_attaché_)

protocol **8.** After the volleyball game ended, the players for the opposing teams followed _____ and shook hands. (_protocol_)

consulate **9.** When the foreign government dignitary was detained in Italy, he immediately called his nation's _____ officers. (_consulate_)

status quo **10.** Will the newly elected representatives from the opposition party challenge the _____, or will it be "business as usual" in the capital? (_status quo_)

FIND THE EXAMPLE

Choose the answer that best describes the action or situation.

_b_ **1.** Someone most likely to be referred to as _Machiavellian_
  a. funny comedian **b.** cunning senator **c.** thoughtful doctor **d.** quiet student

_a_ **2.** An example of a soldier following proper _protocol_
  a. saluting a general **b.** reading a book **c.** eating dinner **d.** writing an e-mail

_d_ **3.** What is most likely to happen when two nations reach an economic _entente_
  a. cessation of war **b.** outbreak of war **c.** misunderstanding **d.** increase in trade

_c_ **4.** Something most likely to require _arbitration_
  a. trivia questions **b.** music lessons **c.** contract disputes **d.** dirty windows

_a_ **5.** Another word for a _covenant_
  a. agreement **b.** diplomat **c.** negotiation **d.** restriction

_c_ **6.** A term that might be used to describe someone who is _discreet_
  a. gossipy **b.** insensitive **c.** self-restrained **d.** rash

_b_ **7.** What someone who yields to the _status quo_ would most likely do
  a. quit abruptly **b.** stay the course **c.** demand changes **d.** revolutionize policy

_c_ **8.** The most likely reason you would visit a _consulate_
  a. to watch a film **b.** to do homework **c.** to get a travel visa **d.** to serve on a jury

_d_ **9.** A place where someone might lead an _insular_ existence
  a. in a huge city **b.** in a dorm **c.** at a birthday party **d.** on a remote island

_c_ **10.** An example of an activity that an _attaché_ might organize
  a. a cultural event **b.** a game of chess **c.** an election **d.** a spelling bee

Excellence

WORD LIST

culminate	eclipse	epitome	impeccable	inimitable
optimum	peerless	quintessence	sublime	zenith

Excellence is an abstract concept with no exact measure. What one person considers excellent, another may not. The taste of a certain food, the story line in a book, the performance of an athlete—any one of these might be described as excellent, depending on who's judging. The words in this lesson provide a vocabulary to express a high level of achievement.

1. **culminate** (kŭl´mə-nāt´) *verb* from Latin *culmen*, "summit"
   a. To reach the highest point or degree
   • His soccer career **culminated** with being named state player of the year.
   b. To come to completion; to end
   • My cousin's long struggle to obtain a travel visa **culminated** in our tearful reunion.

   culmination *noun* The establishment of the nature preserve was the **culmination** of years of lobbying by environmental groups.

2. **eclipse** (ĭ-klĭps´) *verb* from Greek *ek-*, "out" + *leipein*, "to leave"
   a. To exceed or go beyond; to diminish others in importance or fame
   • Alexander the Great **eclipsed** other conquerors of his time by defeating the forces of Greece, Persia, and Egypt.
   b. To obscure or darken
   • The skyscrapers **eclipsed** our view of the lake.

   solar eclipse

   > An *eclipse* is also an event in which the moon moves between the sun and the Earth, hiding the sun from view.

3. **epitome** (ĭ-pĭt´ə-mē) *noun* from Greek *epi-*, "into" + *temnein*, "to cut"
   An example; a perfect representative of a type
   • Albert Einstein is the **epitome** of a great physicist.

   epitomize *verb* Andy Warhol's art **epitomizes** the essence of twentieth-century pop culture.

4. **impeccable** (ĭm-pĕk´ə-bəl) *adjective* from Latin *in-*, "not" + *peccare*, "to sin"
   Having no flaws; perfect; incapable of wrongdoing
   • After ten years of living in Switzerland, Nathan spoke **impeccable** French and German.

5. **inimitable** (ĭ-nĭm´ĭ-tə-bəl) *adjective* from Latin *in-*, "not" + *imitari*, "to imitate"
   Impossible to imitate or copy; unique
   • The song was an excellent choice to showcase the singer's **inimitable** style.

6. **optimum** (ŏp´tə-məm) from Latin *optimus*, "best"
   a. *adjective* Most favorable or advantageous; best
   • The car was designed with four-wheel drive for **optimum** handling in poor driving conditions.
   b. *noun* The point at which something is most favorable
   • His concentration was at its **optimum** early in the morning.

   optimize *verb* Marcus installed storm windows to **optimize** the efficiency of his home's furnace.

The plural of *optimum* is *optima* or *optimums*.

7. **peerless** (pîr´lĭs) *adjective* from Latin *per*, "equal" + English *-less*, "without"
   Having no match; incomparable
   • Mahatma Gandhi was a **peerless** spiritual and political leader.

8. **quintessence** (kwĭn-tĕs´əns) *noun* from Latin *quinta*, "fifth" + *essentia*, "essence"
   The purest essence of something; the most typical example
   • The fictional character Dracula is often viewed as the **quintessence** of evil.

   quintessential *adjective* The Eiffel Tower is the **quintessential** tourist attraction in Paris.

9. **sublime** (sə-blīm´) from Latin *sublimis*, "uplifted"
   a. *adjective* Impressive; awe inspiring; supreme
   • The **sublime** saxophonist Charlie "Bird" Parker was a genius at jazz improvisation.
   b. *noun* Something awe inspiring
   • The students' poetry ranged from the awkward to the **sublime**.

10. **zenith** (zē´nĭth) *noun* from Arabic *samt (ar-ra's)*, "path (over one's head)"
    The peak
    • At the **zenith** of his power, the man controlled a worldwide financial empire.

Zenith has several astronomical meanings related to a high point.

WORD ENRICHMENT

The fifth essence

Alchemy was a mystical endeavor that gradually evolved into chemistry. In the ancient world, alchemists believed that everything was made of four fundamental essences: earth, water, air, and fire. It was also believed that there was a fifth, more subtle, essence, which contributed to heavenly bodies but was hidden in earthly matter. Extracting this fifth essence from matter became one goal of alchemy. The essence was known in Latin as *quintessence*, for *quint* means "five" in that ancient language.

WRITE THE CORRECT WORD

Write the correct word in the space next to each definition. Use each word only once.

Zenith **1.** the peak

Peerless **2.** having no match

Culminate **3.** to reach completion

Optimum **4.** best

Inimitable **5.** impossible to imitate

Sublime **6.** awe inspiring

eclipse **7.** to exceed or surpass

Quintessence **8.** the purest essence

epitome **9.** a defining example

Impeccable **10.** having no flaws

COMPLETE THE SENTENCE

Write the letter for the word that best completes each sentence.

_C_ **1.** Aimee realized that she was running her best time ever and would easily _____ her previous record.
   a. optimize **b.** epitomize **c.** eclipse **d.** culminate

_b_ **2.** If you are _____, you have no equals.
   a. impeccable **b.** peerless **c.** eclipsed **d.** sublime

_d_ **3.** The _____ of our research was the publication of an article about our findings.
   a. optimum **b.** eclipse **c.** epitome **d.** culmination

_b_ **4.** After you reach the _____, the only way to go is down.
   a. optimum **b.** zenith **c.** quintessence **d.** eclipse

_a_ **5.** The professor's flawless research credentials could only be described as _____.
   a. impeccable **b.** culminated **c.** quintessential **d.** epitomized

_a_ **6.** Billie Holiday's _____ combination of voice and style can never be copied.
   a. inimitable **b.** eclipsed **c.** culminated **d.** quintessential

_d_ **7.** To _____ their chances of winning, the football team studied videos of their opponents in action.
   a. epitomize **b.** culminate **c.** eclipse **d.** optimize

_b_ **8.** The movements of a cat are the _____ of grace.
   a. culmination **b.** epitome **c.** peerless **d.** eclipse

_C_ **9.** Jeeves, the valet in a series of comic novels by P. G. Wodehouse, is the _____ of a gentleman servant.
   a. zenith **b.** eclipse **c.** quintessence **d.** optimum

_d_ **10.** Standing in front of Niagara Falls is truly a(n) _____ experience.
   a. culminated **b.** optimum **c.** eclipsed **d.** sublime

Challenge: Julie's years of study _____ in her first fashion show, and any doubts she had about her career choice were _____ by the audience's enthusiastic applause.
_C_ **a.** optimized…epitomized **b.** inimitable…sublime **c.** culminated…eclipsed

Lesson 17 109

Agustín Portillo

On the large canvas, people appear to be laughing at a party. The women wear elegant gowns, and the men wear suits and ties. **(1)** The people's skin is portrayed with *sublime* skill, in a range of hues. Yet, there is something about them that hints they are not the happy partygoers they seem to be. Their faces often express loneliness, disappointment, or discomfort. **(2)** Even as they appear to laugh, their happiness seems to be *eclipsed* by other feelings. Who are they really? The artist leaves the answer to the viewer.

The painting was done by visual artist Agustin Portillo. The figures on the canvas are actual people that Portillo has seen—around the city, on the subway, or in magazines. He brings them together as part of the party crowd, and each face reflects something he sensed in that individual.

Portillo's style of painting is called "expressionism." **(3)** In this artistic tradition, the *quintessence* of a person is revealed through the distortion of the human figure. Instead of rendering people as they appear in life, their emotions are given form by exaggerating their features, such as a cheek, an eye, a frown line, or a skin tone. In this way, inward emotion is given outward form. **(4)** The effect of Portillo's style on viewers is *optimized* by the size of the paintings, which are usually five to six feet high. Portillo says that he wants the people's faces to be on a human scale so that viewers can walk up and "meet" the people he has painted.

Portillo started painting in this expressionist style in the early 1990s. **(5)** In his *inimitable* way, he brought the people of his native Mexico City to life on canvas, just as he also portrays people in the United States. He said he has been fascinated by the colors, forms, and shapes that make up life in the U.S.

(6) Portillo was influenced by many styles of art, from the *peerless* works of the classical masters to the Mexican muralists, such as Diego Rivera and Jose Clemente Orozco. The muralists combined expressionism with a profound sense of social justice, which Portillo shares.

His passionate nature and determination to change what he perceives as wrongs in society was first expressed on the streets of Mexico City. Moving beyond imagery to genuine activism, Portillo organized a hunger strike in front of the Palace of Fine Art to protest what he saw as the injustice of the government towards artists. **(7)** The *epitome* of a political activist, he remained firm in his resolve, and willing to accept the consequences. **(8)** The string of events *culminated* in his leaving his native country for a fellowship in Chicago. Chicago became his new home in 2001.

Portillo then captured and interpreted what he saw in the United States. **(9)** The diversity he saw is *impeccably* portrayed in vibrant colors on his canvases. His desire for social change is still very much alive and is evident in his paintings. Sometimes the message is subtle, and sometimes it is very clear.

Agustin Portillo seems intent on combining expressive and beautiful art with the hope for a better life. **(10)** He has yet to reach the *zenith* of his career, so we can look forward to many more fascinating works of art.

Each sentence below refers to a numbered sentence in the passage. Write the letter of the choice that gives the sentence a meaning that is closest to the original sentence.

_____ **1.** The people's skin is portrayed with _____ skill, in a range of hues.
   a. impressive   **b.** obscure   **c.** most favorable   **d.** typical

_____ **2.** Even as they appear to laugh, their happiness seems to be _____ by other feelings.
   a. matched   **b.** represented   **c.** exposed   **d.** exceeded

_____ **3.** In this artistic tradition, the _____ of a person is revealed through the distortion of the human figure.
   a. incomparability   **b.** quaintness   **c.** purest essence   **d.** impressiveness

b   **4.** The effect of Portillo's style on viewers is ———— by the size of the paintings, which are usually five to six feet high
     a. made worse   **b.** made as good as possible   **c.** exceeded   **d.** unmatched

C   **5.** In his ———— way, he brought the people of his native Mexico City to life on canvas.
     a. copycat   **b.** perfect   **c.** matchless   **d.** final

a   **6.** Portillo was influenced by many styles of art, from the ———— works of the classical masters to the Mexican muralists.
     a. incomparable   **b.** old-fashioned   **c.** latest   **d.** boring

C   **7.** The ———— of a political activist, he remained firm in his resolve, and willing to accept the consequences.
     a. exact opposite   **b.** close synonym   **c.** perfect example   **d.** mirror image

C   **8.** The string of events ———— in his leaving his native country.
     a. began   **b.** peaked   **c.** resulted   **d.** ended

a   **9.** The diversity of America is ———— portrayed in vibrant colors on his canvases.
     a. flawlessly   **b.** competently   **c.** inadequately   **d.** decently

b   **10.** He has yet to reach the ———— of his career.
     a. end   **b.** height   **c.** middle   **d.** lowest point

Indicate whether the statements below are TRUE or FALSE according to the passage.

F   **1.** Portillo believes that his art and his social activism should be kept separate.

T   **2.** Portillo's style of expressionistic art exaggerates features, thereby revealing character traits.

F   **3.** Portillo did not find interesting subjects to paint in the United States.

WRITING EXTENDED RESPONSES

The passage you have read describes an excellent visual artist. Choose someone who is superb in another field. Then, in a persuasive essay, show how you think your subject has achieved this excellence. You should write an essay of at least three paragraphs. Include two or more examples and justify your choices. Use a minimum of three lesson words in your essay and underline them.

WRITE THE DERIVATIVE

Complete the sentence by writing the correct form of the word shown in parentheses. You may not need to change the form that is given.

Sublimely   **1.** In a famous Hans Christian Andersen tale, an emperor is captivated by a nightingale that sings ————. *(sublime)*

zenith   **2.** The sun reached its ———— just past noon today. *(zenith)*

inimitable

3. Choreographer Twyla Tharp is known for her ——— offbeat, but technically brilliant, style of dance. *(inimitable)*

peerless

4. For many years, the ——— New York Yankees dominated professional baseball. *(peerless)*

culmination

5. The ——— of summer camp was always a field day, highlighted by a picnic and a soccer game. *(culminate)*

optimize

6. For the group project, we tried to assign tasks in a way that would ——— the use of each person's skills. *(optimum)*

impeccable

7. Even the most ——— organized travel agent can't control the weather. *(impeccable)*

epitomized

8. The Beatles ——— rock music for an entire generation. *(epitome)*

quintessential

9. Robert Peary was a ——— explorer—courageous, determined, and energetic. *(quintessence)*

eclipses

10. It seems that every year an athlete ——— a previously set world record. *(eclipse)*

FIND THE EXAMPLE

Choose the answer that best describes the action or situation.

_a_ **1.** A *quintessential* characteristic of a good detective
   a. cleverness   **b.** athletic ability   **c.** ease of manner   **d.** police credentials

_c_ **2.** The most likely reaction to a *sublime* performance
   a. polite applause   **b.** walking out   **c.** standing ovation   **d.** yawns and stretches

_d_ **3.** Something or someone that usually reaches a *zenith*
   a. a calendar   **b.** a crosswalk   **c.** a window   **d.** a mountain climber

_b_ **4.** Something that is usually considered the *culmination* of senior year
   a. grades   **b.** graduation   **c.** job   **d.** pop quiz

_b_ **5.** Generally, the best way to *optimize* your grades
   a. find a hobby   **b.** study   **c.** take a break   **d.** cooperate

_d_ **6.** Something that is true of an *inimitable* style
   a. can't be successful   **b.** is the best   **c.** can't be equaled   **d.** can't be copied

_a_ **7.** Most likely to upset an *impeccable* housekeeper
   a. dust   **b.** doorbell ringing   **c.** new carpet   **d.** flowers

_c_ **8.** What something *peerless* will never be
   a. well received   **b.** imperfect   **c.** equaled   **d.** friendless

_c_ **9.** How a leader might feel if his or her power were *eclipsed*
   a. proud   **b.** fulfilled   **c.** angry   **d.** strong

_c_ **10.** Something that *epitomizes* strength and power
   a. the open sea   **b.** a light bulb   **c.** a fox   **d.** feather

Disagreement and Conflict

WORD LIST

affront	altercation	bellicose	breach	contentious
decimate	dissension	rancor	retribution	schism

Different people usually have diverse needs or points of view, which may at times result in disagreement. Sometimes we even experience internal conflict—tension or discord within ourselves—about what we believe or do. The words in this lesson will help you refine how you speak and write about disagreement and conflict.

1. **affront** (ə-frŭnt´) from Latin *ad-*, "to" + *frons*, "face"
   a. *verb* To insult intentionally and openly
   • Richard **affronted** Peggy by greeting everyone in the group but her.
   b. *noun* An open or intentional offense, slight, or insult
   • Michael considered it a personal **affront** when Shakila harshly criticized his writing.

2. **altercation** (ôl´tər-kā´shən) *noun* from Latin *altercari*, "to quarrel"
   A noisy or an intense quarrel
   • The restaurant manager asked the two patrons to settle their **altercation** outside.

3. **bellicose** (bĕl´ĭ-kōs´) *adjective* from Latin *bellum*, "war"
   Warlike in manner or temperament; eager to fight; aggressive
   • **Bellicose** tribes often inspired fear and loathing in the neighboring villages.

   bellicosity or **bellicoseness** The **bellicosity** of the protesters outside the building prevented the workers from being able to leave.

altercation

4. **breach** (brēch) from Old England *brec*, "a breaking"
   a. *noun* A break in friendly relations; an estrangement
   • In 1808, when James Monroe challenged President Madison for the party's nomination, a **breach** in their friendship ensued.
   b. *noun* A violation of a law, an obligation, or a promise
   • There was never a **breach** of the peace treaty signed in 1621 between the pilgrims and the Wampanoag tribe.
   c. *verb* To violate a law, an obligation, or a promise
   • The tenant **breached** the rental contract by moving out and refusing to pay the rent she owed.

> Another definition of *breach* is "an opening, a tear, or a rupture; a gap or rift."

5. contentious (kən-tĕn´shəs) *adjective* from Latin *com-*, "together" + *tendere*, "to stretch; to strive"
   a. Given to quarreling; argumentative
   • The **contentious** partners often argued about the management of their business.
   b. Involving or likely to cause argument; controversial
   • Because Drew was so inclined to argue, I made sure to avoid bringing up any potentially **contentious** issues.

6. decimate (dĕs´ə-māt´) *verb* from Latin *decem*, "ten"
   To destroy or kill a large part of a group
   • In the 1300s, the bubonic plague **decimated** the population of Europe.

   decimation *noun* Repeated hurricanes caused the **decimation** of the orange crop in Florida.

> *Decimate* originally referred to killing every *tenth* person, a method used by the Roman army to punish mutineers.

7. dissension (dĭ-sĕn´shən) *noun* from Latin *dis-*, "not" + *sentire*, "to feel"
   Difference of opinion; disagreement; discord
   • **Dissension** among top campaign officials contributed to the candidate's defeat.

   dissent *verb* It takes bravery to **dissent** in the face of pressure from friends.

   dissent *noun* The general was concerned about **dissent** among his troops.

8. rancor (răng´kər) *noun* from Latin *rancere*, "to stink; to be rotten"
   Bitter, long-lasting resentment; deep-seated ill will; enmity
   • The **rancor** between Javier and Ben even affected their friends, who felt forced to take sides.

   rancorous *adjective* The next congressional session may be especially **rancorous** because several key senators have stated opposing positions on important issues.

9. retribution (rĕt´rə-byoo´shən) *noun* from Latin *re-*, "back" + *tribuere*, "to grant"
   a. Something justly deserved
   • It seemed like the perfect **retribution** when Kevin slipped and fell into the stream right after laughing at Marla for doing the same.
   b. Something given or demanded in repayment, especially as punishment or revenge
   • The angry man demanded a huge monetary settlement as **retribution** for the damage done to his reputation.

   retributive *adjective* The ancient Greeks viewed **retributive** justice as a fitting and effective way to prevent crime.

10. schism (skĭz´əm) *noun* from Greek *skhizein*, "to split"
   A separation or division into opposing groups or factions; discord or discontent
   • There was such disagreement over the issue that it caused a **schism** in the organization, and the two groups never met together again.

WRITE THE CORRECT WORD

Write the correct word in the space next to each definition. Use each word only once.

retribution **1.** deserved punishment

schism **2.** a split within a group

affront **3.** an obvious insult

decimate **4.** to destroy a large part of

dissension **5.** difference of opinion; discord

breach **6.** a violation

altercation **7.** a noisy disagreement

bellicose **8.** aggressive

rancor **9.** bitter resentment

contentious **10.** quarrelsome

COMPLETE THE SENTENCE

Write the letter for the word that best completes each sentence.

_a_ **1.** As the _____ between the debaters intensified, their remarks became more and more insulting.
   a. rancor **b.** decimation **c.** retribution **d.** breach

_c_ **2.** Dudley, always on the defensive, felt it to be a personal _____ if anyone asked him to explain his actions.
   a. schism **b.** retribution **c.** affront **d.** decimation

_a_ **3.** Do you agree with people who say that you should never raise _____ issues at family gatherings?
   a. contentious **b.** retributive **c.** decimating **d.** bellicose

_d_ **4.** Up until a few decades ago, hunting, habitat destruction, and pesticides were _____ the population of our national bird, the bald eagle.
   a. breaching **b.** affronting **c.** dissenting **d.** decimating

_c_ **5.** The United States Civil War resulted from the _____ between the North and the South.
   a. affront **b.** retribution **c.** schism **d.** decimation

_b_ **6.** The _____ ended quickly, once everyone realized how silly the argument was.
   a. retribution **b.** altercation **c.** decimation **d.** breach

_b_ **7.** Several senators openly _____, as their party proposed the new legislation.
   a. affronted **b.** dissented **c.** breached **d.** decimated

_d_ **8.** Some animals, although shy by nature, may instinctively become _____ if you approach their young.
   a. retributive **b.** decimating **c.** schismatic **d.** bellicose

_a_ **9.** Ronda demanded _____ for her pain and suffering.
   a. retribution **b.** altercation **c.** decimation **d.** rancor

_d_ **10.** A _____ of trust is often fatal to a friendship.
   a. retribution **b.** schism **c.** dissension **d.** breach

Challenge: "Please be civil to each other," pleaded the organization's administrator, who knew that altercations can lead to _____, which can then cause a permanent _____.
_b_ **a.** affronts…retribution **b.** rancor…schism **c.** decimation…bellicosity

Windmill Battles

As the problems associated with burning fossil fuels become more apparent, scientists, businesspeople, and others are working to come up with alternate sources of power.

Of course it's easy to say, "We should do things differently." **(1)** But changing a system that has been in place for many years is bound to be a *contentious* process. Many businesses thrive on fossil fuels. **(2)** For some, the idea of changing to alternate energy sources is an *affront*, for it threatens their livelihood.

But imagine a technology that could provide power without these problems, from a source that won't run out and does not need to be drilled or mined. And using this technology could create jobs, too. Believe it or not, this is already happening. Wind power is the fastest-growing source of electricity in the United States. **(3)** But of course, no issue this significant is free of *rancor*.

(4) Some of the *dissension* over wind power comes from obvious sources. Coal, oil, natural gas, and nuclear energy companies do not want another source of competition. **(5)** But "wind farms," which are large groups of massive windmills, have created *schisms* among people who normally agree on many environmental issues. **(6)** When entrepreneurs offer a proposal for a new wind farm, it's often just a matter of time before a *breach* develops. Most environmentalists favor wind power as one way to reduce pollution. But others who are concerned with the safety of birds or bats—some of them endangered—point out that the huge, rapidly spinning blades on modern windmills kill flying animals. **(7)** These nature-lovers worry that wind farms could *decimate* populations of these creatures. Environmentalists in favor of wind power contend, however, that continuing to burn fossil fuels could play a role in wiping out some of those very same species.

(8) Though people on all sides of this issue have been known to be *bellicose*, landowners have been particularly vocal. Those who don't want their property value decreased or their scenic views marred often object to wind farms. **(9)** Protests against a recently proposed wind farm in Massachusetts included several *altercations* between pro-wind-farm environmentalists and anti-wind-farm landowners. Some people concerned with the welfare of birds sided with the landowners.

Solutions to complicated problems are rarely simple. Widespread use of wind power may be a solution to pollution, yet it creates problems of its own. Or it may be just one part of a complex patchwork of solutions to the world's energy issues. As with any major decision, people must weigh the risks and the benefits, the costs versus the rewards. One thing is clear, however. **(10)** If alternate sources of power aren't developed soon, Mother Nature will eventually seek *retribution*.

Each sentence below refers to a numbered sentence in the passage. Write the letter of the choice that gives the sentence a meaning that is closest to the original sentence.

_____ **1.** Changing a system that has been in place for many years is bound to be a(n) _____ process.
  a. insulting **b.** loud **c.** controversial **d.** vengeful

_____ **2.** For some, the idea of changing to alternate energy sources is a(n) _____, for it threatens their livelihood.
  a. split **b.** insult **c.** argument **d.** contest

_____ **3.** But of course, no issue this significant is free of _____.
  a. hostility **b.** extinction **c.** punishment **d.** insults

_____ **4.** Some of the _____ over wind power comes from obvious sources.
  a. disrespect **b.** bitterness **c.** hubbub **d.** disagreement

___b___ **5.** Wind farms have created _____ among people who normally agree.
    a. competition   **b.** divisions   **c.** punishments   **d.** compensation

___a___ **6.** It's often just a matter of time before a _____ develops.
    a. split   **b.** debate   **c.** congress   **d.** solution

___c___ **7.** These nature-lovers worry that wind farms could _____ these creatures.
    a. annoy   **b.** punish   **c.** kill many of   **d.** blow dry

___d___ **8.** People on all sides of this issue have been known to be _____.
    a. likely to chant   **b.** ready to eat   **c.** eager for help   **d.** eager for confrontation

___b___ **9.** Protests included several _____ between pro-wind-farm environmentalists and anti-wind-farm landowners.
    a. compromises   **b.** loud arguments   **c.** wrestling matches   **d.** incidents

___a___ **10.** If alternate sources of power aren't developed soon, Mother Nature will eventually seek _____.
    a. repayment   **b.** fur   **c.** lava   **d.** controversy

Indicate whether the statements below are TRUE or FALSE according to the passage.

___F___ **1.** Generating electricity from wind produces large amounts of pollution.

___F___ **2.** People who care about nature never disagree about energy issues.

___T___ **3.** Landowners are one group of people who often protest wind farms.

FINISH THE THOUGHT

Complete each sentence so that it shows the meaning of the italicized word.

1. There was so much *rancor* that _____

2. In an act of *retribution*, _____

WRITE THE DERIVATIVE

Complete the sentence by writing the correct form of the word shown in parentheses. You may not need to change the form that is given.

___bellicosity___ **1.** Warren's _____ made reasoning with him impossible. (*bellicose*)

___rancorous___ **2.** The _____ argument about who was right accomplished absolutely nothing. (*rancor*)

___contentiously___ **3.** "I dare you to prove me wrong," she said _____. (*contentious*) _dissent_   **4.** In some authoritarian governments, political _____ is punished. *(dissension)*

affront   **5.** The diplomat considered it an _____ to his integrity when the prime minister offered him a bribe. *(affront)*

decimation   **6.** The _____ of the local raccoon population was attributed to a rabies epidemic. *(decimate)*

schism   **7.** The _____ within the company resulted in the establishment of two separate divisions. *(schism)*

retributed   **8.** The requirement that he fix the window he broke is an example of _____ justice. *(retribution)*

breached   **9.** The legal dispute centered around whether the contract had been _____. *(breach)*

altercation   **10.** The batter was ejected from the game after an _____ with the umpire. *(altercation)*

FIND THE EXAMPLE

Choose the answer that best describes the action or situation.

_a_   **1.** A defining characteristic of an *affront*
     a. intent   **b.** secrecy   **c.** tact   **d.** volume

_b_   **2.** Something that one could *breach*
     a. a saying   **b.** a treaty   **c.** a memory   **d.** a war

_d_   **3.** Something that could have a *schism*
     a. an individual   **b.** a lamp   **c.** a lake   **d.** an organization

_c_   **4.** Something that has *decimated* human populations throughout history
     a. cows   **b.** sunlight   **c.** disease   **d.** trees

_c_   **5.** The most likely venue for an *altercation*
     a. piano concert   **b.** ballet recital   **c.** sports arena   **d.** library

_b_   **6.** The most likely reason for *dissension*
     a. obvious facts   **b.** differing opinions   **c.** oral traditions   **d.** strong agreement

_a_   **7.** Something that is likely to make a person *contentious*
     a. stress   **b.** luck   **c.** rest   **d.** vitamins

_d_   **8.** A comment that indicates *rancor*
     a. Pass the toast.   **b.** I trust you.   **c.** Mel is nice.   **d.** You disgust me.

_b_   **9.** Someone most likely to decide matters of *retribution*
     a. salesperson   **b.** judge   **c.** engineer   **d.** tutor

_d_   **10.** Someone most likely to be *bellicose*
     a. teacher   **b.** counselor   **c.** violinist   **d.** warrior

Taking Tests

SAT Critical Reading Tests

The new SAT, first administered in 2005, has a Critical Reading section that presents both short and long reading passages, each of them followed by multiple-choice questions. The strategies below can help you answer such questions successfully.

Strategies

1. *Scan the passage and the test items first.* This will enable you to look for specific information as you read.

2. *Read at an appropriate rate.* Read through the passage once to get the overall idea. Then reread it again slowly to make sure you understand it.

3. *Determine the main idea as you read.* The main idea may or may not be directly stated in the passage, but identifying it is critical to understanding what you read.

4. *Identify supporting details.* Details that support main points are often queried in test items.

5. *Be prepared to make inferences and draw conclusions.* These may involve making predictions or generalizations based on what you have read, or drawing logical conclusions from the information provided.

6. *Be prepared to make judgments.* Critical reading involves making evaluative judgments about ideas; fact and opinions; or an author's attitude, style, or tone.

7. *Refer to the passage to find information.* You do not need to memorize information from the passage, since you may go back to it if necessary.

Practice

Read the following passage. Answer the questions based on what is stated or implied in the passage. For each question, choose the best answer and write the letter of the answer you choose in the space provided.

Most people, if asked to list the rights conferred by U.S. citizenship, would place the right to vote high on their list. Yet approximately five million U.S. citizens are not eligible to vote in federal elections, and thus cannot enjoy full and equal participation in the nation's political life. How can this possibly be fair?

In addition to the 48 contiguous states plus Alaska and Hawaii, the United States includes several overseas dependencies. Guam, the U.S. Virgin Islands, and American Samoa are designated as territories of the United States, while Puerto Rico and the Northern Mariana Islands are U.S. Commonwealths. With minor exceptions, residents of all of these islands are U.S. citizens at birth, but they do not have the right to vote in national elections. Any of these residents who moved to one of the 50 states, however, would be entitled to all of the same rights enjoyed by any state resident, including the right to vote in national elections.

To understand what is responsible for this anomaly, it is necessary to review the U.S. Constitution—the document that defines the powers of our state and national governments. As currently interpreted, the Constitution stipulates that only a U.S. citizen residing in a *state* is eligible to vote for presidents, senators, and congressional representatives. Thus, citizens who reside in places other than the 50 states are not eligible to vote for these national offices. (For the same reason, residents of Washington, D.C., still do not have voting representation in Congress. However, in 1963, the Twenty-third Amendment to the Constitution was ratified, allowing District residents to vote for president and vice president.)

Despite the inequality in voting rights, the territories and commonwealths derive many benefits from their relationship with the United States. Foremost is the granting of U.S. citizenship and nationality. Also important are guarantees of fundamental freedoms, such as freedom of speech and religion. Each of the territories and commonwealths has the right to local self-government, and elects its own governor and legislature. All benefit from trade advantages, direct economic assistance, and favorable tax treatment.

The relationship between the United States and most of its overseas dependencies is not likely to change much in the foreseeable future. Many of the dependencies are significantly smaller than the smallest state. None of them has a viable political movement in favor of statehood. Puerto Rico, on the other hand, has a larger population than 24 of the 50 states and more land than Delaware and Rhode Island. In 1998, exactly 100 years after Spain ceded Puerto Rico to the United States, a referendum indicated that 46.5% of the island's voters were in favor of statehood. Perhaps one day Puerto Rico will become the 51st state; if so, its citizens will become full and equal participants in the political life of the nation.

_____ **1.** Which sentence best states the author's main point in this passage?
   a. Of all U.S. dependencies, the one most likely to become a state is Puerto Rico.
   b. There is a problem with the Constitution of the United States.
   c. Citizens living in U.S. dependencies cannot vote in national elections.
   d. Full political participation must always include the right to vote.
   e. U.S. citizenship benefits residents of the nation's overseas dependencies.

_____ **2.** In the phrase "To understand what is responsible for this *anomaly*," the word *anomaly* means
   a. terrible situation.   **d.** unavoidable error.
   b. something mentioned previously.   **e.** political climate.
   c. deviation from the rule.

_____ **3.** From the information given in this passage, you can conclude that residents of U.S. dependencies
   a. hope to bring their families to one of the 50 states.
   b. are all unhappy with current U.S. voting eligibility requirements.
   c. except Puerto Rico want to gain the right to vote in any election.
   d. are not interested in politics.
   e. could be granted the right to vote in national elections by a Constitutional amendment.

_____ **4.** What is probably the most important reason for the author's contention that Puerto Rico may one day become a state?
   a. Almost half of its citizens have shown an interest in becoming a state.
   b. It has a large population.
   c. It is closer to the North American mainland than any of the other U.S. dependencies.
   d. It has a land area that is actually larger than some states.
   e. The United States already has one island state (Hawaii) and two states that do not border the other 48 states (Hawaii and Alaska).

Honesty and Dishonesty

WORD LIST

apocryphal	bona fide	candor	cant	charlatan
chicanery	feign	insidious	rectitude	veritable

Have you ever heard an *apocryphal* story? Been surprised at somebody's *candor*? Met a model of *rectitude*? Have you ever *feigned* interest in something that actually bored you? The words in this lesson address different levels of truth and honesty, or the lack thereof.

1. apocryphal (ə-pŏk´rə-fəl) *adjective* from Greek *apo-*, "away" + *kruph*, "to hide"
   a. Doubtful; of questionable origin, authorship, or authenticity
   • The **apocryphal** manuscript was full of expressions that were not in use at the time it was supposedly written.
   b. False; fictitious or erroneous
   • Some people claim that there is gold buried in the hills at the edge of town, but others believe the story to be **apocryphal.**

2. bona fide (bō´nə fīd´) *adjective* from Latin *bonus*, "good" + *fides*, "faith"
   a. Authentic; genuine; not counterfeit or copied
   • After extensive examination, the museum declared that the stone arrowheads were **bona fide** ancient Native American artifacts.
   b. Done in good faith without any attempt to deceive; sincere
   • Was that a **bona fide** bid, or was it an attempt to raise the price so the auction house can make more money on the sale?

bona fide artifacts

3. candor (kăn´dər) *noun* from Latin *candere*, "to shine"
   Honesty, frankness, or sincerity of expression; openness
   • The governor was known for her **candor,** whether she was giving compliments, offering criticism, or admitting her mistakes.

   candid *adjective* In the military, officers of lower rank often request permission to be **candid** before expressing opinions to superiors.

4. cant (kănt) *noun* from Latin *cantare*, "to sing"
   a. Hypocritically moralistic language
   • We were tired of hearing the corrupt bureaucrat's **cant** about honest government.
   b. Monotonous speech filled with platitudes
   • Audience members at the political rally were eager to hear the candidates' plans for reform and were disappointed that the speeches were nothing but **cant** and empty rhetoric.
   c. The special vocabulary of a sect, group, or profession; jargon
   • A number of English words originated in the **cant** of nineteenth-century prisoners.

> *Cant* has several other meanings. One is "the whining, singsong speech of beggars." Another is "an angle, tilt, or slope."

5. **charlatan** (shär´lə-tən) *noun* from Italian *ciarlateno,* combination of *ciarlare,* "to prattle" + *cerratano,* an inhabitant of Cerreto, Italy, known for its quacks
A person who falsely claims to have special knowledge or ability; a quack or fraud
- The man had posed as a doctor for years before he was exposed as a **charlatan.**

6. **chicanery** (shĭ-kā´nə-rē, chĭ-kā´nə-rē) *noun* from Old French *chicaner,* "to quibble"
A deception by trickery; a trick
- The con man earned his money through various **chicaneries,** until he ended up in jail.

7. **feign** (fān) *verb* from Latin *fingere,* "to shape or form"
To pretend or represent falsely
- Uncle Eddy **feigned** sleep so the children would leave him alone.

8. **insidious** (ĭn-sĭd´ē-əs) *adjective* from Latin *in-,* "in" + *sedere,* "to sit"
   a. Working or spreading harmfully in a subtle or stealthy way
      - Some **insidious** diseases become well established in the body before symptoms become apparent.
   b. Beguiling or alluring but secretly harmful; treacherous
      - The **insidious** double agent tricked even the most experienced spies into giving her vital national security information.

9. **rectitude** (rĕk´tĭ-tōōd´) *noun* from Latin *rectus,* "straight"
Moral uprightness; righteousness
- If you claim to be an example of **rectitude,** you should avoid associating with lawbreakers.

   rectify *verb* To correct; to set right
   - Joel regretted his mistake and wanted to **rectify** it as soon as possible.

10. **veritable** (vĕr´ĭ-tə-bəl) *adjective* from Latin *verus,* "truth"
Real or genuine; actual
- My hosts treated me so well that I felt like a **veritable** king.

   verify *verb* To prove or determine the truth of
   - "Before we change course, let's **verify** the location and heading of the hurricane," advised the skipper.

WORD ENRICHMENT

Sitting words

As you already know, the word *insidious* comes from the Latin word *sedere,* which means "to sit." Many other English words come from this root. *Sedentary* means "accustomed to sitting or taking little exercise." *Sediment* is "material that settles at the bottom of a liquid"; in other words, it ends up "sitting" at the bottom. A *siege* often involves soldiers surrounding and blockading a city and then sitting around, letting the lack of supplies take its toll on the city's inhabitants. *Saddle,* which refers to a type of seat, comes from the Old English word *sadol,* which stems from the same Indo-European root as *sedere.*

WRITE THE CORRECT WORD

Write the correct word in the space next to each definition. Use each word only once.

feign	**1.** to pretend
candor	**2.** frankness; openness
insidious	**3.** subtle but harmful
rectitude	**4.** righteousness
veritable	**5.** real; actual

apocryphal	**6.** doubtful or false
chicanery	**7.** trickery; deception
Bona Fide	**8.** done in good faith
charlatan	**9.** a quack or fraud
cant	**10.** speech full of platitudes

COMPLETE THE SENTENCE

Write the letter for the word that best completes each sentence.

b **1.** This _____ wouldn't be as tiresome if we hadn't heard the same speech earlier this week.
  a. candor   **b.** cant   **c.** chicanery   **d.** rectitude

a **2.** Maura is a(n) _____ genius in math, able to multiply seven-digit numbers in her head.
  a. veritable   **b.** apocryphal   **c.** insidious   **d.** candid

d **3.** The mayor's reputation was unfairly ruined by _____ rumors.
  a. candid   **b.** veritable   **c.** bona fide   **d.** insidious

a **4.** Al tried to _____ confidence as he stood anxiously at the podium.
  a. feign   **b.** rectify   **c.** verify   **d.** cant

c **5.** Some politicians find it difficult to express controversial views _____.
  a. insidiously   **b.** apocryphally   **c.** candidly   **d.** veritably

b **6.** She's not just someone who likes karate movies—she's a(n) _____ black belt.
  a. apocryphal   **b.** bona fide   **c.** feigned   **d.** candid

d **7.** Most of the legend of Camelot is _____, but King Arthur is a historical figure.
  a. bona fide   **b.** candid   **c.** veritable   **d.** apocryphal

a **8.** The man offering free investment advice proved to be nothing but a _____.
  a. charlatan   **b.** chicanery   **c.** rectitude   **d.** cant

c **9.** When natural disasters strike, people usually look to their leaders to _____ the situation.
  a. verify   **b.** cant   **c.** rectify   **d.** feign

a **10.** Some people argue that advertising is nothing but expensive _____.
  a. chicanery   **b.** rectitude   **c.** charlatan   **d.** candor

Challenge: The philosophy class debated whether _____ friendship with one person in order to help another person was ethical, or just another example of rationalized _____.
b
  a. canting…candor   **b.** feigning…chicanery   **c.** feigning…rectitude

An Alligator in My Bathroom

On the day of the final exam, a group of philosophy students enters the classroom to find that their teacher has written just one question on the chalkboard: "Why?"

All the students, except one, begin writing furiously. The lone, calm student writes two words, turns in his paper, and then leaves. **(1)** When the grades are announced, the teacher says that most of the papers were full of *cant*. Only one student got an A. What was that one student's perceptive, appropriate answer? It was "Why not?"

Maybe you have heard this story before, or perhaps you have heard that alligators live in the New York City sewer system, or that car-sized goldfish live near dams, or that eating fizzing candy with cola will make your stomach explode. **(2)** These stories are *apocryphal* tales known as "urban legends" or "contemporary legends." **(3)** Regardless of what they are called, they provide us with *veritable* volumes of fanciful tales and intriguing rumors.

Such legends circulate among people of all ages. **(4)** Those who repeat the stories are not knowingly using *chicanery* to deceive their friends, family, or coworkers. **(5)** Rather, most people believe that they are reporting *bona fide* events. The stories usually start with something like, "This happened to my cousin's friend."

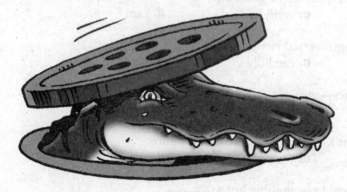

Researchers who study urban legends say that, as people repeat the stories, they simplify the stories' origins. For example, a source described as a "friend's cousin's friend" becomes a "cousin's friend." As a result, the stories often seem "close" enough to the current teller to be true. **(6)** Apparently this simplification is done, not to *feign* a story's origin and without conscious thought. **(7)** Through this somewhat *insidious* process, fiction is turned into something that resembles fact.

Why are urban legends so attractive? Researchers say that, like fairy tales, the stories usually entertain while conveying an important message. **(8)** Many tales *candidly* address topics that may embarrass or frighten people. Stories about ghosts are just one example. But scary legends do more than make campfires fun; the stories also warn against the dangers of parking in remote areas or entering an abandoned house alone.

(9) Other urban legends teach good behavior by showing the rewards of *rectitude*. One example is the tale of the boy who returns an elderly woman's lost purse and then inherits a million dollars from her.

In some ways, telling urban legends is an art form. Researchers find that most people use their imaginations to make the stories more interesting. Today, however, urban legends spread quickly via the Internet, and because people usually just forward the stories in e-mails without adding to them. Much creativity is lost in the process. **(10)** Another relevant downside is that the Internet also attracts *charlatans*. People have been caught *intentionally* spreading all sorts of false information, especially when there is monetary gain involved.

The bottom line? It's usually fine to have a good laugh (or scare) over an urban legend, but don't go basing any serious decisions on something that your friend said he or she heard, even if it supposedly came from that friend's cousin's friend.

Each sentence below refers to a numbered sentence in the passage. Write the letter of the choice that gives the sentence a meaning that is closest to the original sentence.

1. The teacher says most of the papers were full of _____ .
   a. obvious fakes   **b.** plagiarism   **c.** honesty   **d.** platitudes

2. These stories are _____ tales known as "urban legends."
   a. doubtful   **b.** righteous   **c.** sincere   **d.** authentic

3. They provide us with _____ volumes of fanciful tales and intriguing rumors.
   a. a lack of   **b.** subtle   **c.** actual   **d.** harmful

___b___ **4.** People who repeat the stories are not knowingly using _____ to deceive friends.
    a. openness   **b.** trickery   **c.** morality   **d.** impostors

___b___ **5.** Rather, most people believe that they are reporting _____ events.
    a. fictitious   **b.** authentic   **c.** righteous   **d.** faked

___d___ **6.** Apparently this is done, not to _____ a story's origin and without conscious thought.
    a. prove   **b.** harm   **c.** reveal   **d.** misrepresent

___c___ **7.** Through this somewhat _____ process, fiction is turned into something that resembles fact.
    a. honest or open   **b.** readily proven   **c.** subtly harmful   **d.** false or erroneous

___b___ **8.** Many tales _____ address topics that may embarrass or frighten people.
    a. secretly   **b.** frankly   **c.** piously   **d.** crudely

___b___ **9.** Other urban legends teach good behavior by showing the rewards of _____.
    a. speed   **b.** morality   **c.** platitudes   **d.** trickery

___d___ **10.** The Internet also attracts _____.
    a. philanthropists   **b.** stories   **c.** preachers   **d.** frauds

Indicate whether the statements below are TRUE or FALSE according to the passage.

___F___ **1.** Urban legends often deal with people's real fears and concerns.

___T___ **2.** Even if they aren't true, legends can have educational value.

___F___ **3.** It's easy to discern when people are telling an urban legend because they are knowingly lying.

WRITING EXTENDED RESPONSES

Do you think that urban legends do more good than harm, or more harm than good? Write a persuasive essay that expresses your point of view. Elaborate on at least two reasons that support your opinion. Your essay should be three or more paragraphs long. Use a minimum of three lesson words in your essay and underline them.

WRITE THE DERIVATIVE

Complete the sentence by writing the correct form of the word shown in parentheses. You may not need to change the form that is given.

cant **1.** In sailor's _____, a "tack" is not something you stick into a bulletin board.
    (*cant*)

rectitude **2.** The bigoted politician was not the example of moral _____ he claimed to be.
    (*rectitude*)

charlatan **3.** The scientist was a _____ who adjusted experimental outcomes to achieve the desired results. *(charlatan)*

bona fide **4.** The silversmith's initials on the back of the handle proved that the silver spoon was a _____ antique. *(bona fide)*

apocryphal **5.** Ever since Elvis died, there have been _____ stories of the famed entertainer showing up at local snack shacks or shopping malls. *(apocryphal)*

chicanery **6.** She said, "I see right through your _____, and I will most certainly not sign that piece of paper." *(chicanery)*

insidiously **7.** The termites worked _____, weakening the structure of the house without making a sound. *(insidious)*

veritable **8.** The lottery winnings made Dean a _____ millionaire. *(veritable)*

feigning **9.** Is _____ interest in a conversation a good way to avoid hurting a friend's feelings, or is it simply deception? *(feign)*

candid **10.** Politicians who give _____ answers to reporters' questions usually distinguish themselves in the eyes of the press and the public. *(candor)*

FIND THE EXAMPLE

Choose the answer that best describes the action or situation.

C **1.** Something you should make sure is *bona fide* before paying lots of money for it
    a. costume jewelry   **b.** Egyptian sand   **c.** Picasso painting   **d.** fifty-year-old steak

b **2.** Something *insidious*
    a. clean air   **b.** disease without symptoms   **c.** exercise bikes   **d.** armed robbery

C **3.** What a *charlatan* attorney would most likely NOT have done.
    a. received fees   **b.** opened an office   **c.** graduated law school   **d.** lied to clients

d **4.** Something most people consider to be *apocryphal*
    a. the planet Jupiter   **b.** the Milky Way   **c.** great white sharks   **d.** Loch Ness Monster

d **5.** An example of *chicanery*
    a. bragging   **b.** protesting   **c.** arguing   **d.** lying

6. A sure sign of a *veritable* blizzard
    b. gray skies   **c.** blowing snow   **d.** strong winds

C **7.** Something that should be *rectified* if possible
    a. a willow tree   **b.** a mistake   **c.** a false prophet   **d.** a song

a **8.** Someone with whom you're most likely to talk *candidly*
    a. best friend   **b.** stranger   **c.** guard   **d.** acquaintance

a **9.** One way to *feign* sleep
    a. pretend to snore   **b.** dream   **c.** run   **d.** whistle

d **10.** A synonym for *cant*
    a. glossary   **b.** literature   **c.** inability   **d.** jargon

Business and Finance

WORD LIST

accrue	arbiter	audit	cartel	collateral
commodity	conglomerate	liquidate	lucrative	security

Business and finance are closely related but refer to different activities.
Business generally refers to the production and delivery of goods
and services for sale. Finance concerns the management of money,
investments, and credit. Like other fields of human endeavor, business
and finance have specialized vocabularies.

1. accrue (ə-krōō´) *verb* from Latin *accrescere*, "to grow"
To increase, accumulate, or come about as a result of growth
• My account **accrued** almost a hundred dollars in interest last year.

accrual *noun* Margo's **accrual** of sick leave over several years allowed
her to receive her full salary during her extended stay in the hospital.

2. arbiter (är´bĭ-tər) *noun*
  a. A person chosen to judge or decide a disputed issue
    • The retired judge served as the **arbiter** of the contract
      disagreement between the union and management.
  b. A person who has the power to judge at will
    • Who made her the **arbiter** of good taste?

arbitrate *verb* I'm feel like I'm always **arbitrating** disagreements
between my two best friends.

arbitration *noun* **Arbitration** settled the dispute.

3. audit (ô´dĭt) from Latin *auditus*, "a hearing"
  a. *verb* To examine, verify, or correct the financial accounts of
    • Corporations are **audited** by independent accounting firms.
  b. *noun* A review of records or financial accounts to check their
      accuracy
    • The IRS **audit** revealed that the man had paid all of his taxes.
  c. *verb* To attend a course without requesting or receiving
      academic credit
    • Tyra **audited** a French class before vacationing in Paris.

audit

4. cartel (kär-tĕl´) *noun* from Latin *carta*, "paper made from papyrus"
A group of independent businesses formed to control production,
pricing, and marketing of goods
• The Organization of Petroleum Exporting Countries (OPEC) is a
  cartel founded in 1960 to control the supply and price of oil.

Cartels are formed by the
producers and suppliers
(rather than the consumers)
of goods. Cartels are illegal in
the United States.

5. collateral (kə-lăt´ər-əl) from Latin *com-*, "together" + *latus*, "side"
   a. *noun* Property that is pledged as security for a loan if the loan is not repaid, the property is taken
   • Eddie used his valuable coin collection as **collateral** for the loan he needed to buy a car.
   b. *adjective* Serving to support or corroborate
   • My sweat-stained shirt and red face were certainly **collateral** evidence that I had run the two miles the coach required.
   c. *adjective* Of a secondary nature; subordinate
   • The town was not directly hit by the hurricane but suffered **collateral** damage as a result of flooding and heavy winds.

6. commodity (kə-mŏd´ĭ-tē) *noun* from Latin *commodus,* "convenient"
   a. An item of trade or commerce, especially an agricultural or a mining product
   • Cocoa is a **commodity** that the United States imports.
   b. Something or someone valuable and useful
   • In today's world, multilingual workers are a valuable **commodity.**

7. conglomerate from Latin *com-,* "together" + *glomerare,* "to wind into a ball"
   a. *noun* (kən-glŏm´ə-rĭt´) A corporation made up of a number of companies that operate in different fields
   • A book publisher may be owned by a **conglomerate** that also owns oil, gas, and manufacturing companies.
   b. *verb* (kən-glŏm´ə-rāt´) To form or gather into a mass or whole
   • Dozens of seagulls seemed to have **conglomerated** into a solid mass on the rock.

8. liquidate (lĭk´wĭ-dāt´) *verb* from Latin *liquidare,* "to melt"
   a. To settle a debt, claim, or other obligation by selling property or goods
   • In order to pay all of its bills, Frank's Furniture was forced to **liquidate** its entire inventory.
   b. To convert assets into cash
   • Bob **liquidated** his stock portfolio and used the money to buy a retirement home.

   liquidation *noun* The **liquidation** of her doll collection netted Annie several thousand dollars.

9. lucrative (loo´krə-tĭv) *adjective* from Latin *lucrum,* "profit"
   Producing wealth; profitable
   • After earning his master's degree, Julio got a **lucrative** position as a software developer.

10. security (sĭ-kyoor´ĭ-tē) *noun* from Latin *securus,* "secure"
   a. A document showing ownership or something owed; a stock or bond
   • That **security** is traded on the New York Stock Exchange.
   b. Something deposited or given as assurance of the fulfillment of an obligation; a pledge; collateral
   • She offered her best pair of earrings as **security** for the loan of her sister's angora sweater.

> *Security* also means "freedom from risk or danger."

Business and Finance

WRITE THE CORRECT WORD

Write the correct word in the space next to each definition. Use each word only once.

Cartel **1.** a group formed to control production

audit **2.** to examine finances

lucrative **3.** profitable

liquidate **4.** to sell off assets

security **5.** a stock or bond

Collateral **6.** something pledged to secure a loan

Conglomerate **7.** to form into a whole

arbiter **8.** the judge in a dispute

accrue **9.** to accumulate

Commodity **10.** a product

COMPLETE THE SENTENCE

Write the letter for the word that best completes each sentence.

_b_ **1.** Was it a(n) _____ opportunity, or a foolish plan destined to lose money?
   a. liquidated   **b.** lucrative   **c.** collateral   **d.** audited

_d_ **2.** The _____ gave each side five minutes to state his side of the case.
   a. cartel   **b.** audit   **c.** conglomerate   **d.** arbiter

_c_ **3.** Even when you've paid your taxes conscientiously, being _____ is unpleasant.
   a. liquidated   **b.** conglomerated   **c.** audited   **d.** accrued

_a_ **4.** The separate businesses combined into a single _____ to create a stronger financial structure.
   a. conglomerate   **b.** liquidation   **c.** commodity   **d.** collateral

_c_ **5.** The bank closed down the failing company and _____ all its assets to raise cash.
   a. accrued   **b.** conglomerated   **c.** liquidated   **d.** arbitrated

_b_ **6.** Since I own my car, I was able to use it as _____ for the loan.
   a. cartel   **b.** collateral   **c.** audits   **d.** accrual

_d_ **7.** _____ often benefit the producers while consumers end up paying more.
   a. Liquidations   **b.** Audits   **c.** Securities   **d.** Cartels

_c_ **8.** Instead of using any vacation time, I let it _____ so I could take a long trip.
   a. liquidate   **b.** conglomerate   **c.** accrue   **d.** audit

_a_ **9.** Lumber and pork bellies are two of the _____ traded on the Chicago Mercantile Exchange.
   a. commodities   **b.** cartels   **c.** conglomerates   **d.** audits

_b_ **10.** Newspapers devote entire sections to the day-to-day price fluctuations of _____.
   a. arbiters   **b.** securities   **c.** cartels   **d.** accruals

Challenge: Some people seem to think that happiness is a _____ that _____ with the number of things you own, but I think the opposite is true.
_b_   **a.** cartel...audits   **b.** commodity...accrues   **c.** conglomerate...arbitrates

Futures Exchanges

The roots of today's futures exchanges go back to ancient times when farmers brought their produce to fairs. In addition to selling what they had, they drew up contracts that bound them to deliver crops at a future time, place, and price.

(1) Futures trading is the basis of today's *commodities* market. Here's a simplified example of how it works: In March, roughly six months before wheat can be harvested, a commodities trader will agree to buy the wheat from farmers at four dollars per bushel. **(2)** A futures contract is drawn up and signed, to be *liquidated* in September when the wheat is available. **(3)** If the selling price of wheat actually turns out to be five dollars in September, a profit of one dollar per bushel *accrues* to the trader. If, however, the September selling price is three dollars per bushel, the trader will have to buy it from the farmers at the contracted price of four dollars, but will have to sell it at the going price of three dollars, thus losing a dollar per bushel. So, depending on how well they can predict the future prices of commodities, these traders either earn profits or incur losses.

Farmers often want to make sure that they can sell their crops at a certain price, so they typically agree to a standardized futures contract. Two types of traders assume the risks of accepting these transactions: "market makers" and "speculators." Market makers tend to be either small firms or individuals. **(4)** Most speculators are similarly small, but some *conglomerates* deal in speculation, too.

(5) Agricultural products, metals, currency, and even *securities* are traded on today's futures market. **(6)** A career in futures trading can be *lucrative* but also risky. **(7)** Traders who have made incorrect predictions

of market trends have lost homes they'd put up as *collateral* for contracts.

(8) Openness in futures trading is the key to keeping prices fair and beyond the influence of *cartels* that might try to control the market by illegally influencing prices or driving out competition.

MARCH SEPTEMBER

Of course, no system is perfect. From time to time, corruption surfaces. **(9)** For this reason, regulatory agencies conduct *audits* of futures transactions. **(10)** Some of the exchanges, such as the Chicago Mercantile Exchange, have committees that *arbitrate* disputes between clients. Finally, the Commodities Futures Trading Commission is supposed to police the whole futures industry.

Commodity exchanges have come a long way from individual farmers who promised to bring future goods to local merchants. Yet today, as in ancient times, the exchanges play a vital role in spreading risk and allocating products in efficient ways, not to mention making profits for the traders who assume the risk of speculating in commodities.

Each sentence below refers to a numbered sentence in the passage. Write the letter of the choice that gives the sentence a meaning that is closest to the original sentence.

_____ C **1.** Futures trading is the basis of today's _____ market.
   a. stock   **b.** corporation   **c.** products   **d.** loan

_____ b **2.** A futures contract is drawn up and signed, to be _____ in September when the wheat is available.
   a. grown   **b.** settled   **c.** examined   **d.** increased

_____ **3.** If the selling price of wheat actually turns out to be five dollars in September, a profit of one dollar per bushel _____ the trader.
   a. is corrected by   **b.** organizes with   **c.** is lost from   **d.** comes to

_____ **4.** Most speculators are similarly small, but some _____ deal in speculation, too.
   a. useful products   **b.** dispute-solvers   **c.** stocks and bonds   **d.** multi-company groups

a 5. Agricultural products, metals, currency, and even _____ are traded on today's futures market.
   a. stocks and bonds   **b.** documents   **c.** examinations   **d.** large corporations

b 6. A career in futures trading can be _____ but also risky.
   a. useful   **b.** profitable   **c.** organized   **d.** secondary

a 7. Traders have lost homes that they'd put up as _____ for contracts.
   a. secure pledges   **b.** corporations   **c.** examinations   **d.** stubborn disputes

d 8. Openness in futures trading is the key to keeping prices fair and beyond the influence of _____ that might try to control the market illegally.
   a. disputes   **b.** problem solvers   **c.** pledges   **d.** groups of businesses

c 9. For this reason, regulatory agencies conduct _____ of futures transactions.
   a. deceptions   **b.** profits   **c.** reviews   **d.** securities

b 10. Some of the exchanges, such as the Chicago Mercantile Exchange, have committees that _____ disputes between clients.
   a. verify   **b.** settle   **c.** question   **d.** copy

Indicate whether the statements below are TRUE or FALSE according to the passage.

F 1. Once a futures contract is set, the price a futures trader pays for a product does not change.

F 2. The roots of futures exchanges go back in time to about 1945.

F 3. Those who pursue futures trading as a career are generally guaranteed a steady income.

FINISH THE THOUGHT

Complete each sentence so that it shows the meaning of the italicized word.

1. I *accrued* _____

2. The *cartel* _____

WRITE THE DERIVATIVE

Complete the sentence by writing the correct form of the word shown in parentheses. You may not need to change the form that is given.

securities **1.** She made her fortune in the _____ market before she became a full-time philanthropist. *(security)*

arbiters **2.** Even with _____ the owners and players couldn't come to an agreement, so all the games for the season were canceled. *(arbiter)* _collateral_   **3.** I can offer this watch as _____. *(collateral)*

lucrative   **4.** Jenna was lucky enough to stumble onto a _____ opportunity. *(lucrative)*

cartels   **5.** Because fixing prices is against the law in the United States, _____ are illegal. *(cartel)*

liquidated   **6.** When the cycling store _____ its inventory, I was able to buy a bike I had been wanting for a long time. *(liquidate)*

accruement   **7.** Many consumers have found themselves deeper in debt because of the _____ of high interest on credit cards. *(accrue)*

audited   **8.** The 1934 Securities and Exchange Act required all publicly traded companies to have their financial information _____. *(audit)*

commodities   **9.** Wheat is one of several agricultural _____ that is grown in many parts of the world. *(commodity)*

conglomerate   **10.** The advantage of a _____ is that the profits from one company can be used to develop another company. *(conglomerate)*

FIND THE EXAMPLE

Choose the answer that best describes the action or situation.

_C_   **1.** The reason most business *cartels* form
    a. to reduce loans   **b.** to deal illegally   **c.** to control prices   **d.** to reduce debt

_a_   **2.** The word most likely to follow the words *Giant Liquidation* in an advertisement
    a. *Sale!*   **b.** *Security!*   **c.** *Opening!*   **d.** *Business!*

_b_   **3.** Something that could realistically be resolved with *arbitration*
    a. illegal sales   **b.** contract dispute   **c.** weather forecast   **d.** marathon winner

_d_   **4.** The *commodity* most likely to be an object of futures trading
    a. toys   **b.** books   **c.** paintings   **d.** soybeans

_d_   **5.** Something that *accrues* over time
    a. youthfulness   **b.** a car's value   **c.** ice in springtime   **d.** dust in corners

_C_   **6.** The most likely name of a *conglomerate*
    a. Sadie's Fashions   **b.** Joe's Groceries   **c.** Omni-Corp   **d.** Surf's Up!

_b_   **7.** The typical subject of an *audit*
    a. temperature records   **b.** financial records   **c.** athletic records   **d.** vinyl records

_a_   **8.** Something always true of *lucrative* work
    a. pays well   **b.** very enjoyable   **c.** somewhat boring   **d.** easy to do

_C_   **9.** Something likely to be accepted as *collateral* for a loan
    a. clothing   **b.** signature   **c.** real estate   **d.** food

_d_   **10.** A type of *security* bought and sold on exchanges around the world
    a. wheat   **b.** checks   **c.** banks   **d.** stocks

Help and Harm

WORD LIST

adulterate	bane	boon	inimical	malevolent
panacea	pernicious	salutary	toxic	vitiate

Just as something that is usually helpful can be harmful, so something that is usually harmful can be helpful. Some bacteria cause disease, but some aid digestion. Bees sting, but they also pollinate flowers and make honey. Medicines and vitamins are helpful, but can be harmful in very high doses. The words in this lesson express different aspects of help and harm.

1. adulterate (ə-dŭl´tə-rāt´) *verb* from Latin *adulterare*, "to pollute"
To make impure by adding improper, inferior, or unnecessary ingredients
• Early forgers **adulterated** gold coins by adding bronze or copper.

adulteration *noun* Because of the **adulteration** of the water supply by sewage, residents were told to boil their water before using it.

2. bane (bān) *noun* from Old English *bana*, "destroyer"
a. A cause of great harm, ruin, or death
• The bubonic plagues of the 1300s were the **bane** of Europe.
b. A source of constant annoyance or frustration
• Flying insects are the **bane** of motorcycle riders.

3. boon (bo͞on) *noun* from Old Norse *bon*, "prayer"
A benefit or blessing, especially one that is timely
• Demand for vacation homes by foreigners has been a **boon** to the Mexican economy.

4. inimical (ĭ-nĭm´ĭ-kəl) *adjective* from Latin *inimicus*, "enemy"
a. Harmful; injurious
• Prolonged lack of sleep is **inimical** to one's health.
b. Unfriendly; hostile
• Some governments foster an atmosphere that is **inimical** to free speech and a free press.

5. malevolent (mə-lĕv´ə-lənt) *adjective* from Latin *mal-*, "bad" + *velle*, "to wish"
a. Having or showing ill will; wishing harm to others; malicious
• Science-fiction stories often feature **malevolent** beings who are planning to take over the earth.
b. Having an evil or a harmful influence
• Racism is a **malevolent** force in society.

malevolence *noun* Although it may seem that she betrayed you by telling your secret, she did not do it with **malevolence,** but with concern for your well being.

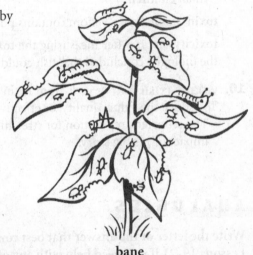
bane

6. panacea (păn´ə-sē´ə) *noun* from Greek *pan-*, "all" + *akos*, "cure"
A remedy for all diseases, evils, or difficulties; a cure-all
• The ginseng root was once thought to be a **panacea** for all health problems.

7. pernicious (pər-nĭsh´əs) *adjective* from Latin *pernicies*, "destruction"
Tending to cause death or great harm
• A **pernicious** 1918 flu epidemic killed more than twenty million people.

perniciousness *noun* Part of carbon monoxide's **perniciousness** is that this poisonous gas is odorless, colorless, and tasteless.

8. salutary (săl´yə-tĕr´ē) *adjective* from Latin *salus*, "health"
a. Helpful or designed to be helpful; remedial
• His writing improved after he followed his teacher's **salutary** advice.
b. Favorable to health; wholesome
• A warm, dry climate often has a **salutary** effect on asthma sufferers.

> *Salute* and *salutation* used to refer to wishing someone good health.

9. toxic (tŏk´sĭk) *adjective* from Old Persian *taxsa*, "arrow"
Poisonous; capable of causing injury or death by chemical means
• Paint chips that contain high levels of lead can be **toxic** if eaten by small children.

toxin *noun* Snake venom contains powerful **toxins**.

toxicity *noun* After measuring the **toxicity** of the river's water, the biologist concluded that fish could not survive in it.

> The ancient practice of putting poison on arrows led to the meaning of the word *toxic*.

10. vitiate (vĭsh´ē-āt´) *verb* from Latin *vitium*, "fault"
To reduce the value, quality, or effectiveness of
• The reporter's reputation for stretching the truth **vitiated** the impact of his big story.

ANALOGIES

Write the letter of the answer that best completes each analogy. Refer to Lessons 19–21 if you need help with any of the lesson words.

_____ **1.** *Arbiter* is to *settle* as _____.
    a. *conglomerate* is to *company*   **c.** *collateral* is to *debt*
    b. *liquidator* is to *buyer*   **d.** *charlatan* is to *deceive*

_____ **2.** *Candor* is to *true* as _____.
    a. *cant* is to *sincere*   **c.** *bane* is to *captured*
    b. *rectitude* is to *wrong*   **d.** *chicanery* is to *deceptive*

_____ **3.** *Lucrative* is to *profit* as _____.
    a. *bona fide* is to *cure*   **c.** *feigned* is to *belief*
    b. *pernicious* is to *harm*   **d.** *adulterated* is to *strength*

_____ **4.** *Bane* is to *boon* as _____.
    a. *apocryphal* is to *actual*   **c.** *panacea* is to *health*
    b. *commodity* is to *wheat*   **d.** *liquidation* is to *sale*

WRITE THE CORRECT WORD

Write the correct word in the space next to each definition. Use each word only once.

Salutary	**1.** helpful or healthful		*Panacea*	**6.** a cure-all	
boon	**2.** a benefit		*Pernicious*	**7.** tending to cause death	
toxic	**3.** poisonous		*malevolent*	**8.** showing ill will	
bane	**4.** a cause of harm or annoyance		*vitiate*	**9.** to reduce in value, quality, or effect	
adulterate	**5.** to make impure		*inimical*	**10.** unfriendly; hostile	

COMPLETE THE SENTENCE

Write the letter for the word that best completes each sentence.

d **1.** If looks could kill, that _____ glance surely would have done me in.
   a. salutary   **b.** adulterated   **c.** vitiated   **d.** malevolent

a **2.** A steady wind is a _____ to sailors.
   a. boon   **b.** bane   **c.** toxin   **d.** vitiation

b **3.** No medicine is a _____ for all ills.
   a. salutation   **b.** panacea   **c.** toxin   **d.** bane

c **4.** After weeks of steady rain, the sunny day had a _____ effect on everyone's spirits.
   a. pernicious   **b.** malevolent   **c.** salutary   **d.** vitiated

c **5.** That chemical is highly _____ to some animals but harmless to others.
   a. salutary   **b.** vitiated   **c.** toxic   **d.** adulterated

b **6.** Many people think that the amount of violence in the media has a(n) _____ effect on society.
   a. salutary   **b.** pernicious   **c.** panacea   **d.** adulterated

a **7.** Our enjoyment of the play was _____ by the poor acoustics in the theater, which made it hard to hear the actors.
   a. vitiated   **b.** salutary   **c.** inimical   **d.** a bane

d **8.** He _____ the sample by accidentally mixing in the wrong solution.
   a. panacea   **b.** saluted   **c.** bane   **d.** adulterated

c **9.** Hunger and lack of sleep are _____ to one's ability to learn.
   a. a boon   **b.** salutary   **c.** inimical   **d.** a panacea

b **10.** Fleas are the _____ of many stray dogs and cats.
   a. boon   **b.** bane   **c.** toxin   **d.** panacea

Challenge: Though I don't know of a _____ for debt, I'm sure we can come up with a _____ measure that will at least improve your financial situation.
c   **a.** bane…pernicious   **b.** toxin…vitiated   **c.** panacea…salutary

Going with the Flow

The dikes break. People flee as water rushes over the land and engulfs their homes. **(1)** For thousands of years, flooding has been the *bane* of the Netherlands. Because more than half the nation's residents live below sea level, the Dutch have built a system of dikes to keep the North Sea out of their living rooms. **(2)** These barriers have not been a *panacea*, however. Recent flooding has caused billions of dollars worth of damage.

Furthermore, the sea is rising. The United Nations' Intergovernmental Panel on Climate Change reports that global warming trends could cause sea levels to rise several feet in the coming century.

(3) This *pernicious* change will make flooding increasingly common, not just in the Netherlands but throughout the world. **(4)** Attempts to protect low-lying island nations or populated coastal areas by building dikes or using pumps may be *vitiated* by the rate at which sea levels are rising. To avoid an unprecedented mass migration from these areas (and a possible refugee crises), solutions that go beyond dikes and pumps are needed to stem the rising tides.

In one intriguing response, the Dutch have decided to simply "go with the flow," or live *on* the water. They are building homes on floating platforms that rise with the tides to counteract flooding. Anchored to piers, these elegant, spacious homes have full staircases and sloping aluminum roofs for protection from the elements. **(5)** Another *boon* of this strategy is that it doesn't use any more of the Netherlands' already densely populated land.

Floating houses can also provide healthful living quarters. **(6)** The industrial pollution and automobile exhaust in densely populated areas are increasingly *inimical* to human health. **(7)** A house floating on the water can offer a more *salutary* environment, with air freshened by relatively clean sea breezes. Some of the floating homes even include rooftop lawns and gardens.

An added benefit to these floating homes is the solution they offer to evade annoying neighbors: Just hire a tugboat and relocate to another pier!

Of course, care must be taken to choose proper building materials for a houseboat. **(8)** *Toxic* chemicals in some construction materials would make this new type of housing harmful to the ocean environment. **(9)** Homes powered by traditional fossil fuels would produce wastes that could *adulterate* the seawater and harm the animals—such as fish, shrimp, and crabs— that live in it. Planners have recommended using solar panels and wind turbines instead of fossil fuel-based power sources. Laws regulating solid waste disposal are important, too. **(10)** Carelessly flushing wastes into the water, even without any *malevolent* intent, can cause serious environmental damage.

Floating homes are becoming more and more popular. Ijburg, a community in the Netherlands that will accommodate several thousand people, is being built on seven artificial islands. It will include schools, hospitals, offices, walkways, and bike paths. Not surprisingly, it will also include houses built on floating supports that "go with the flow."

Each sentence below refers to a numbered sentence in the passage. Write the letter of the choice that gives the sentence a meaning that is closest to the original sentence.

1. For thousands of years, flooding has been the _____ of the Netherlands.
   a. pollution source
   b. poisonous trend
   c. great cure-all
   d. cause of harm

2. These barriers have not been a _____, however.
   a. cure-all
   b. chemical
   c. benefit
   d. force

3. This _____ change will make flooding increasingly common.
   a. polluted
   b. healthful
   c. harmful
   d. beneficial

4. Attempts to protect low-lying island nations or populated coastal areas by using dikes or pumps may be _____ by the rate at which sea levels are rising.
   a. made harmful
   b. made healthier
   c. made poisonous
   d. made ineffective

b   **5.** Another _____ of this strategy is that it doesn't use any more of the Netherlands' already densely populated land.
    a. remedy   **b.** benefit   **c.** poison   **d.** pollution

a   **6.** Industrial pollution and automobile exhaust are increasingly _____ to human health.
    a. injurious   **b.** remedial   **c.** beneficial   **d.** healthful

c   **7.** A house floating on the water can offer a more _____ environment, with air freshened by relatively clean sea breezes.
    a. harmful   **b.** curable   **c.** healthful   **d.** impure

b   **8.** _____ chemicals in some construction materials would make this new type of housing harmful to the ocean environment.
    a. Helpful   **b.** Poisonous   **c.** Healthful   **d.** Evil

c   **9.** Homes powered by traditional fossil fuels would produce wastes that could _____ the seawater and harm the animals that live in it.
    a. crush   **b.** weaken   **c.** pollute   **d.** reduce

a   **10.** Carelessly flushing wastes into the water, even without any _____ intent, can cause serious environmental damage.
    a. curable   **b.** conscious   **c.** improper   **d.** harmful

Indicate whether the statements below are TRUE or FALSE according to the passage.

F   **1.** In the reading passage, "going with the flow" means not worrying about the effects of climate change.

T   **2.** Floating homes have several advantages besides their ability to resist flooding.

T   **3.** Floating homes are a panacea for the flooding problems of the Netherlands.

WRITING EXTENDED RESPONSES

Would you like to live in a floating home? Why or why not? Using what you learned from the reading passage and any other relevant knowledge you may have, write an expository essay explaining your preference. Your essay should be at least three paragraphs long and contain two or more supporting points. Use a minimum of three lesson words in your essay and underline them.

WRITE THE DERIVATIVE

Complete the sentence by writing the correct form of the word shown in parentheses. You may not need to change the form that is given.

vitiated   **1.** Heat and dehydration _____ my strength before I was even halfway through the race. (*vitiate*)

toxin   **2.** Would there be more _____ in our air, water, and food if it weren't for environmental regulations and the threat of lawsuits? (*toxic*) _salutary_ **3.** Pet ownership can have a _____ effect on the psyche of people who live alone. *(salutary)*

adulteration **4.** The _____ of herbal remedies with pesticides and other toxic substances is a worldwide problem. *(adulterate)*

panacea **5.** Some political candidates promise that their programs will be a _____ for society's ills. *(panacea)*

pernicious **6.** Many think that advertising campaigns that market unhealthy food to children are having a _____ effect on their diets. *(pernicious)*

inimical **7.** Substandard prison conditions are _____ to prisoners, the justice system, and, ultimately, all of society. *(inimical)*

boon **8.** The unexpected increase in demand was a _____ for the electronics company. *(boon)*

malevolence **9.** Large predators kill their prey because of hunger, not _____ . *(malevolent)*

bane **10.** My long commute has become the _____ of my workday. *(bane)*

FIND THE EXAMPLE

Choose the answer that best describes the action or situation.

_d_ **1.** The likely name for a product claiming to be a *panacea*
  a. Grade A Eggs   **b.** Sharp's Pencils   **c.** Seaside Taffy   **d.** Claude's Amazing Tonic

_b_ **2.** A *bane* to someone with a headache
  a. quiet room   **b.** loud noise   **c.** good rest   **d.** aspirin

_a_ **3.** A *salutary* suggestion for someone with the flu
  a. fluids and rest   **b.** wind and rain   **c.** walking and running   **d.** chills and coughs

_d_ **4.** Something *inimical* to one's eyesight, over time
  a. beautiful sights   **b.** good nutrition   **c.** just enough sleep   **d.** too little light

_b_ **5.** Something most likely to *vitiate* a company's advertising campaign
  a. ads   **b.** scandal   **c.** demand   **d.** consumers

_d_ **6.** A *malevolent* computer program
  a. spreadsheet   **b.** word processor   **c.** game   **d.** virus

_a_ **7.** A sign you would be likely to see near a *toxic*-waste dump
  a. Do Not Enter!   **b.** Welcome!   **c.** Free Fishing!   **d.** Camp Here!

_d_ **8.** A *boon* to both doctor and patient
  a. nursing shortage   **b.** crowded ward   **c.** lack of insurance   **d.** effective medicine

_d_ **9.** The most *pernicious* organism to most people
  a. bumblebee   **b.** singing cricket   **c.** salamander   **d.** pneumonia bacteria

_c_ **10.** A form of *adulteration* that maintains the shelf life of foods
  a. adding medicine   **b.** adding milk   **c.** adding preservatives   **d.** adding toxins

Prefixes, Roots, and Suffixes

The Prefixes *inter-*, *intra-*, and *intro-*

When added to a Latin combining root or a base word, the prefixes *inter-*, *intra-*, and *intro-* form words that reflect the meanings of their word parts. Recall that a *prefix* is a word part that attaches to the beginning of the main word and a *root* is the main word part.

The meaning of each of these prefixes is given in the table below, along with an example. The meaning of *extra-* (sometimes spelled *extro-*), which contrasts with *intro-*, is also given.

Prefix	Prefix Meaning	Root	Word	Word Meaning
inter-	between, among	cellular	intercellular	between, among cells
intra-	within	cellular	intracellular	within a cell
intro-	in; inward	-vert- (turn)	introvert	a private person; turned inward
extra-	beyond; outside	galactic	extragalactic	beyond or outside the galaxy

You can use your knowledge of prefixes to help you understand unknown words, but remember that this process may only hint at a word's meaning, rather than resulting in a literal meaning. But you can combine this information with the context of a sentence to formulate a possible definition for the unknown word. Then you can ensure the accuracy of a definition by checking it in the dictionary.

Practice

You can combine the use of context clues with your knowledge of these prefixes to make intelligent guesses about the meanings of words. Each of the sentences below contains a word formed with the prefix *inter-*, *intra-*, or *intro-*. Read each sentence and try to infer what the word in italics means. Then check your definition with the one that you find in the dictionary, remembering to choose the definition that best fits in the sentence.

1. Since she could not eat while in the hospital, she was given nutrients *intravenously*.

My definition _____

Dictionary definition _____

2. The results of the *intramural* tennis competitions at the University of Michigan determined which of its teams would compete with other universities.

My definition _____

Dictionary definition _____

3. The official's timely *intervention* in the argument prevented it from turning into a brawl.

My definition _____

Dictionary definition _____

4. The patient's *intracranial* activity was monitored by special equipment.

My definition _____

Dictionary definition _____

5. The tedium of the long lecture was broken when a student *interjected* a joke.

My definition _____

Dictionary definition _____

6. Occasionally, Carmen liked to take time out of her daily routines for *introspection* about her life goals.

My definition _____

Dictionary definition _____

7. The rows of corn were *interspersed* with rows of bean.

My definition _____

Dictionary definition _____

8. Science-fiction movies often show *intragalactic* travel.

My definition _____

Dictionary definition _____

9. The physicist studied *intramolecular* forces.

My definition _____

Dictionary definition _____

10. The *introrse* anthers of the lily faced its stem.

My definition _____

Dictionary definition _____

11. An insect can crawl into the smallest *interstice*.

My definition _____

Dictionary definition _____

12. At the *interurban* conference, the mayors discussed solutions to housing problems.

My definition _____

Dictionary definition _____

The Root -spec-

WORD LIST

auspices	auspicious	circumspect	despicable	introspective
perspicuous	specious	spectacle	specter	spectrum

The word root *-spec-* means "look." To *inspect* is "to look at carefully." Glasses may be called *spectacles*. Even the word *spy* comes from *–spec-*. Most English words with this root are taken from the Latin verb *specere*, "to look." However, other sources are the Latin verb *spectare*, meaning "to watch," and the Indo-European root *-spek-*.

1. auspices (ô′spĭ-sĭz) *plural noun* from Latin *avis*, "bird" + *spec*, "look"
Sponsorship, support, or protection
• The lecture series was organized under the **auspices** of the Department of Education.

> "Under the *auspices* of" is a common phrase.

2. auspicious (ô-spĭsh′əs) *adjective* from Latin *avis*, "bird" + *spec*, "look"
a. Favorable; promising success
• The clear, sunny day was an **auspicious** one for their wedding.
b. Marked by success; prosperous
• "On this **auspicious** occasion, I would like to thank all the volunteers who worked so hard to make my campaign a success," said the newly elected congressman.

3. circumspect (sûr′kəm-spĕkt′) *adjective* from Latin *circum-*, "around" + *spec*, "look"
Cautious; prudent; mindful of circumstances and potential consequences
• The **circumspect** politician returned any gifts he received, for he was wary of being accused of taking bribes.

circumspection *noun* A little **circumspection** is wise when sending e-mails, for you never know who might end up reading them.

4. despicable (dĭ-spĭk′ə-bəl) *adjective* from Latin *de-*, "down" + *spec*, "look"
Deserving of scorn, contempt, or a low opinion
• Cheating is a **despicable** act.

despise *verb* I simply **despise** cruelty to animals.

5. introspective (ĭn′trə-spĕk′tĭv) *adjective* from Latin *intro-*, "in" + *spec*, "look"
Contemplating one's own thoughts and feelings; self-examining
• Poets and novelists are often **introspective** people.

introspect *verb* Keeping a journal is one way to **introspect** about the direction of one's life.

introspection *noun* The decision to marry should be preceded by a considerable amount of **introspection**.

introspective

6. **perspicuous** (pər-spĭk´yōō-əs) *adjective* from Latin *per-*, "through"
+ *spec*, "look"
Clearly expressed; easy to understand
 • The media praised the president's **perspicuous** outline of reforms to
 the health-care system.

 perspicuity *noun* **Perspicuity** is a quality greatly appreciated
 in teachers.

7. **specious** (spē´shəs) *adjective* from Latin *species*, "appearance," based
on *spec*, "look"
Seemingly true, but actually false
 • The beautifully written theory about the existence of life on Mars
 was, nevertheless, **specious**.

 speciousness *noun* If you ignore his charm and listen to
 the **speciousness** of his arguments, you won't vote for that politician.

8. **spectacle** (spĕk´tə-kəl) *noun* from Latin *spec*, "look"
 a. An impressive public performance or display
 • The **spectacle** of those daring acrobats almost took our
 breath away.
 b. A public display of bad behavior
 • The child made a **spectacle** of herself by throwing a tantrum in the
 toy store.

> *Spectacle* can also mean "an impressive sight," as in "The Grand Canyon is quite a *spectacle*."

9. **specter** (spĕk´tər) *noun* from Latin *spec*, "look"
 a. A ghost or spirit
 • In Dickens's *A Christmas Carol*, Jacob Marley's **specter** appears to
 warn Scrooge of the evil of his ways.
 b. A haunting or disturbing image or possibility
 • The **specter** of civil war looms over the country.

 spectral *adjective* The night fog gave her a **spectral** appearance.

10. **spectrum** (spĕk´trəm) *noun* from Latin *spec*, "look"
 a. A band showing different wavelengths of color or sound, arranged
 in order
 • A rainbow shows the colors of the **spectrum** in the form of an arc.
 b. A broad range of related qualities or ideas
 • The actress's many performances showed she was capable of
 displaying the entire **spectrum** of human emotions.

> The plural of *spectrum* can be *spectrums* or *spectra*.

WORD ENRICHMENT

Auspicious birds

In ancient Rome, an *auspex* was a person who observed the flight
patterns of birds to predict whether it was a favorable time to do something,
such as conduct a marriage ceremony. From this manner of predicting by
observing birds, comes the word *auspicious*. In a similar way, the word
auspice means "protection or support." Today, when we refer to something
being done "under the auspices" of an organization, we mean that it receives
the support and sponsorship of that body.

WRITE THE CORRECT WORD

Write the correct word in the space next to each definition. Use each word only once.

Spectrum **1.** a range of qualities

Introspective **2.** self-examining

auspices **3.** patronage; support

despicable **4.** deserving of scorn

Spectacle **5.** an impressive display

Specter **6.** ghost or spirit

Perspicuous **7.** easy to understand

Circumspect **8.** cautious; prudent

auspicious **9.** favorable

Specious **10.** seeming to be true but actually false

COMPLETE THE SENTENCE

Write the letter for the word that best completes each sentence.

_C_ **1.** The ancient Romans often looked to the skies to determine whether it was a(n) _____ day for an important undertaking.
   a. introspective   **b.** perspicuous   **c.** auspicious   **d.** specious

_d_ **2.** In a rare _____ moment, the businesswoman reflected on her hectic life.
   a. perspicuous   **b.** spectral   **c.** specious   **d.** introspective

_C_ **3.** If you observe this classroom for a while, you will see the whole _____ of children's behavior.
   a. specter   **b.** introspection   **c.** spectrum   **d.** auspices

_a_ **4.** _____ writing includes vivid verbs and exact modifiers.
   a. Perspicuous   **b.** Circumspect   **c.** Specious   **d.** Despicable

_a_ **5.** The _____ of widespread famine galvanized the relief agency into action.
   a. specter   **b.** circumspection   **c.** perspicuity   **d.** introspection

_C_ **6.** The medical studies were performed under the _____ of the National Institute of Health.
   a. perspicuity   **b.** speciousness   **c.** auspices   **d.** spectacle

_b_ **7.** Spitting in public is a(n) _____ habit.
   a. auspicious   **b.** despicable   **c.** circumspect   **d.** specious

_b_ **8.** By wearing ripped jeans to the formal event, Bill made a _____ of himself.
   a. specter   **b.** spectacle   **c.** spectrum   **d.** perspicuity

_d_ **9.** The _____ conclusions of the article were not supported by the facts cited in it.
   a. perspicuous   **b.** circumspect   **c.** specious   **d.** auspicious

_d_ **10.** The cautious diplomat was known to be _____ when conducting negotiations.
   a. spectral   **b.** auspicious   **c.** specious   **d.** circumspect

Challenge: The _____ of the second debater's compelling reasoning revealed the _____ of the arguments that had been put forth by the first speaker.
_a_   **a.** spectacle…auspices   **b.** specter…circumspection   **c.** perspicuity…speciousness

Lesson 22 143

Fireworks: Fun or folly?

Sparkling against the night sky, fireworks have been used to celebrate everything from the English wedding of King Henry VII in 1486 to the 100th anniversary of the Statue of Liberty, 500 years later. **(1)** Almost all of us have enjoyed the beautiful *spectacle* of a fireworks show.

Legend has it that over a thousand years ago, a Chinese cook accidentally mixed saltpeter (a cleaner), sulfur (used to light fires), and charcoal, thereby creating an impressive explosion of flames and sparks. He also noticed that if this specific mixture was contained in a cylinder, such as a bamboo tube, and ignited, it made a loud noise. **(2)** From that time on, the Chinese used fireworks to celebrate *auspicious* occasions. The explosions were believed to frighten away evil spirits.

On July 4, 1777, the first celebration of United States' independence included a brilliant fireworks display. **(3)** However, *introspective* viewers might have wondered whether they should be enjoying such festivities, when the survival of the new nation was far from secure. In fact, the Revolutionary War would not end for another six years.

(4) In the late 1700s and 1800s, it was discovered that adding metal chlorides to the original chemical mixture produced a *spectrum* of colors. Barium produced a brilliant green, strontium a vivid red, and copper compounds a pale blue. More recently, magnesium has been added to brighten the colors.

(5) As much as we enjoy fireworks festivities, the *specter* of injury, or even death, looms over them. Aerial fireworks can be particularly dangerous, for they may land in unintended places. In one incident, 81-year-old Lillian Herring of Hawaii died when an aerial firework set fire to her home. In another, a 25-year-old man died while setting off a display. **(6)** While these deaths were accidental, individual firecrackers have sometimes been used for *despicable* acts, such as deliberately starting fires.

(7) Such incidents have led to public pressure to ban private fireworks displays and to only permit displays that are organized under the *auspices* of a city or county. In fact, some states do not permit individuals to purchase or use fireworks at all, limiting their function entirely to public displays.

Even with restrictions on the use of fireworks, there are people who would like to see all fireworks banned. **(8)** However, politicians are *circumspect* about going that far. **(9)** Even though the naysayers charge that arguments for keeping fireworks are *specious,* fireworks enjoy a great deal of support. One reason may be tourism. Honolulu, Hawaii, is famous for its New Year's Eve display. But because of accidents like the one that killed Lillian Herring, there were calls from many local residents to ban fireworks. **(10)** In a *perspicuous* presentation of the issue, the *Honolulu Star Bulletin* described the results of a survey. Almost 40 percent of Hawaiian residents favored banning fireworks, while 95 percent of tourists favored having no limits on them at all.

Tourism is an important consideration in other places as well. When fireworks were eliminated from Chinese New Year celebrations in New York City, merchants in Chinatown complained that they lost a lot of business.

Actually, according to medical reports, injuries from fireworks have been declining steadily, as safer mechanisms and tighter regulations have been instituted. What would the Fourth of July be without the spectacle of green, blue, and red colors filling the sky? Fireworks are still as thrilling to us as they were to those who celebrated the first Independence Day in 1777.

Each sentence below refers to a numbered sentence in the passage. Write the letter of the choice that gives the sentence a meaning that is closest to the original sentence.

1. Almost all of us have enjoyed the beautiful _____ of a fireworks show.
   a. scary explosions   **b.** promising success   **c.** dazzling colors   **d.** public display

2. The Chinese used fireworks to celebrate _____ occasions.
   a. successful   **b.** religious   **c.** ghostly   **d.** self-reflective

3. However, _____ viewers might have wondered whether they should be enjoying such festivities.
   a. critical   **b.** self-examining   **c.** supporting   **d.** cautious

b **4.** In the late 1700s and 1800s, it was discovered that adding metal chlorides to the original chemical mixture produced a _____ of colors.
  a. brightness   **b.** range   **c.** spirit   **d.** unison

d **5.** As much as we enjoy fireworks festivities, the _____ of injury, or even death, looms over them.
  a. seeming truth   **b.** serious display   **c.** eerie ghost   **d.** haunting possibility

c **6.** Individual firecrackers have sometimes been used for _____ acts.
  a. impressive   **b.** a wide range of   **c.** contemptible   **d.** ghostly

a **7.** Such incidents have led to public pressure to ban private fireworks displays and to only permit displays that are organized under the _____ of a city or county.
  a. sponsorship   **b.** range of qualities   **c.** clear expression   **d.** employees

d **8.** However, politicians are _____ about going that far.
  a. favorable   **b.** self-examining   **c.** zealous   **d.** cautious

b **9.** Even though the naysayers charge that arguments for keeping fireworks are _____, fireworks enjoy a great deal of support.
  a. disgusting   **b.** false   **c.** too cautious   **d.** clear

a **10.** In a _____ presentation of the issue, the *Honolulu Star Bulletin* described the results of a survey.
  a. clearly expressed   **b.** seemingly true   **c.** nearly successful   **d.** carefully worded

Indicate whether the statements below are TRUE or FALSE according to the passage.

T **1.** In many places in the U.S., fireworks are banned altogether.

F **2.** The ancient Chinese added chemicals to the original fireworks mixture to produce colors.

T **3.** Fireworks displays often increase tourism.

FINISH THE THOUGHT

Complete each sentence so that it shows the meaning of the italicized word.

1. People should be *circumspect* when _____

2. Because the argument was *specious* _____

WRITE THE DERIVATIVE

Complete the sentence by writing the correct form of the word shown in parentheses. You may not need to change the form that is given.

Spectrum **1.** A wide _____ of opinions was expressed at the community meeting.
  (*spectrum*)

Speciousness **2.** The _____ of Cal's argument was difficult to detect because of his calm, rational presentation. _(specious)_

Introspection **3.** Anne's two-week solo camping trip gave her ample time for _____. _(introspective)_

Auspicious **4.** The ancient Chinese regarded eclipses as _____ events. _(auspicious)_

Circumspectly **5.** After the doctor told him of the risks of having high cholesterol levels, Kyle started to eat more _____. _(circumspect)_

despise **6.** I _____ malicious gossip. _(despicable)_

Specter **7.** Until the early 1900s, the _____ of widespread infant mortality was a constant presence in human life. _(specter)_

auspices **8.** The charity drive was conducted under the _____ of the Society for the Prevention of Cruelty to Animals. _(auspices)_

Perspicuity **9.** With considerable _____, the bestselling book explained the advantages and disadvantages of globalization. _(perspicuous)_

Spectacle **10.** We stopped to watch the _____ of the street performer juggling swords. _(spectacle)_

FIND THE EXAMPLE

Choose the answer that best describes the action or situation.

_c_ **1.** What you might do if you see a _specter_
  a. laugh   **b.** cough   **c.** scream   **d.** dance

_c_ **2.** A _spectrum_
  a. a sunset   **b.** Northern lights   **c.** a rainbow   **d.** a stereo

_d_ **3.** Someone who often works under the _auspices_ of a university
  a. congressperson   **b.** banker   **c.** mayor   **d.** researcher

_a_ **4.** A way to make a _spectacle_ in a fancy restaurant
  a. sing loudly   **b.** order several courses   **c.** pay in cash   **d.** wear nice clothes

_b_ **5.** The professional most likely to be thought of as _introspective_
  a. school teacher   **b.** artist   **c.** politician   **d.** marketing manager

6. An activity that might be enjoyed by a _circumspect_ person
  jumping   **b.** hang gliding   **c.** bicycle riding   **d.** rock climbing

_c_ **7.** A _despicable_ act
  a. swimming   **b.** studying   **c.** cheating   **d.** sharing

_a_ **8.** Something that should always be written in a _perspicuous_ manner
  a. instructions   **b.** poetry   **c.** proverbs   **d.** letter

_a_ **9.** An _auspicious_ beginning to a business negotiation
  a. argument   **b.** rude comment   **c.** tripping and falling   **d.** funny joke

_d_ **10.** Where you are most likely to encounter _specious_ claims
  a. term paper   **b.** class lecture   **c.** the news   **d.** infomercial

 146 **The Root _-spec-_**

The Root -plí-

WORD LIST

complicity	deploy	explicate	explicit	implicate
implicit	inexplicable	replica	supple	supplicant

The root *-pli-*, sometimes spelled *-plic-* or *-ploy-*, comes from the Latin verb *plicare*, which means "to fold." The root appears in many English words, including *employer, multiply, reply,* and *triplicate.* Think about how the meanings of these words and the lesson words are literally or figuratively related to folding.

1. **complicity** (kəm-plĭs´ĭ-tē) *noun* from Latin *com-*, "together" + *plic,* "fold"
   Involvement as an accomplice in a crime or wrongdoing
   • Judges and juries often try to weigh degrees of **complicity** when determining jail sentences for convicted criminals.

   complicit *adjective* Hal didn't realize that by helping a fugitive hide from the police, he was legally **complicit** in the crime.

2. **deploy** (dĭ-ploi´) *verb* from Latin *dis-*, "apart" + *ploy,* "fold"
   a. To position troops or people strategically or systematically
   • The commander **deployed** security officers along the parade route.
   b. To put into use or action
   • Skydivers receive instruction in altitude awareness so that they will know exactly when to **deploy** their parachutes.

   deployment *noun* The National Guard unit returned home from a long and dangerous **deployment.**

deploy

3. **explicate** (ĕk´splĭ-kāt´) *verb* from Latin *ex-*, "out" + *plic,* "fold"
   To explain; to make clear the meaning of something
   • The lecturer **explicated** the technological, political, and economic factors that have given rise to globalization.

   explicable *adjective* Ancient people attributed to evil spirits many events that are now **explicable** through scientific evidence.

   explication *noun* Her thesis was an **explication** of the symbolism in Ernest Hemingway's novels and short stories.

4. **explicit** (ĭk-splĭs´ĭt) *adjective* from Latin *ex-*, "out" + *plic,* "fold"
   a. Fully and clearly expressed; leaving nothing implied
   • Legal contracts should be **explicit** about the obligations of all parties concerned.
   b. Readily observable
   • The removal of roadblocks was an **explicit** sign that the floodwaters had receded from the road ahead.

5. implicate (ĭm′plĭ-kāt′) *verb* from *im-*, "in" + *plic*, "fold"
  a. To involve or connect intimately or incriminatingly
   • Several large checks made out to the official **implicated** her in the bribery scandal.
  b. To have as a consequence; to entail
   • The extensive termite damage **implicated** costly repairs to the house.

implication *noun* The judge's decision to award damages to the inventor of the computer technology had **implications** for many high-tech firms.

As you can see, the word *implication* is related to both *implicate* and *implicit*. *Implication* can mean "a connection or involvement," "a consequence," or "an implied meaning or suggestion."

6. implicit (ĭm-plĭs′ĭt) *adjective* from *im-*, "in" + *plic*, "fold"
  a. Implied or understood though not directly expressed
   • Showing a product in a movie is an **implicit** form of advertisement.
  b. Unquestioning; without doubt or reservation
   • I had **implicit** faith that Captain Gregory would get us home safely.

implication *noun* He resented even the **implication** that he'd hurt someone on purpose.

7. inexplicable (ĭn-ĕk′splĭ-kə-bəl) *adjective* from *in-*, "not" + *ex-*, "out" + *plic*, "fold"
Difficult or impossible to explain or account for
 • I was confused by the **inexplicable** events in the story, such as the sun rising in the west, not in the east."

8. replica (rĕp′lĭ-kə) *noun* from *re-*, "back" + *plic*, "fold"
  a. A copy or reproduction of a work of art, especially one made by the original artist
   • She agreed to make a **replica** of her famous statue for the lobby of city hall.
  b. A copy or reproduction, especially one that is smaller than the original
   • The boy won a scale-model **replica** of a sports car, complete with a ten-horsepower electric engine.

replicate *verb* The way in which genes are **replicated** is well understood today due to modern research technology.

9. supple (sŭp′əl) *adjective* from *sub-*, "under" + *plic*, "fold"
  a. Easily bent; limber; pliant
   • The **supple** limbs of the young tree drooped from the weight of the ice.
  b. Changing or yielding readily; compliant; adaptable
   • Ever **supple** in temperament, Jasmine's favorite reply was, "Okay, fine with me."

suppleness *noun* Oil glands ensure the **suppleness** of the skin.

10. supplicant (sŭp′lĭ-kənt) *noun* from *sub-*, "under" + *plic*, "fold"
A person who asks, prays, or begs humbly and earnestly
 • The **supplicant** knelt in the church and made heartfelt pleas for his daughter's recovery.

supplicate *verb* The noble knight **supplicated** the king to have mercy on the people.

supplication *noun* The **supplications** fell on deaf ears.

Think about why the etymology of *supple* is the same as that of *supplicant*.

WRITE THE CORRECT WORD

Write the correct word in the space next to each definition. Use each word only once.

replica **1.** a reproduction

supple **2.** easily bent

implicit **3.** not stated directly

supplicant **4.** one who pleads

complicity **5.** involvement in crime

inexplicable **6.** impossible to explain

deploy **7.** to put into action

explicit **8.** clearly expressed

implicate **9.** to incriminate

explicate **10.** to explain

COMPLETE THE SENTENCE

Write the letter for the word that best completes each sentence.

__d__ **1.** Sven was sentenced to six months in prison for his _____ in the theft.
   a. explication   **b.** explicitness   **c.** replica   **d.** complicity

__a__ **2.** The general _____ the troops along the border.
   a. deployed   **b.** implicated   **c.** explicated   **d.** supplicated

__c__ **3.** The doctors were baffled by her _____ loss of hearing.
   a. supple   **b.** implicit   **c.** inexplicable   **d.** explicit

__a__ **4.** A(n) _____ of Rodin's famous sculpture _The Thinker_ sat in front of the library.
   a. replica   **b.** supplicant   **c.** implication   **d.** deployment

__b__ **5.** The professor _____ what she considered to be the deeper meaning of the poem.
   a. implicated   **b.** explicated   **c.** supplicated   **d.** deployed

__d__ **6.** His memos and e-mails _____ him in the insider-trading scandal.
   a. explicated   **b.** replicated   **c.** supplicated   **d.** implicated

__c__ **7.** Steel is more _____ than fiberglass, so it is a better material for the construction of skyscrapers.
   a. complicit   **b.** inexplicable   **c.** supple   **d.** explicit

__c__ **8.** Is _____ violence in movies really appropriate for _anyone_?
   a. deployed   **b.** complicit   **c.** explicit   **d.** explicated

__a__ **9.** Hannah had _____ trust in her best friend.
   a. implicit   **b.** complicit   **c.** replicated   **d.** explicated

__b__ **10.** From a distance, Mom's kneeling position made her look like a(n) _____ as she planted tulip bulbs in the garden.
   a. deployment   **b.** supplicant   **c.** implication   **d.** complicity

Challenge: Harold was found to be _____ in the elaborate fraud scheme, and his involvement had serious _____ for the future of his career.
__a__   **a.** complicit…implications   **b.** implicated…explications   **c.** explicit…supplications

Animal Babies

Little ducklings tag along behind a person instead of their mother. Baby monkeys prefer a soft doll to an adequate food supply. **(1)** Although these behaviors may seem *inexplicable* at first, they are fairly well understood.

"Imprinting" is the instinctual process by which animals bond with their mother, another caregiver, or—in less frequent examples—something else entirely. For many species the imprinting process is the key to survival. It is especially important in birds that leave the nest soon after they hatch—ducks, in particular. **(2)** Scientists have pointed out quite *explicitly* what is required for duck imprinting: It seems that the birds imprint on the most visible moving object in their immediate environment. This is normally the ducklings' mother, but the cute little creatures can imprint on just about anything. **(3)** Scientists know this because they have imprinted ducklings to humans, *replicas* of ducks, and even old boots.

There is, however, a critical period, or "time window," for imprinting. Ducks and geese must form these attachments when they are between twenty-four and forty-eight hours old. **(4)** If they successfully imprint, they will follow a mother (or something else) with *implicit* trust.

(5) Just as interesting, imprinting can cause some birds to act like *supplicants*. Konrad Lorenz, a famous researcher, found that jackdaws  that had imprinted on him tried to gain his approval by presenting him with fresh, juicy earthworms!

Another thought-provoking example of manipulated imprinting has been used for centuries in China, where farmers rely on ducks to get rid of snails that harm their crops. The farmers have the birds imprint on a piece of wood, which they then put in a snail-infested part of a rice paddy. **(6)** By moving the stick, the farmers can *deploy* the snail-munching ducks in as many areas as needed, eliminating the need to spend money on toxic pesticides.

Researchers have also studied imprinting in monkeys. In one study, a "mother figure" made of wire was equipped to provide food for a baby monkey, while a cuddlier terrycloth "mother" provided no food. Experimenters found that the monkeys preferred the terrycloth model. It seems that, to these monkeys, softness is more important than the ability to provide sustenance. **(7)** *Suppleness*, warmth, and a rocking motion were also found to be crucial for stimulating imprinting in monkeys.

(8) These findings have several significant *implications*. One is the importance of critical periods in animal development. **(9)** For obvious reasons, pet shops and animal shelters should provide new owners with full *explication* of baby animals' needs and developmental stages. Another key conclusion drawn from imprinting research is the necessity for mammals to have a nurturing touch. Studies have shown that it is critical for human babies, as well as for young monkeys, to be held and touched. **(10)** In settings such as orphanages, staff members who don't do this may be unwittingly *complicit* in providing a less than optimum environment for the children.

Animals and people share many things, including the planet Earth and a surprising amount of DNA. We also have some of the same needs, especially when we are young and helpless.

Each sentence below refers to a numbered sentence in the passage. Write the letter of the choice that gives the sentence a meaning that is closest to the original sentence.

_____ C **1.** These behaviors may seem _____ at first.
    a. adaptable   **b.** implied   **c.** unexplainable   **d.** obvious

_____ C **2.** Scientists have pointed out quite _____ what is required for duck imprinting.
    a. pleadingly   **b.** flexibly   **c.** clearly   **d.** hopefully

_____ b **3.** Scientists have imprinted ducklings to _____ of ducks.
    a. expressions   **b.** models   **c.** movements   **d.** beggars

_____ a **4.** They will follow a mother (or something else) with _____ trust.
    a. unquestioning   **b.** unexplained   **c.** limited   **d.** adaptable

a **5.** Imprinting can cause some birds to act like _____.
    a. silly geese   **b.** criminal helpers   **c.** graceful dancers   **d.** humble pleaders

d **6.** By moving the stick, the farmers can _____ the ducks in as many areas as needed.
    a. flexibly bend   **b.** duplicate all   **c.** bond with   **d.** strategically position

b **7.** _____, warmth, and a rocking motion were also found to be crucial for stimulating imprinting in monkeys.
    a. Earnestness   **b.** Pliability   **c.** Clarity   **d.** Security

b **8.** These findings have several significant _____.
    a. explanations   **b.** consequences   **c.** studies   **d.** reproductions

c **9.** Pet shops and animal shelters should provide new owners with full _____ of baby animals' needs.
    a. duplication   **b.** positioning   **c.** explanation   **d.** involvement

d **10.** In settings such as orphanages, staff members who don't do this may be unwittingly _____ in providing a less than optimum environment for the children.
    a. implied   **b.** yielding   **c.** productive   **d.** involved

Indicate whether the statements below are TRUE or FALSE according to the passage.

F **1.** Birds and mammals are not born with imprinting instincts.

T **2.** Both baby monkeys and baby humans need to be held and touched.

F **3.** Humans have figured out ways to influence the imprinting process in other species.

WRITING EXTENDED RESPONSES

Why is imprinting adaptive and beneficial? In other words, how does imprinting help young animals—and therefore whole species—survive? Think about what you learned from the reading passage. You may also draw on relevant personal knowledge, experience, and common sense. Write an expository essay that explains why imprinting is important for survival. Your essay should be at least three paragraphs long. Use a minimum of three lesson words in your essay and underline them.

WRITE THE DERIVATIVE

Complete the sentence by writing the correct form of the word shown in parentheses. You may not need to change the form that is given.

inexplicable   **1.** Though science has made amazing leaps, there is still much in our huge universe that remains _____, at least for now. (*inexplicable*)

replica   **2.** The craftsman built a miniature _____ of the U.S.S. *Constitution*. (*replica*)

supplility   **3.** The _____ of the leather seats was one appealing feature of the luxury car. (_supple_)

deployment   **4.** The rapid _____ of troops intimidated the opposing army. (_deploy_)

complicite   **5.** Because she drove the getaway car, Alice was _____ in the crime. (_complicity_)

explicated   **6.** Although the events were unusual, they were _____. (_explicate_)

implications   **7.** "The _____ of my time machine are mind-boggling!" roared the exhilarated physicist. (_implicate_)

explicitly   **8.** The teacher _____ stated that the students were to use at least ten sources for their research papers. (_explicit_)

implication   **9.** The _____ of our conversation was that I should go home if it was raining. (_implicit_)

supplicated   **10.** "Instead of saying 'I _____ for betrothal and received a highly favorable response,' you could have just said, 'She said yes.'" (_supplicant_)

FIND THE EXAMPLE

Choose the answer that best describes the action or situation.

_d_   **1.** Something a _supplicant_ would say
    a. No, thanks.   **b.** Yes, you may.   **c.** I'll have that one.   **d.** Please, I beg you.

_c_   **2.** The person who does NOT need to be especially _supple_
    a. ballet dancer   **b.** high jumper   **c.** accountant   **d.** acrobat

_c_   **3.** Something that produces _replicas_
    a. pen   **b.** snowstorm   **c.** copier   **d.** oven

_d_   **4.** A likely source of an _implicit_ understanding
    a. specific language   **b.** detailed contract   **c.** instruction manual   **d.** facial expression

_a_   **5.** One way to be _complicit_ in a food fight
    a. yell "Join in!"   **b.** leave the cafeteria   **c.** eat heartily   **d.** say "Stop wasting food."

_b_   **6.** Something _inexplicable_ to the average kindergartener
    a. letters   **b.** trigonometry   **c.** numbers   **d.** finger painting

_d_   **7.** A word that describes _explicit_ directions
    a. assumed   **b.** vague   **c.** implied   **d.** clear

_c_   **8.** Something that would most likely require _explication_
    a. a stop sign   **b.** a smile   **c.** a theory   **d.** a bicycle

_c_   **9.** Someone most likely to be _deployed_ in a region that had suffered an earthquake
    a. pro athlete   **b.** barber   **c.** relief worker   **d.** housekeeper

_d_   **10.** Something that would most strongly _implicate_ a suspect in a jewel theft
    a. love of jewelry   **b.** job in a factory   **c.** solid alibi   **d.** possession of the jewels

The Roots -fid- and -jur-

WORD LIST

adjudicate	affidavit	confidant	conjure	fealty
fiancé	fidelity	infidel	jurisprudence	perjure

The root *-fid-* means "faith" or "trust" and comes from the Latin word *fidelis* (or *fidus*), meaning "faithful." The root *-jur-* means "law" or "right" and, in an extension of that meaning, "judge." It comes from the Latin *jurare*, "to take an oath." In a legal proceeding, a person takes an oath to tell the truth or to judge fairly. The common words *faith, fidelity,* and *confidential* come from *-fid-*. Such words as *judge* and *jury* come from *-jur-*.

1. **adjudicate** (ə-jōō´dĭ-kāt´) *verb* from Latin *ad-*, "to" + *jur*, "judge"
   a. To hear and settle a case through a judicial procedure
   • A judge was asked to **adjudicate** a case involving a restaurant's lack of facilities for handicapped persons.
   b. To settle a dispute
   • It seems as if my cousin is constantly **adjudicating** his children's quarrels.

   adjudication *noun* The two neighbors' dispute over land rights is still under **adjudication** in the courts.

2. **affidavit** (ăf´ĭ-dā´vĭt) *noun* from Latin *ad-*, "to" + *fid*, "trust"
   A written statement made under oath before an official
   • The woman signed an **affidavit** stating that she had witnessed the accident.

3. **confidant** (kŏn´fĭ-dănt´) *noun* from Latin *con-*, "with" + *fid*, "trust"
   A person trusted with secrets or private matters
   • A husband and wife are usually close **confidants**.

   confide *verb* Don't **confide** your innermost feelings to those who gossip.

confidant

4. **conjure** (kŏn´jər) *verb* from Latin *con-*, "together" + *jur*, "judge"
   a. To produce or summon, as if by magic
   • In an Arabian tale, Aladdin **conjured** up a genie by rubbing an oil lamp.
   b. To call to mind an image or a memory
   • The smell of cookies **conjured** up memories of my mother's kitchen.

   conjurer *noun* How did that **conjurer** pull a rabbit from an empty hat?

5. fealty (fē´əl-tē) *noun* from Latin *fid,* "trust"
Faithfulness; allegiance
• Public officials should be appointed on the basis of competence, not **fealty** to a political party.

6. fiancé (fē´än-sā´) *noun* from Latin *fid,* "faith"
A man to whom a woman is engaged be married
• It is customary in some cultures for a **fiancé** to give his intended bride a ring.

fiancée *noun* A **fiancée** is a woman engaged to be married to a man.

7. fidelity (fĭ-dĕl´ĭ-tē) *noun* from Latin *fid,* "faith"
a. Faithfulness to obligations, duties, or vows
• A company's board of directors is charged with **fidelity** to the interests of the company's stockholders.
b. The degree to which a sound or image is accurately reproduced
• Sound equipment now produces recordings that have great **fidelity** to the original music.

8. infidel (ĭn´fĭ-dəl) *noun* from Latin *in-,* "not" + *fid,* "faith"
A person who does not accept a particular faith or religion
• During the Crusades of the Middle Ages, Muslims and Christians called each other **infidels.**

9. jurisprudence (jŏŏr´ĭs-prōōd´ns) *noun* from Latin *jur,* "law"
+ *prudentia,* "knowledge"
The philosophy and science of law or a division of the law
• The field of medical **jurisprudence** is growing, as solving crimes depends upon increasingly complex laboratory work.

10. perjure (pûr´jər) *verb* from Latin *per-,* "detrimental to" + *jur,* "law"
To deliberately lie or testify falsely under oath
• Those who **perjure** are guilty of a crime.

perjury *noun* The defending lawyer accused the witness of **perjury.**

ANALOGIES

Write the letter of the answer that best completes each analogy. Refer to Lessons 22–24 if you need help with any of the lesson words.

_____ **1.** *Explicit* is to *clear* as _____ .
    a. *specious* is to *correct*   **c.** *auspicious* is to *favorable*
    b. *despicable* is to *likeable*   **d.** *perspicuous* is to *noticeable*

_____ **2.** *Fidelity* is to *betray* as _____ .
    a. *spectacle* is to *hide*   **c.** *spectrum* is to *range*
    b. *affidavit* is to *swear*   **d.** *complicity* is to *guilt*

_____ **3.** *Replicated* is to *copy* as _____ .
    a. *specious* is to *space*   **c.** *introspective* is to *mind*
    b. *conjured* is to *summon*   **d.** *fiancé* is to *marriage*

_____ **4.** *Adjudicate* is to *dispute* as _____ .
    a. *perjure* is to *trial*   **c.** *supplicant* is to *knees*
    b. *implicate* is to *victim*   **d.** *deploy* is to *army*

WRITE THE CORRECT WORD

Write the correct word in the space next to each definition. Use each word only once.

Confidant **1.** a trusted person

fealty **2.** allegiance

Jurisprudence **3.** the study of law

Fiance' **4.** an engaged man

affidavit **5.** a written statement made under oath

adjudicate **6.** to settle a court case

Perjure **7.** to lie under oath

fidelity **8.** faithfulness

Conjure **9.** to produce or summon

Infidel **10.** a person who doesn't accept a religion

COMPLETE THE SENTENCE

Write the letter for the word that best completes each sentence.

_b_ **1.** Seeing children play on the swing set _____ up memories of my childhood playground.
   a. perjured   **b.** conjured   **c.** adjudicated   **d.** fealty

_C_ **2.** My _____ proposed to me at a romantic restaurant overlooking the ocean.
   a. infidel   **b.** affidavit   **c.** fiancé   **d.** jurisprudence

_d_ **3.** The case of food poisoning brought against the restaurant will be _____ in court.
   a. confided   **b.** perjured   **c.** conjured   **d.** adjudicated

_C_ **4.** The man _____ himself when he gave false testimony under oath in the trial.
   a. conjured   **b.** adjudicated   **c.** perjured   **d.** confided

_a_ **5.** The only person who knew Ellen planned to quit her job was her closest _____.
   a. confidant   **b.** fidelity   **c.** affidavit   **d.** fealty

_a_ **6.** Because his speech was critical of their religious practices, the congregation denounced him as a(n) _____.
   a. infidel   **b.** confidant   **c.** fiancé   **d.** jurisprudence

_d_ **7.** Fulfilling an oath of _____, the Japanese samurai fought for his lord.
   a. affidavit   **b.** adjudication   **c.** perjury   **d.** fealty

_b_ **8.** Law school students spend much of their days studying _____.
   a. confidants   **b.** jurisprudence   **c.** fealty   **d.** infidels

_a_ **9.** According to the _____ you signed, you witnessed the defendant shoplifting the jewelry.
   a. affidavit   **b.** fiancée   **c.** perjury   **d.** conjurer

_d_ **10.** Showing great _____, the dog refused to abandon the side of its injured master.
   a. adjudication   **b.** confidant   **c.** jurisprudence   **d.** fidelity

Challenge: Husbands and wives, who are assumed to be close _____, cannot testify about each other in court, lest their _____ —or lack of it—interfere with the discovery of truth.

_b_   **a.** infidels…perjury   **b.** confidants…fidelity   **c.** fiancés…fidelity

Powerhouse of Her Time

(1) Do you *conjure* up images of timid women when you think about the Middle Ages? If so, then you probably haven't heard of Eleanor of Aquitaine. A powerful and an adventurous woman, she was the wife of two kings and the mother of two others.

Born around 1122, Eleanor was the daughter of the Duke of Aquitaine. Aquitaine was a province in present-day France known for its wealth and culture. Eleanor's father, proud of her intelligence, provided her with an excellent education.

When her father died, she was his heir. **(2)** His will provided that the king of France—to whom the duke had sworn *fealty*—care for Eleanor. In those times, a rich heiress provided important power and money. **(3)** So the king promptly made Eleanor the *fiancée*, and then wife, of his son. Only a few days after the wedding, Eleanor's father-in-law died, and she became the queen of France, wife of Louis VII.

(4) Louis treated his wife as a respected *confidant*, consulting with her on state matters. But Eleanor had a taste for adventure. **(5)** When Louis went to fight *"infidels"* in the Second Crusade, Eleanor insisted on going along. Since she also supplied a thousand men from Aquitaine to the cause, Louis let her have her way. During this time, Eleanor became friendly with her uncle, Raymond of Poitiers.

In a dispute, she actually sided with Raymond against her husband. This strained Louis and Eleanor's marriage to the breaking point, so Louis decided to take her back to France. **(6)** On their way, they visited the pope, who tried to *adjudicate* their quarrel. Soon after, though, Eleanor demanded a divorce from Louis. **(7)** Without modern-day *jurisprudence*, the couple simply needed to persuade the church to grant them an annulment. **(8)** It is doubtful that the couple even supplied anything resembling an *affidavit* certifying the grounds for divorce.

Eleanor did not remain single for long. Six weeks later she married King Henry II of England, and became queen of another country. Henry was often involved in disputes. **(9)** He had a running feud with the archbishop, Thomas of Becket, and accused Becket of an act equivalent to *perjury*. Eventually the king brought about Becket's murder.

Predictably, Henry and Eleanor, both extremely strong personalities, clashed. **(10)** Although she bore him eight children, she had little political *fidelity* to him. In fact, she led three of their sons in a revolt. In response, Henry imprisoned her in the Tower of London for fifteen years!

When Henry died, Eleanor was released, and Henry's son Richard the Lionhearted became king. Eleanor helped to govern England while Richard fought in the Crusades. In his absence, she governed effectively, and even resisted his brother John's treasonous efforts to seize the throne. But after Richard died, she acted as an important adviser to John, who then inherited the throne.

Well into her seventies, Eleanor made strenuous trips to arrange the marriages of her grandchildren. She also spent time in her native Aquitaine, helping to develop a code of chivalry that empowered women. Queen, politician, and cultural leader, Eleanor was indeed a woman ahead of her times.

Each sentence below refers to a numbered sentence in the passage. Write the letter of the choice that gives the sentence a meaning that is closest to the original sentence.

1. Do you _____ images of timid women when you think about the Middle Ages?
- **a.** strike down
- **b.** call to mind
- **c.** settle in court
- **d.** make fun of

2. His will provided that the king of France—to whom the duke had sworn _____—care for Eleanor.
- **a.** loyalty
- **b.** to pay
- **c.** judgment
- **d.** a lie

3. So the king promptly made Eleanor the _____, and then wife, of his son.
- **a.** star pupil
- **b.** coworker
- **c.** cook
- **d.** engaged woman

4. Louis treated his wife as a respected _____.
- **a.** business partner
- **b.** trusted person
- **c.** magician
- **d.** religious official

___d___ **5.** When Louis went to fight _____, Eleanor insisted on going.
    a. trusted friends   **b.** liars   **c.** invaders   **d.** nonbelievers

___c___ **6.** On their way, they visited the pope, who tried to _____ their quarrel.
    a. summon   **b.** prolong   **c.** settle   **d.** pledge loyalty to

___c___ **7.** Without modern-day _____, the couple simply needed to persuade the church to grant them an annulment.
    a. telephones   **b.** faithfulness   **c.** legal science   **d.** distractions

___a___ **8.** It is doubtful that the couple even supplied anything resembling an _____ certifying the grounds for divorce.
    a. written statement   **b.** book report   **c.** lie under oath   **d.** medical prescription

___b___ **9.** He had a running feud with the archbishop, Thomas of Becket, and accused Becket of an act equivalent to _____.
    a. burglary   **b.** lying under oath   **c.** studying science   **d.** settling a quarrel

___c___ **10.** Although she bore him eight children, she had little political _____ to him.
    a. connection   **b.** clout   **c.** loyalty   **d.** sworn written statements

Indicate whether the statements below are TRUE or FALSE according to the passage.

___F___ **1.** Eleanor was willing to stay home while Louis fought in the Second Crusade.

___T___ **2.** Eleanor clashed with both of her husbands.

___T___ **3.** The evidence suggests that Eleanor had considerable skill in leadership and governing.

FINISH THE THOUGHT

Complete each sentence so that it shows the meaning of the italicized word.

1. My *confidant* _____

2. He will *adjudicate* _____

WRITE THE DERIVATIVE

Complete the sentence by writing the correct form of the word shown in parentheses. You may not need to change the form that is given.

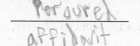

___Perjured___ **1.** Because the witness _____ himself, he now faces criminal charges. *(perjure)*

___affidavit___ **2.** Everything in your _____ suggests that you had no intention of paying my client for the building materials he provided. *(affidavit)*

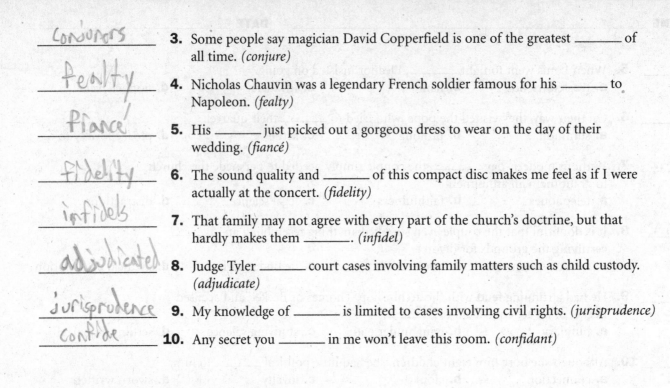

conjurers   **3.** Some people say magician David Copperfield is one of the greatest _____ of all time. *(conjure)*

fealty   **4.** Nicholas Chauvin was a legendary French soldier famous for his _____ to Napoleon. *(fealty)*

fiancé   **5.** His _____ just picked out a gorgeous dress to wear on the day of their wedding. *(fiancé)*

fidelity   **6.** The sound quality and _____ of this compact disc makes me feel as if I were actually at the concert. *(fidelity)*

infidels   **7.** That family may not agree with every part of the church's doctrine, but that hardly makes them _____. *(infidel)*

adjudicated   **8.** Judge Tyler _____ court cases involving family matters such as child custody. *(adjudicate)*

jurisprudence   **9.** My knowledge of _____ is limited to cases involving civil rights. *(jurisprudence)*

confide   **10.** Any secret you _____ in me won't leave this room. *(confidant)*

FIND THE EXAMPLE

Choose the answer that best describes the action or situation.

_c_   **1.** A likely discussion topic in a roomful of *fiancé(e)s*
     a. math equations   **b.** horse racing   **c.** wedding plans   **d.** stock market

_d_   **2.** The people most likely to have pledged *fidelity* to each other
     a. sworn enemies   **b.** a group of actors   **c.** judge and lawyer   **d.** a married couple

_a_   **3.** An example of a person who might need to read an *affidavit*
     a. an attorney   **b.** a toddler   **c.** an astronaut   **d.** a musician

_b_   **4.** Something that a *confidant* would be entrusted to do
     a. take notes   **b.** keep a secret   **c.** sell used cars   **d.** hit a game-winning shot

_c_   **5.** What two people who call each other *infidels* are most likely to disagree on
     a. where to eat   **b.** favorite movie   **c.** how to pray   **d.** the cost of an item

_d_   **6.** What a vassal might have received from his feudal lord, in exchange for *fealty*
     a. cruel punishment   **b.** a new car   **c.** military service   **d.** a parcel of land

_a_   **7.** Something that would convince a witness NOT to commit *perjury*
     a. It's a crime.   **b.** It's rude.   **c.** It's tiring.   **d.** It's difficult to do.

_c_   **8.** An example of something that a school principal might *adjudicate*
     a. a final exam   **b.** a lunch menu   **c.** a fight   **d.** the senior prom

_b_   **9.** What someone with an interest in *jurisprudence* would most likely study
     a. the Civil War   **b.** bankruptcy law   **c.** chemistry   **d.** investigative journalism

_d_   **10.** An example of something that a *conjurer* might seem to pull out of thin air
     a. an excuse   **b.** a funny joke   **c.** an anecdote   **d.** a bouquet of flowers

Prefixes, Roots, and Suffixes

The Prefixes *ambi-* and *para-*

The prefixes in this feature deal with location. *Ambi-*, from Latin, means "around" or "both." The common word *ambition* came from the Roman practice of going around to campaign, or ask for votes. *Para-*, from Greek, means "beside." For example, at one time, *paragraph* marks were put beside the writing (graph). *Para-* can also mean "similar to," "beyond," or "assistant to."

Prefix	Prefix Meaning	Word	Word Meaning
ambi-	around, both	ambidextrous	using both hands
para-	beside, similar to	paralegal	a person assisting a lawyer

Practice

You can combine the use of context clues with your knowledge of these prefixes to make intelligent guesses about the meanings of words. Each of the sentences below contains a word formed with the prefix *ambi-* or *para-*. Read each sentence and try to infer what the word in italics means. Then check your definition with the one that you find in the dictionary, remembering to choose the definition that best fits in the sentence.

1. The directions we had were *ambiguous,* so we didn't know where to take our next turn.

   My definition _____

   Dictionary definition _____

2. *Paralinguistic* phenomena, such as pauses and tone of voice during speech, communicate many messages.

   My definition _____

   Dictionary definition _____

3. After having spent several months in bed, it was good to see that Sergei was *ambulatory* once again.

   My definition _____

   Dictionary definition _____

4. The use of fictionalized *parajournalism* disturbs some critics, but others feel that it is a healthy, creative outlet.

   My definition _____

   Dictionary definition _____

5. *Paranormal* phenomena, such as ghostly voices, have been discredited.

My definition _____

Dictionary definition _____

6. Shannon felt *ambivalent* about going on the roller coaster ride, and missed out while she was trying to decide.

My definition _____

Dictionary definition _____

7. With its soft music, beautiful décor, and candlelight, the restaurant's *ambiance* was lovely.

My definition _____

Dictionary definition _____

8. Those lines are *parallel* and will never intersect.

My definition _____

Dictionary definition _____

9. Certain worms are *parasites* that can lodge within human organs and then feed off the organs.

My definition _____

Dictionary definition _____

Review Word Elements

Reviewing word elements helps you to remember them and use them in your reading. Below, write the meanings of the word elements you have studied.

Word	Word Element	Type of Element	Meaning of Word Element
spectator	*spec*	root	_____
interact	*inter-*	prefix	_____
pliant	*pli*	root	_____
intramural	*intra-*	prefix	_____
fidelity	*fid*	root	_____
jurisdiction	*jur*	root	_____

The Roots -val- and -vince-

WORD LIST

ambivalence	avail	countervailing	evaluate	evince
invaluable	prevail	valedictorian	valiant	vanquish

The Latin roots -val- and -vail- pertain to strength. The root -val- means "strength" or "value." It comes from the verb *valere*, "to be strong." The root -vince-, sometimes spelled -van-, means "conquer." It comes from the verb *vincere*, "to conquer." The words in this lesson will help you better understand, discuss, and write about strength, victory, and many other subjects.

1. **ambivalence** (ăm-bĭv′ə-ləns) *noun* from Latin *ambi-*, "both" + *val*, "strength"
   a. The presence of conflicting or opposing ideas or feelings
      • Sanjay felt **ambivalence** toward his difficult but worthwhile job.
   b. Uncertainty or indecisiveness as to which course to follow
      • My **ambivalence** about what to order annoyed the waitress.

   ambivalent *adjective* Though she would have preferred unbridled enthusiasm, it was clear that he was **ambivalent** about their vacation.

ambivalence

2. **avail** (ə-vāl′) from Latin *ad-*, "to" + *vail*, "strength"
   a. *verb* To be of use or advantage to; to help
      • Maribel **availed** herself of every opportunity to improve her vocabulary.
   b. *noun* Use, benefit, or advantage
      • Joshua labored to solve the calculus problem to no **avail**; he just couldn't solve it.

> *To no avail* and *to avail oneself of* are common phrases.

3. **countervailing** (koun′tər-vāl′ĭng) *adjective* from Latin *counter-*, "against" + *vail*, "strength"
   Acting against something so as to cancel its effect; counteractive
   • To repel the invaders, the locals formed what they hoped would be a **countervailing** force.

   countervail *verb* Do the benefits of cell phones **countervail** the increase in car accidents?

4. **evaluate** (ĭ-văl′yoo-āt′) *verb* from Latin *ex-*, "out" + *val*, "value"
   To judge or determine the value of
   • Tests are supposed to **evaluate** student progress.

   evaluation *noun* My supervisor at work gave me a good **evaluation**.

5. **evince** (ĭ-vĭns´) *verb* from Latin *ex-*, "out" + *vince*, "conquer"
To show or demonstrate clearly
- The judges **evinced** great surprise at the beginning gymnast's exceptional performance.

6. **invaluable** (ĭn-văl´yōō-ə-bəl) *adjective* from Latin *in-*, "very" + *val*, "value"
Priceless; having a value too great to be measured
- "Your help has been **invaluable** to us," said the charity's founder to the donor.

7. **prevail** (prĭ-vāl´) *verb* from Latin *pre-*, "before" + *vail*, "strength"
   a. To be greater in strength or influence; to triumph; to win out
      - After three years of fighting off invaders, the tribe finally **prevailed**.
   b. To be in use or effect; to be current
      - Eating turkey on Thanksgiving is a tradition that **prevails** in the United States.
   c. To persuade successfully
      - They **prevailed** upon us to let people stay at our home during the conference.

   prevailing *adjective* Believe it or not, the **prevailing** opinion among students is that school uniforms should be required.

> The third definition of *prevail* is often used with *on*, *upon*, or *with*.

8. **valedictorian** (văl´ĭ-dĭk-tôr´ē-ən) *noun* from Latin *val*, "worth" + *dict*, "say"
The student who has the highest academic rank in a class and who usually delivers the graduation speech
- The **valedictorian** expressed thanks to the faculty and everyone else who contributed to the school's creative environment.

   valedictory *noun* A closing or farewell statement or address
   - In a famous **valedictory** at the end of his second term, President George Washington talked about the need for a strong federal government.

   valedictory *adjective* The **valedictory** address was delivered by a famous graduate.

9. **valiant** (văl´yənt) *adjective* from Latin *val*, "strength"
Brave; possessing courage and boldness
- In the 1960s, some **valiant** American citizens lost their lives while struggling for civil rights.

   valiance *noun* Firefighters demonstrate **valiance** on the job regularly.

10. **vanquish** (văng´kwĭsh) *verb* from Latin *van*, "conquer"
To defeat; to overcome, conquer, or subdue
- So far this season, Seth has **vanquished** all his wrestling opponents.

WRITE THE CORRECT WORD

Write the correct word in the space next to each definition. Use each word only once.

Valiant	**1.** brave	
invaluable	**2.** priceless	
avail	**3.** to be of use to; help	
evaluate	**4.** to judge	
Valedictorian	**5.** the student with the highest academic ranking	

evince	**6.** to demonstrate clearly	
ambivalence	**7.** conflicting feelings	
Vanquish	**8.** to defeat	
Countervailing	**9.** acting against something	
Prevail	**10.** to be in use or effect	

COMPLETE THE SENTENCE

Write the letter for the word that best completes each sentence.

C **1.** In her speech, the _____ encouraged fellow students to ask the question, "How do I want to be remembered?"
  a. valiance   **b.** ambivalence   **c.** valedictorian   **d.** evaluation

d **2.** Felicia's parents felt great _____ when their daughter left home for college, for they were proud yet sad to see her go.
  a. valedictory   **b.** valiance   **c.** avail   **d.** ambivalence

a **3.** An official will _____ your driving skills before giving you a license.
  a. evaluate   **b.** countervail   **c.** evince   **d.** vanquish

C **4.** Paul couldn't quite reach the mountain's peak, but his climb was a(n) _____ effort, especially considering his sprained ankle.
  a. prevailing   **b.** ambivalent   **c.** valiant   **d.** countervailing

b **5.** I tried to _____ myself of every opportunity to learn Spanish.
  a. prevail   **b.** avail   **c.** evince   **d.** vanquish

d **6.** Because it's the only picture I have of my grandmother, it is _____ to me.
  a. countervailing   **b.** valedictory   **c.** ambivalent   **d.** invaluable

b **7.** Though the coach didn't say anything, her face _____ disgust at the foul call.
  a. availed   **b.** evinced   **c.** countervailed   **d.** vanquished

a **8.** In fairy tales, the forces of good usually _____ over the forces of evil.
  a. prevail   **b.** avail   **c.** evaluate   **d.** evince

d **9.** The doctor had to make sure not to prescribe _____ medication.
  a. prevailing   **b.** valiant   **c.** evinced   **d.** countervailing

C **10.** At one time, the Roman Empire could _____ any enemy on the battlefield.
  a. evaluate   **b.** evince   **c.** vanquish   **d.** avail

Challenge: "General, how does one _____ whether a soldier has performed _____ enough to earn a commendation?" asked the reporter.

_____ **a.** evaluate…valiantly   **b.** avail…ambivalently   **c.** vanquish…valiantly

Coltan: Modern Gold Rush

Can mining for gold make a person rich? Thousands of people who raced to California during the gold rush of the mid-1800s thought so. **(1)** But an honest *valedictory* to that period would have to include some negative aspects. **(2)** History's verdict on "gold fever" amounts to a mixed *evaluation*. The gold rush did make a few people wealthy. However, most of them were not hard-working miners but businesspeople who supplied the miners with products and services. And the gold rush also brought environmental destruction, accidental poisoning, and lawlessness.

Today, there is a new "rush," not for gold, but for an ore called columbite-tantalite, also known as columbo-tantalite, but more often abbreviated to "coltan." It is not found in California, however, but in Central Africa. In a region of the world that suffers from widespread poverty, it would seem that any marketable natural resource would be beneficial. **(3)** Yet the mining of this ore has sparked *ambivalent* reactions and worse.

Coltan is found in vast quantities in the eastern part of the Democratic Republic of the Congo. When refined into a heat-resistant metallic powder, called tantalum, it has unique abilities to hold electrical charges. **(4)** This superconductive material is *invaluable* for use in cellular phones and other technologies.

Coltan is mined by labor-intensive, exhausting methods. Companies hire thousands of laborers to dig, day in and day out. Workers often use only shovels to dig large craters, stripping away the soil to expose the ore underneath. In the process, they destroy the land. **(5)** It has been hard to *prevail* upon mining organizations to use methods that are environmentally sound.

The result has been widespread destruction of farmland and rain forest. Coltan-rich areas are often reduced to piles of dead trees surrounded by rivers muddied by eroded soil. **(6)** Companies *evince* little interest in saving such land for future cultivation.

Animal life has suffered from other coltan-related causes, too. The destruction of forests and farmland leaves people with fewer food sources. **(7)** People may search for food supplies to no *avail*. People have had to hunt animals, some of which are endangered. Rare species of both gorillas and okapis are diminishing, victims of lost habitats and of starving humans.

Because the mining of coltan is lucrative, many people fight to control it. In fact, the search for coltan is reportedly fueling lawlessness and a long-term civil war. Fighting forces seize coltan-rich areas. **(8)** These militias force farmers off the land and *vanquish* any resistance. Then these rebels mine the valuable mineral for their own profit.

(9) Worldwide, *valiant* efforts have been made to draw attention to these ongoing issues. In 2001, environmental advocates released negative reports across the globe. In addition, a campaign of "No blood on my cell phone" called for people to not buy phones containing coltan. This was followed by initiatives within the coltan industry to use nondestructive sources of the ore. Yet, the situation is complex. **(10)** Economic needs often *countervail* environmental and long-term humanitarian concerns. Many workers survive by mining, purifying, transporting, and selling coltan. Some used to be farmers, but, as one lamented while standing next to a piece of ruined land, "Coltan is our only way of making a living now. . . . There's nothing else to do here."

Each sentence below refers to a numbered sentence in the passage. Write the letter of the choice that gives the sentence a meaning that is closest to the original sentence.

_____C **1.** An honest _____ to that period would have to include some negative aspects.
  a. final defeat   **b.** assessed tax   **c.** closing speech   **d.** secret value

_____b **2.** History's verdict on "gold fever" amounts to a mixed _____.
  a. benefit   **b.** judgment   **c.** signal   **d.** discussion

_____b **3.** Yet the mining of this ore has sparked _____ reactions and worse.
  a. joyful   **b.** conflicting   **c.** intelligent   **d.** destructive

___d___ **4.** This superconductive material is _____ for use in cellular phones.
    a. undecided   **b.** displayed   **c.** brave and valiant   **d.** important and valuable

___b___ **5.** It has been hard to _____ companies to use methods that are environmentally sound.
    a. persuade   **b.** conquer   **c.** help   **d.** demonstrate

___c___ **6.** Companies _____ little interest in saving such land for future cultivation.
    a. judge   **b.** require   **c.** demonstrate   **d.** expect

___a___ **7.** People may search for food supplies to no _____.
    a. effect   **b.** successful persuasion   **c.** appraisal   **d.** indecisiveness

___d___ **8.** These militias force farmers off the land and _____ any resistance.
    a. negotiate   **b.** value   **c.** judge   **d.** crush

___b___ **9.** _____ efforts have been made to draw attention to these ongoing issues.
    a. Conflicting   **b.** Courageous   **c.** Halfhearted   **d.** Judged

___c___ **10.** Economic needs often _____ environmental and humanitarian concerns.
    a. judge   **b.** help support   **c.** work against   **d.** display

Indicate whether the statements below are TRUE or FALSE according to the passage.

___F___ **1.** Mining during the California gold rush produced great wealth for many.

___F___ **2.** Most people who mine coltan use it to make jewelry.

___T___ **3.** Indirect casualties of coltan mining include people and endangered species.

WRITING EXTENDED RESPONSES

What is your opinion about coltan mining in Africa? In a persuasive essay of at least three paragraphs, state whether you favor continued coltan mining, and then explain the reasons for your stance. Be sure to address the concerns that someone on the "other side" of the issue might raise. Support your arguments with facts and logic. Use at least three lesson words in your essay and underline them.

WRITE THE DERIVATIVE

Complete the sentence by writing the correct form of the word shown in parentheses. You may not need to change the form that is given.

___Prevailing___ **1.** The _____ wind will be coming from the northwest. (*prevail*)

___invaluable___ **2.** These paintings by Rembrandt are _____. (*invaluable*)

___countervail___ **3.** Our defensive efforts effectively _____ their offense. (*countervailing*) _valedictory_ **4.** Before retiring, the president delivered a _____ to his employees. (_valedictorian_)

ambivalent **5.** The action movie was exciting but shallow, so when my friend asked me what I thought about it, I felt _____ . (_ambivalence_)

avail **6.** I tried to race indoors before the rainstorm began, but it was to no _____ . (_avail_)

vanquished **7.** Words of encouragement _____ the toddler's fears, and she took her first step. (_vanquish_)

evinces **8.** A volunteer usually _____ an unselfish spirit. (_evince_)

valiant **9.** Thanks to the rescuers' _____ efforts, the trapped animal was saved. (_valiant_)

evaluated **10.** The doctor _____ her patient before making a diagnosis. (_evaluate_)

FIND THE EXAMPLE

Choose the answer that best describes the action or situation.

_a_ **1.** A person most likely to be _valiant_ while at work
a. paramedic **b.** chess master **c.** ballet dancer **d.** accountant

_d_ **2.** A common occasion when one person would _prevail_ over another
a. dancing **b.** study session **c.** lunch **d.** tennis match

_c_ **3.** Something that normally _evinces_ sadness
a. a joke **b.** a smile **c.** tears **d.** hiccups

_b_ **4.** Something that would _countervail_ swelling
a. a punch **b.** some ice **c.** a bruise **d.** a noise

_a_ **5.** Something an _ambivalent_ person would say
a. I can't decide. **b.** Definitely. **c.** Pass the butter. **d.** Absolutely not.

_c_ **6.** Someone most likely to _vanquish_ you on the basketball court
a. knowledgable fan **b.** chemistry teacher **c.** NBA player **d.** senior citizen

_d_ **7.** The person most likely to formally _evaluate_ an employee
a. freelancer **b.** volunteer **c.** visitor **d.** supervisor

_b_ **8.** Something definitely true of a _valedictorian_
a. was a good athlete **b.** got good grades **c.** had clean hair **d.** was very quiet

_a_ **9.** Something _invaluable_
a. cure for cancer **b.** stick of gum **c.** a nice dinner **d.** pencil sharpener

_b_ **10.** The item most likely to _avail_ a child who is suffering from a cold
a. harsh music **b.** cough syrup **c.** school work **d.** germs

The Roots -quisit-, -rog-, and -sag-

WORD LIST

abrogate	conquistador	inquisitive	interrogate	perquisite
presage	quest	requisite	sagacity	surrogate

A major theme throughout human history is the quest for wisdom. The Latin roots in this lesson relate to questioning, searching, and understanding. *-Quisit-*, *-quist-*, and *-quest-* mean "search" or "seek" and come from the Latin verb *quaerere*, "to seek." The root *-rog-* means "ask" or "propose" and comes from the Latin verb *rogare*, "to ask." *-Sag-* means "wisdom" or "knowledge" and comes from *sapere*, "to be wise," and its related forms.

1. **abrogate** (ăb´rə-gāt´) *verb* from Latin *ab-*, "away" + *rog*, "ask"
   To abolish, do away with, repeal, or cancel, especially by authority
   • During World War II, Nazi Germany **abrogated** its treaty with Russia and attacked this former ally.

   abrogation *noun* Does the prosecution of reporters who refuse to name their confidential sources demonstrate an **abrogation** of freedom of the press?

2. **conquistador** (kŏng-kē´stə-dôr´, kŏn-kwĭs´tə-dôr´) *noun* from Latin *com-*, "completely" + *quist*, "seek"
   A conqueror, especially one of the Spanish soldiers who defeated the native civilizations of Mexico, Central America, or Peru in the 1500s
   • The famous **conquistador** Ponce de León searched for the mythical Fountain of Youth in an area that he named "Florida."

3. **inquisitive** (ĭn-kwĭz´ĭ-tĭv) *adjective* from Latin *in-*, "into" + *quisit*, "seek"
   a. Eager for knowledge; inclined to investigate
   • "It's my job to be **inquisitive**, ma'am," explained the detective.
   b. Excessively curious; inclined to ask questions; nosy
   • The **inquisitive** six-year-old questioned her aunt about every detail of her day.

   inquisitiveness *noun* Aunt Lulu's **inquisitiveness** trapped us at the dinner table for hours.

4. **interrogate** (ĭn-tĕr´ə-gāt´) *verb* from Latin *inter-*, "between" + *rog*, "ask"
   To question formally and officially
   • Government agents **interrogated** the suspected smugglers.

   interrogation *noun* Special rules govern police **interrogations**.

Interrogation in progress

5. **perquisite** (pûr´kwĭ-zĭt) *noun* from Latin *per-*, "through" + *quisit*, "seek"
   a. A benefit of employment besides one's salary; a fringe benefit
   • Use of the company jet was a **perquisite** of the CEO position.
   b. Something claimed as an exclusive right
   • At one time, politics were the **perquisite** of the rich.
   c. A tip; a gratuity
   • Though the waiter's wage was low, he made more from **perquisites**.

The word *perquisite* is often abbreviated to "perk," as in "Tuition reimbursement is one of the *perks* of the job."

6. **presage** from Latin *pre-*, "before" + *sag*, "knowledge"
   a. *noun* (prĕs´ĭj) An indication or a warning of a future event; an omen
   • The Romans thought that birds' flight patterns were **presages** of success or failure in battle.
   b. *noun* (prĕs´ĭj) A feeling or an intuition of what is going to occur
   • This morning I experienced the **presage** that I would have a pop quiz in math class.
   c. *verb* (prē sāj´, prĭ sāj´, pres ij´) To indicate or warn of in advance; to foretell or predict
   • In the late 1800s, impressionist techniques **presaged** the development of abstract art.

7. **quest** (kwĕst) from Latin *quest*, "seek"
   a. *noun* A search or pursuit; the act of seeking something
   • The philosopher vowed never to abandon his **quest** for truth.
   b. *verb* To seek or pursue
   • The knight **quested** for the hidden treasure.

A *quest* can be physical, mental, emotional, spiritual, or a combination.

8. **requisite** (rĕk´wĭ-zĭt) from Latin *re-*, "back" + *quisit*, "seek"
   a. *adjective* Required; essential
   • It is extremely dangerous to go rock climbing without the **requisite** supplies and equipment.
   b. *noun* Something essential or indispensable; a requirement
   • Knowledge of Spanish was **requisite** for the job in Peru.

9. **sagacity** (sə-găs´ĭ-tē) *noun* from Latin *sag*, "knowledge"
   Wisdom; sound judgment
   • The **sagacity** of Dr. Gund made him a sought-after resource for many.

   sagacious *adjective* **Sagacious** officials guided the public treasury from deficit to surplus.

10. **surrogate** (sûr´ə-gĭt) from Latin *sub-*, "under" + *rog*, "ask"
    a. *noun* One who takes the place of another; a substitute
    • The graduate student served as a surprisingly good **surrogate** for the vacationing professor.
    b. *adjective* Substitute; taking the place of another
    • Over the years, the kindly teacher acted as a **surrogate** parent for many students.

WORD ENRICHMENT

Sagacity and sage

The root *sag*, which is the basis of *presage* and *sagacity*, is also used to form the word *sage*, "a person of wisdom, experience, and good judgment." The herb *sage*, however, used to flavor meat, comes from a different root. It is taken from the same source as the word *saliva*.

WRITE THE CORRECT WORD

Write the correct word in the space next to each definition. Use each word only once.

Perqusite **1.** a fringe benefit

inquisitive **2.** eager for knowledge

Conquistador **3.** a Spanish conqueror

interrogate **4.** to question formally

abrogate **5.** to cancel or repeal

Presage **6.** an omen

Surrogate **7.** a substitute

requisite **8.** required; essential

Sagacity **9.** wisdom

quest **10.** a search or pursuit

COMPLETE THE SENTENCE

Write the letter for the word that best completes each sentence.

_c_ **1.** In some animal species, if parents die or are incapacitated, other animals assume the role of _____ and raise the young.
   a. perquisites   **b.** requisites   **c.** surrogates   **d.** presages

_b_ **2.** If you enjoy writing, learning about the world, and talking with people, being a newspaper reporter has many _____.
   a. interrogations   **b.** perquisites   **c.** requisites   **d.** presages

_b_ **3.** The small, pink buds on the trees _____ the coming of spring.
   a. abrogated   **b.** presaged   **c.** quested   **d.** interrogated

_a_ **4.** Most young children are highly _____ about the world around them.
   a. inquisitive   **b.** abrogated   **c.** interrogated   **d.** requisite

_c_ **5.** The arrogant, competitive CEO was known as "the corporate _____."
   a. perquisite   **b.** presage   **c.** conquistador   **d.** requisite

_a_ **6.** People who are inflamed with anger often do not behave with _____.
   a. sagacity   **b.** requisition   **c.** abrogation   **d.** perquisites

_d_ **7.** She filled out all the _____ forms and applications for receiving assistance.
   a. inquisitive   **b.** abrogated   **c.** sagacious   **d.** requisite

_d_ **8.** Some cities now require videos of police _____ to assure that there are no abuses.
   a. abrogations   **b.** perquisites   **c.** presages   **d.** interrogations

_c_ **9.** Gandhi's _____ for justice involved nonviolent resistance.
   a. interrogation   **b.** sagacity   **c.** quest   **d.** surrogate

_d_ **10.** All of the group members lost confidence in their leader when she _____ their agreement.
   a. interrogated   **b.** quested   **c.** presaged   **d.** abrogated

Challenge: Although many _____ came with being the wife of the president, the First Lady was _____ enough to know that an ostentatious style would alienate the public.

_c_   **a.** quests…inquisitive   **b.** requisites…abrogating   **c.** perquisites…sagacious

A Voice from Peru

Studying the past is like solving a puzzle. Using old diaries, letters, or even paintings, historians try to piece together what daily life was like. In 1908, a crucial puzzle piece of Peruvian history was unexpectedly found.

(1) Many books describe how Spanish *conquistadors* defeated the Incas and other civilizations in the 1500s. But hundreds of years later, a man in a Danish library stumbled upon a book that tells the story from the "other" side.

The book, titled *The First New Chronicle and Good Government,* was written in 1615 by Felipe Guaman Poma de Ayala, a native of Peru. In it, Ayala describes the situation in which indigenous peoples found themselves after the Spanish took over their homeland. The book offers a rare opportunity to view these events through the eyes of a native of the Americas.

Ayala begins by describing the Inca Empire that thrived in Peru and beyond until Francisco Pizarro arrived in 1532. **(2)** Of Pizarro's *quest* to claim Incan land and riches, Ayala wrote, "They were like a desperate man: foolish, crazy, and out of their minds with greed for silver and gold." (sic)

(3) At first, as an *inquisitive* young boy, Ayala trusted the newcomers. He learned to speak Spanish and began translating for the explorers, whom he found very odd in appearance. He wrote, "To our Indian eyes, the Spaniards looked as if they were shrouded like corpses. Their faces were covered with wool, leaving only the eyes visible, and the caps they wore resembled little red pots on top of their heads."

(4) The *perquisites* of his job as a translator included witnessing important historical events. Much of what he saw or heard about, though, was tragic for the Peruvian culture. He describes how Pizarro and his men captured an Incan ruler, Atahualpa, who had welcomed the Spaniards in peace: "The Spaniards began to fire their muskets and charged upon the Indians, killing them like ants. At the sound of the explosions . . . the [Incas] were terror-stricken." Countless Incas were killed, and "the king was left very sad . . . . sitting on the ground, his throne and kingdom gone."

(5) This sorry image of a former king *presaged* decades of Incan suffering under their conquerors. Taken prisoner, Atahualpa sought to buy his freedom with gold. **(6)** Pizarro accepted many tons of Incan treasure, but then *abrogated* the agreement and killed the Incan king anyway.

The Incas lost control of their land. **(7)** Their leaders were beaten, imprisoned, *interrogated* about potential rebellions, and then, if they were lucky, sent away.

(8) Europeans became the *surrogate* kings of the Incas, who were forced to labor in the gold and silver mines. Within forty years, 80 percent of the Inca population had died, victims of Spanish violence, abuse, and diseases.

Later in life, Ayala looked back at what the Spanish had done. **(9)** He questioned the *sagacity* of his choice to support them and began to speak out for native rights. He also wrote a book and sent it to the king of Spain.

(10) Ayala's writing listed changes he believed were *requisite* to improve the lives of Peruvians. No one knows if the king even read it, but many modern historians value its insights.

PERU

Each sentence below refers to a numbered sentence in the passage. Write the letter of the choice that gives the sentence a meaning that is closest to the original sentence.

___C___ **1.** Many books describe how Spanish _____ defeated the Incas.
  a. requirements **b.** benefits **c.** conquerors **d.** wise men

___b___ **2.** Of Pizarro's _____ Incan land and riches, Ayala was critical.
  a. wise advice on **b.** mission to get **c.** questions about **d.** substitutes for

___a___ **3.** At first, as a _____ young boy, Ayala trusted the newcomers.
  a. curious **b.** required **c.** wise **d.** helpful

___b___ **4.** The _____ of his job as a translator included witnessing historical events.
  a. requirements **b.** benefits **c.** questions **d.** conquerors

___a___ **5.** This sorry image of a former king _____ decades of Incan suffering.
  a. symbolized   **b.** required   **c.** quickly repealed   **d.** warned of

___a___ **6.** Pizarro accepted many tons of Incan treasure, but then _____ the agreement
      and killed the Incan king.
  a. canceled   **b.** questioned   **c.** searched   **d.** replaced

___c___ **7.** Their leaders were beaten, imprisoned, _____ about potential rebellions, and
      then, if they were lucky, sent away.
  a. abused   **b.** searched   **c.** questioned   **d.** voided

___d___ **8.** Europeans became the _____ kings of the Incas, who were forced to work in
      the gold and silver mines.
  a. repealed   **b.** wise   **c.** curious   **d.** substitute

___b___ **9.** He questioned the _____ of his choice to support them.
  a. cancellation   **b.** wisdom   **c.** requirements   **d.** benefits

___c___ **10.** Ayala's writing listed changes he believed were _____ to improve the lives
      of Peruvians.
  a. cancelled   **b.** sought   **c.** required   **d.** substituted

Indicate whether the statements below are TRUE or FALSE according to the passage.

___T___ **1.** Ayala's attitude toward the Spanish conquistadors changed over time.

___T___ **2.** Ayala's book could be considered an exception to the rule "History is written by
      the winners."

___F___ **3.** The Spanish either enslaved or killed any indigenous person they encountered.

FINISH THE THOUGHT

Complete each sentence so that it shows the meaning of the italicized word.

1. He went on a *quest* to _____

2. Since I appreciate the *sagacity* of your advice, _____

WRITE THE DERIVATIVE

**Complete the sentence by writing the correct form of the word shown in
parentheses. You may not need to change the form that is given.**

___Surrogate___ **1.** The regent to an underage king or queen serves as a type of _____ parent,
      especially in the area of political policy. *(surrogate)*

___abrogation___ **2.** This _____ of my constitutional rights is an outrage! *(abrogate)*

quest   **3.** What started as a simple trip to the mall turned into a tedious, exhausting, all-day _____ for the "perfect" pair of shoes. *(quest)*

inquisitiveness   **4.** "The domesticated feline's _____ led to its demise" is a fancy way of saying "curiosity killed the cat." *(inquisitive)*

perks   **5.** One of the _____ of working for an airline is reduced-rate travel. *(perquisite)*

sagacious   **6.** Rather than working with a brash young upstart, we would prefer an experienced, _____ leader. *(sagacity)*

conquistadors   **7.** Spanish _____ came from a surprising variety of social and religious backgrounds. *(conquistador)*

requisite   **8.** We filled out the _____ forms to file the insurance claim. *(requisite)*

presage   **9.** Yesterday's drop in barometric pressure _____ the storm. *(presage)*

interrogation   **10.** Suspects in a crime are often subjected to _____. *(interrogate)*

FIND THE EXAMPLE

Choose the answer that best describes the action or situation.

_c_   **1.** Something that is typically *requisite* in a college application
     a. family history   **b.** musical talent   **c.** your grades   **d.** sample poetry

_d_   **2.** An adjective that does NOT describe the *conquistadors*
     a. bold   **b.** power hungry   **c.** greedy   **d.** timid

_b_   **3.** Something that might *presage* a health problem
     a. energy   **b.** tiredness   **c.** an agreement   **d.** burial

_d_   **4.** An action that would most likely result in the *abrogation* of a worker's employment contract
     a. surpassing goals   **b.** taking vacation   **c.** being rude   **d.** harassing coworkers

_a_   **5.** A human *quest* that has already been completed or achieved
     a. for flight   **b.** for peace   **c.** for fairness   **d.** for travel to the sun

_d_   **6.** An *inquisitive* thing to say
     a. Who cares?   **b.** Don't ask.   **c.** I like hawks.   **d.** How does that work?

_b_   **7.** A habit that best leads to *sagacity*
     a. shouting   **b.** listening   **c.** humming   **d.** napping

_c_   **8.** A likely *perquisite* of working for a college
     a. higher grades   **b.** huge salary   **c.** reduced tuition   **d.** free products

_a_   **9.** Something a *surrogate* always is
     a. substitute   **b.** superior   **c.** superficial   **d.** solid

_c_   **10.** The person most likely to be *interrogated*
     a. company boss   **b.** sleeping child   **c.** accused criminal   **d.** sprinting athlete

The Roots -greg-, -here-, and -sim-

WORD LIST

adhere	aggregate	cohere	dissimulate	egregious
ensemble	facsimile	gregarious	inherent	semblance

The three word roots in this lesson pertain to "togetherness." *-Greg-* means "flock," as in a flock of sheep; *-here-* means "stick; sticky"; and *-sim-* (or *-sem-*) means "similar; alike." *-Greg-* comes from the Latin word *grex* and is used in words such as *congregation*, a "flock" of worshippers. *-Here-* comes from the Latin verb *haerere*, "to stick." The word *adhere* contains this root. *-Sim-* comes from *similis*, Latin for "similar."

adhere

1. **adhere** (ăd-hîr´) *verb* from Latin *ad-*, "to" + *here*, "stick"
   a. To stick tightly to a surface
      • The bandage **adhered** to my skin and was difficult to remove.
   b. To be loyal or devoted to something
      • It is not always easy to consistently **adhere** to a set of beliefs.
   c. To carry out a plan or program without straying from it
      • I strictly **adhere** to my exercise routine.

   adherence *noun* **Adherence** to a schedule is important when working on a long-term project.

   adherent *noun* The prince's **adherents** remained loyal even when he was defeated in battle.

2. **aggregate** from Latin *ad-*, "to" + *greg*, "flock"
   a. *adjective* (ăg´rĭ-gĭt) Total; amounting to a whole
      • **Aggregate** sales were up for the holiday season.
   b. *noun* (ăg´rĭ-gĭt) A total composed of different parts
      • The corporation is an **aggregate** of several different companies.
   c. *verb* (ăg´rĭ-gāt´) To add up; to gather into a mass, sum, or whole
      • Please **aggregate** your inventory from each factory and report the total value.

   > *Aggregate* can also mean the materials, such as sand and stone, used to make concrete.

3. **cohere** (kō-hîr´) *verb* from Latin *co-*, "together" + *here*, "stick"
   a. To stick together in a mass that resists separation
      • The crumbly dough will **cohere** if you press it into a ball.
   b. To be internally consistent and have logically linked parts
      • The essay **cohered** nicely around the central thesis.

   cohesion *noun* The plot lacked **cohesion** and was hard to follow.

   cohesive *adjective* My **cohesive** family always gathers for holidays.

   coherent *adjective* Genevieve's argument was so **coherent** that the opposing debate team could find nothing to refute.

   > *Cohesiveness* and *coherence* are nouns that have meanings similar to that of *cohesion*. The difference between *cohesive* and *coherent* is that *coherent* is generally used to mean "internal consistency."

4. dissimulate (dĭ-sĭm´yə-lāt´) *verb* from Latin *dis-*, "apart"
+ *sim*, "similar"
To disguise under a fake appearance; to conceal feelings or intentions
• He **dissimulated** his disappointment over not being elected class
president, claiming he never really wanted the position.

dissimulation *noun* Cooper's **dissimulation** irritated his friends, who
wanted to know how he really felt about the plan.

5. egregious (ĭ-grē´jəs) *adjective* from Latin *e-*, "out" + *greg*, "flock"
Conspicuously bad or offensive
• The student's paper was filled with **egregious** misspellings and
punctuation errors, and her teacher insisted that she revise it.

6. ensemble (ŏn-sŏm´bəl) *noun* from Latin *in-*, "in" + *sim*, "similar"
A whole unit or group composed of complementary or
coordinated parts
• An orchestra is an **ensemble** made up of many musicians and a
variety of instruments.

> An *ensemble* can be an outfit, a set of furniture, or a group of musicians, dancers, or other performers.

7. facsimile (făk-sĭm´ə-lē) *noun* from Latin *facere*, "to make" +
sim, "similar"
An exact copy or reproduction
• The **facsimile** of the Declaration of Independence appeared on the
inside cover of the history book.

> A *fax* (an abbreviation of *facsimile*) is a copy of a document sent by a fax machine.

8. gregarious (grĭ-gâr´ē-əs) *adjective* from Latin *greg*, "flock"
Sociable; seeking and enjoying the company of others
• **Gregarious** people often enjoy attending parties.

gregariousness *noun* Politicians must have some **gregariousness**, for
their success depends on being known and liked by many people.

9. inherent (ĭn-hîr´ənt) *adjective* from Latin *in-*, "in" + *here*, "stick"
Inborn; naturally a part of something; intrinsic
• The photographer has an **inherent** ability to capture her subject's
emotion.

10. semblance (sĕm´bləns) *noun* from Latin *sim*, "similar"
  a. An outward or a token appearance
  • Despite feeling hurt, Mary tried to keep a **semblance** of dignity.
  b. A very small amount; the barest trace
  • There wasn't even a **semblance** of humor in that so-called comedy.

ANALOGIES

On the answer line, write the letter of the answer that best completes
each analogy. Refer to lessons 25–27 if you need help with any of the
lesson words.

_____ **1.** *Ambivalent* is to *certain* as _____ .
  a. *gregarious* is to *sociable*   **c.** *inquisitive* is to *curious*
  b. *surrogate* is to *substitute*   **d.** *egregious* is to *excellent*

_____ **2.** *Evince* is to *demonstrate* as _____ .
  a. *aggregate* is to *separate*   **c.** *adhere* is to *stick*
  b. *abrogate* is to *agree*   **d.** *prevail* is to *conduct*

174   **The Roots -greg-, -here-, and -sim-**

WRITE THE CORRECT WORD

Write the correct word in the space next to each definition. Use each word only once.

_____cohere_____ **1.** to be internally consistent

_____inherent_____ **2.** inborn; natural

_____adhere_____ **3.** to stick tightly to

_____egregious_____ **4.** noticeably bad

_____ensemble_____ **5.** a group composed of coordinated parts

_____Semblance_____ **6.** an outward appearance

_____aggregate_____ **7.** to add up

_____Facsimile_____ **8.** an exact copy

_____dissimulate_____ **9.** to disguise; to conceal feelings

_____gregarious_____ **10.** sociable

COMPLETE THE SENTENCE

Write the letter for the word that best completes each sentence.

__C__ **1.** No doubt Albert Einstein had a(n) _____ ability for mathematics.
   a. egregious   **b.** coherent   **c.** inherent   **d.** gregarious

__a__ **2.** A theory lacking any _____ of proof would gain little attention from scientists.
   a. semblance   **b.** dissimulation   **c.** gregariousness   **d.** adherent

__b__ **3.** Duct tape is often used to repair things because it _____ to almost any surface.
   a. dissimulates   **b.** adheres   **c.** coheres   **d.** aggregates

__a__ **4.** _____ people tend to have lots of friends.
   a. Gregarious   **b.** Facsimile   **c.** Egregious   **d.** Inherent

__d__ **5.** A string quartet is a type of _____ .
   a. dissimulation   **b.** facsimile   **c.** semblance   **d.** ensemble

__d__ **6.** The reviewer was very critical of the actor's _____ performance.
   a. inherent   **b.** cohesive   **c.** aggregate   **d.** egregious

__C__ **7.** To determine your profit, _____ your sales receipts, then subtract your expenses.
   a. cohere   **b.** adhere   **c.** aggregate   **d.** dissimulate

__a__ **8.** To prove his identity, he had to present a(n) _____ of his birth certificate.
   a. facsimile   **b.** aggregation   **c.** ensemble   **d.** dissimulation

__b__ **9.** When asked an embarrassing question, he preferred to _____ rather than reveal his true feelings.
   a. aggregate   **b.** dissimulate   **c.** adhere   **d.** cohere

__d__ **10.** A(n) _____ argument is more likely to persuade an audience than a disjointed one is.
   a. gregarious   **b.** egregious   **c.** dissimulated   **d.** cohesive

Challenge: The performance by the music _____ was so _____ that one critic called it a musical disaster.
__a__
   a. ensemble...egregious   **b.** ensemble...gregarious   **c.** aggregate...cohesive

Identical Pairs

Even if you don't personally know any identical twins, you have likely seen them on television or in the movies, though you may not have been aware of it. Brothers Cole and Dylan Sprouse split the role of Cullen Crisp, Jr., in the movie *Kindergarten Cop*. And most everyone is familiar with sisters Mary Kate and Ashley Olsen, who both played the role of Michelle on the show *Full House* and went on to make many movies together. **(1)** Identical twin *ensembles* are popular in Hollywood because sharing a role eases the burden on young actors. **(2)** If either member of these pairs chooses to *dissimulate* by appearing as the other twin, well, who would be the wiser?

Unlike fraternal twins, identical twins share exactly the same genetic material because they develop from a single egg that splits in two after fertilization. (Fraternal twins develop from two separate eggs.) **(3)** Identical twins are not simply *facsimiles* of each other, however. They typically develop differently, even before birth. So, while identical twins share eye and hair color, and many other traits, they do not always have the same birth weight. Their fingerprints, also partially determined by prenatal conditions, are different, too.

Mirror twins are identical twins who separated nine to twelve days after their development began. They are identical, but on opposite sides. If one is right-handed, the other tends to be left-handed. And if they have cowlicks in their hair, they have them on opposite sides of their heads.

Of course, what happens after a person is born is also important to development. **(4)** If twins are raised in the same household, their parents typically *adhere* to the same schedules and a similar approach to play, sleep, and feeding. This common experience leads to further similarities. But twins vary just as other siblings do and are unique individuals. **(5)** Some share a *cohesive* relationship with each other, whereas others prefer to be more independent.

(6) Studies comparing identical and fraternal twins show, in *aggregate*, that identical twins are more similar to each other than fraternal twins are, not only in appearance but in personal preferences and characteristics as well. **(7)** Identical twins tend to share such traits as *gregariousness* and optimism.

(8) The study of identical twins who are raised apart is fascinating to scientists, for it provides clues that help determine whether certain traits are *inherent* or shaped by environmental factors. Such twins sometimes have strangely similar habits. For example, both may favor unusual behaviors such as twisting rubber bands around their wrists or reading magazines backward.

Alexander Dumas's novel *The Man in the Iron Mask* is about an unusual pair of twins. According to legend, Louis XIV of France had an identical twin brother who was kept hidden by their father to avoid questions about who would inherit the throne. **(9)** When the cruel Louis became king, his treatment of his unfortunate twin was *egregious*, for he supposedly locked his brother away and forced him to wear a horrible disguise. **(10)** Eventually, a *semblance* of justice was done . . . but you'll have to read the novel to find out the ending for yourself!

Each sentence below refers to a numbered sentence in the passage. Write the letter of the choice that gives the sentence a meaning that is closest to the original sentence.

_____ **1.** Identical twin _____ are popular in Hollywood because sharing a role eases the burden on young actors.
 a. staff   **b.** crew   **c.** writers   **d.** groups

_____ **2.** If either member of these pairs chooses to _____ by appearing as the other twin, well, who would be the wiser?
 a. copy   **b.** be loyal   **c.** fake a disguise   **d.** stick together

_____ **3.** Identical twins are not simply _____ each other.
 a. exact copies of   **b.** sick of   **c.** consistent with   **d.** traces of

_____d_____ **4.** If twins are raised in the same household, their parents typically _____ the same schedules and a consistent approach.
    a. admire   **b.** conceal   **c.** reproduce   **d.** stick to

_____b_____ **5.** Some share a(n) _____ relationship with each other.
    a. fake   **b.** close   **c.** distant   **d.** token

_____a_____ **6.** Studies comparing identical and fraternal twins show, in _____, that identical twins are more similar to each other than fraternal twins are.
    a. total   **b.** crowds   **c.** social settings   **d.** small amounts

_____d_____ **7.** Identical twins tend to share such traits as _____ and optimism.
    a. badness   **b.** healthiness   **c.** appearance   **d.** sociability

_____c_____ **8.** The study of identical twins who are raised apart provides clues that help determine whether certain traits are _____ or shaped by environmental factors.
    a. consistent   **b.** social   **c.** intrinsic   **d.** rare

_____a_____ **9.** When the cruel Louis became king, his treatment of his unfortunate twin was _____.
    a. conspicuously bad   **b.** loyal and devoted   **c.** complementary   **d.** internally consistent

_____a_____ **10.** Eventually, a(n) _____ of justice was done.
    a. monument   **b.** total   **c.** disguising   **d.** appearance

Indicate whether the statements below are TRUE or FALSE according to the passage.

_____T_____ **1.** Identical twins sometimes share TV roles.

_____F_____ **2.** *Fraternal* describes twin brothers only.

_____T_____ **3.** Scientists find the study of twins to be useful in trying to determine which traits are genetic and which ones develop as a result of our environment.

WRITING EXTENDED RESPONSES

Do you think that you would like to be an identical twin? Write an expository essay detailing what you think the pros and cons would be. (If you are, in fact, an identical twin, you may state the pros and cons based on your experience.) Your essay should be at least three paragraphs long and include supporting details. Use a minimum of three lesson words in your essay and underline them.

WRITE THE DERIVATIVE

Complete the sentence by writing the correct form of the word shown in parentheses. You may not need to change the form that is given.

__Facsimiles__ **1.** Some _____ can be very difficult to distinguish from the originals. (*facsimile*)

__Coherency__ **2.** The argument lacked _____ and fell apart like a house of cards in an earthquake. (*cohere*) _inherently_   **3.** Many philosophers have argued about whether people are _____ good or evil. (_inherent_)

semblance   **4.** In order to infiltrate a gambling ring, the undercover agent had to maintain a convincing _____ of wealth. (_semblance_)

adherement   **5.** _____ to the rules of the camp was required of all the campers. (_adhere_)

aggregate   **6.** Cement is an _____ made of powdered lime, silica, and several other hard substances. (_aggregate_)

dissimulation   **7.** Known for her _____, Linda rarely revealed her true feelings. (_dissimulate_)

ensemble   **8.** To complete his unusual _____, Harkness bought a striped shirt to go with his favorite pair of checkered pants. (_ensemble_)

egregiously   **9.** Monica was disappointed that she had performed _____ in her first recital. (_egregious_)

gregariousness   **10.** Ms. King's _____ was a great advantage as she campaigned for mayor. (_gregarious_)

FIND THE EXAMPLE

Choose the answer that best describes the action or situation.

_d_   **1.** An example of a popular, lighthearted _dissimulation_
   a. pajamas   **b.** camcorder   **c.** schoolwork   **d.** clown costume

_b_   **2.** Something _inherent_ to successful musicians
   a. aggressive agent   **b.** good ear for pitch   **c.** recording contract   **d.** retirement plan

_c_   **3.** Something that lacks any _semblance_ of order
   a. lunch line   **b.** file cabinet   **c.** garbage pile   **d.** table of contents

_a_   **4.** An example of an _ensemble_
   a. a band   **b.** a van   **c.** a skirt   **d.** a singer

_b_   **5.** The most _egregious_ thing
   a. white lie   **b.** treasonous act   **c.** volunteer work   **d.** charitable act

_d_   **6.** Something you probably _adhere_ to
   a. conjectures   **b.** jokes   **c.** rumors   **d.** beliefs

   that is illegal to make _facsimiles_ of
                           b. e-mail   **c.** documents   **d.** money

_c_   **8.** The mathematical operation you would most likely use to _aggregate_ your income
   a. division   **b.** square root   **c.** addition   **d.** subtraction

_c_   **9.** Something that _coheres_
   a. soup   **b.** confetti   **c.** clay   **d.** ink

_b_   **10.** An outlet for _gregariousness_
   a. a solo flight   **b.** a dinner party   **c.** an operation   **d.** a chess tournament

178   **The Roots** _-greg-, -here-,_ and _-sim-_

Prefixes, Roots, and Suffixes

The Word Elements *astro-*, *geo-*, *hydro-*, *-mar-*, and *-terra-*

The five word elements in this feature deal with natural physical features. *Astro-*, *geo-*, and *hydro-* come from Greek. Each one can be used as a prefix or as a root. The roots *-mar-* and *-terra-* come from Latin. The meanings of each element are given in the table below.

Element	Type	Meaning	Word	Word Meaning
astro-, astro	prefix, root	star	astronomy	the study of outer space
geo-, geo	prefix, root	earth	geography	the study of Earth's features
hydro-, hydro	prefix, root	water	hydroelectric	generating electricity using water
mar	root	sea	mariner	one who navigates a ship
terra	root	earth	territory	land

Practice

You can combine the use of context clues with your knowledge of these word elements to make intelligent guesses about meanings. Each of the sentences below contains a word formed with the word element *astro*, *geo*, *hydro*, *mar*, or *terra*. Read each sentence and try to infer what the word in italics means. Then check your definition with the one you find in the dictionary, remembering to choose the definition that best fits in the sentence.

1. After suffering from seasickness for the entire week of our voyage, I was glad to be back on *terra firma.*

My definition _____

Dictionary definition _____

2. *Submarine* warfare was an important element of World War II.

My definition _____

Dictionary definition _____

3. Sailors in the time of Columbus often relied on *astronavigation.*

My definition _____

Dictionary definition _____

4. He is a specialist in *geophysics.*

My definition _____

Dictionary definition _____

5. The specialists in *hydrobiology* took samples from the pond at regular intervals.

My definition _____

Dictionary definition _____

6. It was difficult to travel through the mountainous *terrain*.

My definition _____

Dictionary definition _____

7. A *maritime* code deals with commerce conducted on the ocean.

My definition _____

Dictionary definition _____

8. The *hydrofoil* skimmed the surface.

My definition _____

Dictionary definition _____

Review Word Elements

Reviewing word elements helps you to remember them and use them in your reading. Below, write the meanings of the word elements you have studied.

Word	Word Element	Type of Element	Meaning of Word Element
ambivalent	*ambi-*	prefix	_____
sagacity	*sag*	root	_____
congregate	*greg*	root	_____
parallel	*para-*	prefix	_____
valiant	*val*	root	_____
adhere	*here*	root	_____
inquisitive	*quisit*	root	_____
invincible	*vinc, vince*	root	_____
dissimulate	*sim*	root	_____
interrogate	*rog*	root	_____
fidelity	*fid*	root	_____
spectacles	*spec, spect*	root	_____
pliant	*pli*	root	_____

Luck and Whím

WORD LIST

alchemy	amulet	capricious	fatalism	propitious
providential	quirk	serendipity	vagary	vicissitude

Much that happens in the universe is beyond our control. Chance events and the whims of others affect us in both significant and subtle ways. The words in this lesson will help you better understand, discuss, and write about luck and whim.

1. **alchemy** (ăl´kə-mē) *noun* from Arabic *al-*, "the" + *kimiya,* "chemistry"

   a. The ancient and medieval chemical art of trying to change metals to gold, cure diseases, or find eternal youth
   • The practice of **alchemy** eventually led to the development of many medicines.

   b. A seemingly magical power or process of change
   • By what **alchemy** does the universe give us an oak tree from an acorn?

   alchemist *noun* In the story, the **alchemist** accidentally changes lead into water.

2. **amulet** (ăm´yə-lĭt) *noun* from Latin *amuletum*
   An object worn, usually around the neck, to bring good luck or protection; a charm
   • The ancient Egyptians often wore **amulets** shaped like scarab beetles.

amulet

3. **capricious** (kə-prĭsh´əs, kə-prē´shəs) *adjective* from Italian *caporiccio,* "fright; sudden start"
   Unpredictable; impulsive; subject to whim
   • Young children often have **capricious** tastes in food, loving something one minute and hating it the next.

   capriciousness *noun* Known for **capriciousness,** the Roman emperor Nero would suddenly imprison the person on whom he had lavished gifts the day before.

4. **fatalism** (fāt´l-ĭz´əm) *noun* from Latin *fatum,* "prophesy; doom"
   The belief that all events are determined in advance by fate or destiny and therefore cannot be changed
   • His **fatalism** showed in his refusal to wear his seatbelt or take his heart medication.

   fatalist *noun* Only a true **fatalist** would shrug and take no action when faced with this dire situation.

   fatalistic *adjective* Lea's **fatalistic** attitude kept her stress level low, but it also kept her from taking full responsibility for her life and making something out of it.

5. **propitious** (prə-pĭsh´əs) *adjective* from Latin *propitius,*
"favorable; gracious"
Presenting favorable circumstances; advantageous; auspicious
• Since John had just been praised for his work, he thought it was a
  propitious moment to ask for a raise.

6. **providential** (prŏv´ĭ-dĕn´shəl) *adjective* from Latin *pro-,* "forward"
+ *videre,* "to see"
Happening favorably, as if through divine intervention; fortunate;
opportune
• The sudden breeze was **providential** because after days of sitting on a
  motionless ship, the sailors were running out of drinking water.

providence *noun* "May **providence** protect you," said the captain to
the new class of police academy graduates.

7. **quirk** (kwûrk) *noun*
   a. An odd or peculiar behavior or mannerism
      • One of my dad's **quirks** is nodding three times whenever he shakes
        someone's hand.
   b. A strange happening
      • It was a **quirk** of fate that the three friends shared the same
        birthday.

quirky *adjective* One of the guitarist's **quirky** mannerisms was
whispering "thank you" to herself whenever she played a good solo.

> *Quirk of fate* is a common phrase.

8. **serendipity** (sĕr´ən-dĭp´ĭ-tē) *noun* from Persian fairy tale, *The Three
Princes of Serendip*
The occurrence of lucky, accidental events or discoveries
• It was pure **serendipity** that Darius and Shauna bumped into each
  other at the mall after not seeing each other for a decade.

serendipitous *adjective* "How **serendipitous** that you would call me
on a whim when I've been trying to track you down all day!"

> In 1754, English author Horace Walpole coined the word *serendipity* based on a Persian fairy tale with heroes who continually encountered accidental good fortune.

9. **vagary** (vā´gə-rē) *noun* from Latin *vagus,* "wandering"
An unexpected impulse, whim, or fancy; an extravagant or erratic
notion or action
• What we saw on our sightseeing tour depended totally on the
  vagaries of our eccentric guide.

10. **vicissitude** (vĭ-sĭs´ĭ-tōod´) *noun* from Latin *vicissim,* "in turn"
   a. A change or variation
      • The fishermen hoped that the weather would undergo only minor
        vicissitudes.
   b. A sudden or unexpected change
      • Winning the lottery is one of those **vicissitudes** that can change
        one's life.
   c. The quality of being changeable; variability
      • Whose life do you think has more **vicissitude,** the average teenager
        or the average adult?

WRITE THE CORRECT WORD

Write the correct word in the space next to each definition. Use each word only once.

amulet **1.** a good luck charm

quirk **2.** a peculiar behavior

Fatalism **3.** belief in destiny

Vagary **4.** an unexpected whim

alchemy **5.** medieval chemical art

Vicissitude **6.** a change or variation

Providential **7.** fortunate

Serendipity **8.** a lucky accident

Propitious **9.** advantageous; favorable

Capricious **10.** impulsive

COMPLETE THE SENTENCE

Write the letter for the word that best completes each sentence.

___d___ **1.** Getting a flat on the first day of a cross-country trip is not a _____ start.
  a. capricious **b.** quirky **c.** fatalistic **d.** propitious

___b___ **2.** _____ often doubles as an excuse for not working hard.
  a. Alchemy **b.** Fatalism **c.** Vagary **d.** Vicissitude

___a___ **3.** She wore an ancient arrowhead _____ around her neck.
  a. amulet **b.** quirk **c.** vicissitude **d.** vagary

___d___ **4.** Tom's discovery of sunken treasure while scuba diving was a clear case of _____.
  a. vagary **b.** alchemy **c.** capriciousness **d.** serendipity

___c___ **5.** _____ was a forerunner of chemistry.
  a. Fatalism **b.** Quirk **c.** Alchemy **d.** Serendipity

___c___ **6.** Sailboat crews must pay close attention to the _____ of ocean currents.
  a. amulets **b.** fatalism **c.** vicissitudes **d.** serendipity

___d___ **7.** To the desperate farmers facing severe drought, the heavy rains seemed _____.
  a. alchemy **b.** quirky **c.** amulet **d.** providential

___b___ **8.** The behavior of a _____ person is unpredictable.
  a. propitious **b.** capricious **c.** serendipitous **d.** providential

___a___ **9.** The success of new products is subject to the _____ of consumer tastes.
  a. vagaries **b.** amulets **c.** providence **d.** fatalism

___b___ **10.** One lab rat had the _____ of always entering the maze through the smallest door.
  a. amulet **b.** quirk **c.** vicissitude **d.** serendipity

Challenge: Some of the beloved professor's many _____ included a propensity to have moments of revelation in movie theaters, and an intense fascination with the history of _____.

___c___   **a.** amulets…vicissitude **b.** vagaries…capriciousness **c.** quirks…alchemy

Alchemy and Chemistry

Would you like to change aluminum pots into gold? Would your silverware look better as "goldware"? **(1)** If you like the idea of changing things into gold, you may be interested in the story of *alchemy*.

In the Western world, one of the main goals of alchemy was to change less valuable metals into gold. For centuries, experimenters and magicians searched for the substance that would make this change possible—a "philosopher's stone." Along the way, alchemists made important discoveries in the field we now call chemistry.

There were alchemists in China, too, but instead of riches, they generally sought eternal life. **(2)** Unwilling to accept death *fatalistically*, emperors drank the alchemists' potions in attempts to live forever. Ironically, some of these potions were poisonous.

The Egyptians, Greeks, and Romans also practiced alchemy. When Rome fell in 476, however, much knowledge was lost to the West. **(3)** It was *providential* that the traditions of alchemy were kept alive in the Arab world.

(4) The Arab inheritance of Greek and Roman alchemy traditions was *propitious* for the development of chemistry. While they still sought ways to make gold, Arab thinkers also made many scientific advances. **(5)** Jabir ibn Hayyan, for example, replaced the *vagaries* of a misinformed philosophy with the rigors of objective experimentation. **(6)** Even so, some of his scientific breakthroughs were probably made *serendipitously*. In any case, Hayyan developed techniques for experimental evaporation, sublimation, and crystallization. Sometimes called "the Father of Chemistry," he wrote about ways to refine metals, dye fabrics, and make glass. Also known as Geber, his writings were used as textbooks in Europe for centuries. **(7)** His long-lasting renown and influence did not save him from the *vicissitudes* of his times, however. In the early 800s, he died while under house arrest because he was allied with a group that fell from power.

In the 1100s, many Arabic scientific writings were translated for use by Europeans, who began to make their own advances in chemistry. Many Europeans, however, continued to search for both the philosopher's stone and for "the panacea"—something that would cure all illness. And despite scientific advances, many alchemists still attempted what we would consider magic. **(8)** Because the study of science wasn't yet removed from the supernatural world, chants, *amulets*, and secret symbols were a central part of alchemy. **(9)** Failed experiments were typically blamed on *capricious* fate or on some soon-to-be-discovered missing ingredient.

(10) Today, thanks to advances in science, the physical world seems a lot less *quirky* and a lot more predictable than it once did. We also now know that making gold, although possible through complex atomic reactions, involves expense greater than the value of the gold itself. Although alchemy may seem intriguing, hard work is a surer road to riches than the "philosopher's stone" ever was.

Each sentence below refers to a numbered sentence in the passage. Write the letter of the choice that gives the sentence a meaning that is closest to the original sentence.

_____ **1.** If you like the idea of changing things into gold, you may be interested in the story of _____.
    a. historical records   **b.** odd, sudden change   **c.** philosophy   **d.** medieval chemical arts

_____ **2.** Unwilling to accept death _____, emperors drank the potions in attempts to live forever.
    a. as destiny   **b.** as reasonable   **c.** as unpredictable   **d.** as lucky

_____ **3.** It was _____ that the traditions of alchemy were kept alive in the Arab world.
    a. random   **b.** peculiar   **c.** fortunate   **d.** accidental

_____ **4.** The Arab inheritance of Greek and Roman alchemy traditions was _____ for the development of chemistry.
    a. unfortunate   **b.** accidental   **c.** peculiar   **d.** advantageous

_____C_____ **5.** Jabir ibn Hayyan replaced the _____ of a misinformed philosophy with the rigors of objective experimentation.
  a. bonuses   **b.** destiny   **c.** whims   **d.** advantages

_____b_____ **6.** Even so, some of his scientific breakthroughs were probably made _____.
  a. by mistake   **b.** by lucky accident   **c.** on a whim   **d.** with a charm

_____d_____ **7.** His renown and influence did not save him from the _____ of his times.
  a. public tastes   **b.** sad destiny   **c.** true morality   **d.** sudden changes

_____a_____ **8.** Because the study of science wasn't yet removed from the supernatural world, chants, _____, and secret symbols were a central part of alchemy.
  a. charms   **b.** decorations   **c.** songs   **d.** accidents

_____C_____ **9.** Failed experiments were typically blamed on _____ fate.
  a. dependable   **b.** predestined   **c.** unpredictable   **d.** evil

_____C_____ **10.** The physical world seems a lot less _____ than it once did.
  a. charmed   **b.** welcoming   **c.** odd and peculiar   **d.** lucky and fortuitous

Indicate whether the statements below are TRUE or FALSE according to the passage.

_____T_____ **1.** Alchemy never achieved its intended goals, but it had value for humanity in other important ways.

_____F_____ **2.** The root of most alchemists' problems was the lack of support for research.

_____T_____ **3.** Arab scholars made important chemical advances.

FINISH THE THOUGHT

Complete each sentence so that it shows the meaning of the italicized word.

1. It is *providential* that _____

2. Due to the *vicissitudes* of the weather, _____

WRITE THE DERIVATIVE

Complete the sentence by writing the correct form of the word shown in parentheses. You may not need to change the form that is given.

_____quirky_____ **1.** I like _____ people more than I like people who are trying to be the same as everyone else. (*quirk*)

_____Vagaries_____ **2.** The _____ of winter travel in the Northern Hemisphere present challenges requiring both flexibility and perseverance. (*vagary*)

_____amulets_____ **3.** Garlic _____ were once believed to offer protection from evil. (*amulet*)

fatalist   **4.** Is a _____ attitude a realistic recognition of one's place in a huge universe, or is it just a failure to admit responsibility? *(fatalism)*

vicissitudes   **5.** Even in the face of many _____ Mohammed Ali managed to "float like a butterfly and sting like a bee." *(vicissitude)*

propitious   **6.** "Here's to a _____ start," said the founder and CEO. *(propitious)*

alchemy   **7.** The critic pointed out the "magical _____" that all could see whenever the two actors were on stage together. *(alchemy)*

Providence   **8.** Some people attribute all good fortune to divine _____ . *(providential)*

Capriciousness   **9.** Professor Crenshaw's _____ kept his students on their toes. *(capricious)*

serendipitous   **10.** A truly important and _____ discovery was that of penicillin. *(serendipity)*

FIND THE EXAMPLE

Choose the answer that best describes the action or situation.

_b_   **1.** Something NOT influenced by human *vagaries*
     a. the stock market   **b.** the sunrise   **c.** consumer habits   **d.** international relations

_d_   **2.** Something that would be a behavioral *quirk*
     a. greeting friends   **b.** eating food   **c.** talking during day   **d.** walking backward

_c_   **3.** A goal of *alchemy*
     a. internal life   **b.** external life   **c.** eternal life   **d.** extraterrestrial life

_a_   **4.** NOT a description of a *capricious* person
     a. predictable   **b.** spontaneous   **c.** whimsical   **d.** impulsive

_c_   **5.** A *fatalistic* saying
     a. I am in control.   **c.** Whatever will be, will be.
     b. Reading brings the world to you.   **d.** It's always darkest before the dawn.

_d_   **6.** An event that would likely seem *providential* to a charitable organization
     a. increased apathy   **b.** global warming   **c.** fire at the office   **d.** enormous donation

_d_   **7.** A usual result of *serendipity*
     a. disappointment   **b.** an injury   **c.** a failure   **d.** a benefit

_a_   **8.** Something *propitious* for a marathon runner
     a. steady tailwind   **b.** large potholes   **c.** high ozone   **d.** freak hailstorm

_a_   **9.** Something that would NOT make a good *amulet*
     a. shark's tooth   **b.** gold ring   **c.** granite boulder   **d.** silver flower

_b_   **10.** The person who is most directly at the mercy of *vicissitudes* in public opinion
     a. fisherman   **b.** politician   **c.** scientist   **d.** doctor

Words About Music

WORD LIST

a cappella	aria	cacophony	cadence	crescendo
dissonance	libretto	motif	sonata	staccato

Ever since our ancestors began banging rhythms on primitive drums, music has been a part of human culture. The importance of this art form is reflected in the number of music-related words in our languages. This lesson teaches words that will help you discuss and understand music.

1. **a cappella** (ä´kə-pěl´ə) from Italian *a*, "in the manner of" + *cappella*, "chapel; choir"
Without instrumental accompaniment
   - *adjective* The **a cappella** group could travel without having to transport musical instruments.
   - *adverb* For the final song, the choir sang **a cappella**.

An *a cappella* group

2. **aria** (ä´rē-ə) *noun* from Latin and Greek *aer*, "air"
A solo vocal piece with instrumental accompaniment, as in an opera
   - The famous opera *Aida* features beautiful **arias** for the lead tenor.

3. **cacophony** (kə-kŏf´ə-nē) *noun* from Greek *kakos*, "bad" + *phone*, "sound"
A harsh, unpleasant, or jarring mixture of sounds
   - She closed the windows to block out the **cacophony** of horns from the traffic jam.

   cacophonous *adjective* The **cacophonous** sound of the orchestra musicians tuning their instruments filled the assembly hall.

4. **cadence** (kād´ns) *noun* from Latin *cadere*, "to fall"
   a. The balance or rhythmic flow of music, speech, poetry, or movement
      - The slow **cadence** of the speaker's voice intensified the somber mood.
   b. The rhythm or beat
      - The marathoner's **cadence** quickened as she reached the finish line.
   c. A progression of chords moving toward a harmonic close or resolution
      - Shawn was awed by the dramatic **cadence** at the end of the symphony.

5. **crescendo** (krə-shěn´dō) *noun* from Latin *crescere*, "to grow; to increase"
   a. A gradual increase in volume or intensity of sound
      - Cynthia ended her violin piece on a **crescendo**.
   b. A buildup of force or intensity
      - The waves reached a **crescendo** and then broke into white foam.

6. dissonance (dĭsʹə-nəns) *noun* from Latin *dis-*, "apart" + *sonare*, "to sound"
  a. A harsh, disagreeable combination of sounds
    • My little brother relished the **dissonance** he created as he pounded on the piano keys.
  b. A lack of agreement, consistency, or harmony; conflict
    • **Dissonance** among the board members resulted in arguments at the meeting.

  dissonant *adjective* The **dissonant** sound of five pianos being tuned in the practice room was very distracting.

7. libretto (lĭ-brĕtʹō) *noun* from Latin *liber*, "book"
  The text of a dramatic musical work, such as an opera
    • Richard Rodgers composed the music and Oscar Hammerstein wrote the **libretto** for *The Sound of Music*.

  librettist *noun* In addition to great musical accomplishments, Mozart was a fine **librettist.**

> The plural of *libretto* is either *librettos* or *libretti.*

8. motif (mō-tēfʹ) *noun* from Latin *movere*, "to move"
  a. A short rhythm or melody repeated or evoked many times in a work of music
    • The **motif** of Beethoven's Fifth Symphony is probably one of the most well-recognized in classical music.
  b. A recurrent thematic element in art or literature
    • In several places throughout the novel, the author used rain to symbolize the **motif** of loss and sadness.
  c. A repeated figure or design in architecture or decoration
    • The **motif** of green leaves was imprinted on the curtains, bedspread, and wall covering.

9. sonata (sə-näʹtə) *noun* from Latin *sonare*, "to sound"
  A composition of three or four independent movements, written for one or more solo instruments, one of which is usually a keyboard instrument
    • The *Moonlight Sonata* for piano begins with a slow movement and ends with a third movement that is lively and energetic.

10. staccato (stə-käʹtō) *adjective* from Old French *destachier*, "to detach"
  Having short, sharp sounds; abrupt and crisp
    • In contrast to the flowing sound of the cello, the piano played **staccato** notes.

WORD ENRICHMENT

Cacophony and its sounds

The word *cacophony* comes from the Greek *kakos*, "bad," and *phone*, "sound." Many other English words contain the root *phone*. For example, *euphony* refers to pleasant sounds. (The prefix *eu-* means "good" in Greek.) This word root also forms the basis of *phonetics*, the study of the sounds of language. When an instrument was invented that allowed us to vocally communicate over great distances it was called the *telephone*. (*Tele-* means "distant" in Greek.)

WRITE THE CORRECT WORD

Write the correct word in the space next to each definition. Use each word only once.

motif **1.** a theme

Cacophony **2.** a harsh, jarring sound

dissonance **3.** a lack of harmony; conflict

Cadence **4.** the rhythm or beat

Sonata **5.** composition for solo instruments

Crescendo **6.** a buildup of force

Staccato **7.** short and sharp

aria **8.** a vocal solo

a cappella **9.** without instruments

libretto **10.** the text of a dramatic musical work

COMPLETE THE SENTENCE

Write the letter for the word that best completes each sentence

_C_ **1.** The performers played a(n) _____ for violin and bass by Jean-Marie Leclair.
   a. cacophony   **b.** staccato   **c.** sonata   **d.** aria

_C_ **2.** One line of the _____ is, "How could you, Don Carsoni, how *could* you!"
   a. dissonance   **b.** cadence   **c.** libretto   **d.** cacophony

_b_ **3.** When the _____ group's tenor vocalist got sick, Joe had to find a replacement.
   a. aria   **b.** a cappella   **c.** dissonance   **d.** libretto

_a_ **4.** The snare drum is a good instrument for delivering crisp, _____ sounds.
   a. staccato   **b.** motif   **c.** aria   **d.** a cappella

_b_ **5.** Some music from the Far East may sound _____ to untrained Western ears.
   a. aria   **b.** dissonant   **c.** cadence   **d.** sonata

_a_ **6.** Chants help people move with the same _____ when rowing or marching.
   a. cadence   **b.** motif   **c.** cacophony   **d.** crescendo

_d_ **7.** "But who will play piano during my _____?" the soloist demanded.
   a. libretto   **b.** dissonance   **c.** cadence   **d.** aria

_d_ **8.** If you want to experience _____, spend some time in the cafeteria during lunch.
   a. motif   **b.** libretto   **c.** sonata   **d.** cacophony

_b_ **9.** That simple, five-note _____ was so catchy, I couldn't get it out of my head.
   a. libretto   **b.** motif   **c.** a cappella   **d.** dissonance

_d_ **10.** The composer built up the music's tension until it was resolved in a final _____.
   a. aria   **b.** sonata   **c.** cadence   **d.** crescendo

Challenge: _____ between one's beliefs and one's actions can build to a _____ of inner conflict and anxiety.

_C_   **a.** Cadence…sonata   **b.** Cacophony…dissonance   **c.** Dissonance…crescendo

Classroom Composer

Irene Britton Smith taught reading in the Chicago Public Schools for forty years. But what many of her students were surprised to learn was that their teacher was also a classical composer.

Smith's evenings, weekends, and summers were spent playing and writing music for the violin, piano, and organ. Her most famous piece is her 1947 Sonata for Violin and Piano.

Born in 1907, Smith grew up at a time when most women weren't expected to go to college or to write serious music, especially if they were African American, as she was. **(1)** But the *a cappella* spirituals and choral works that people sang in her church instilled in her a deep love of music. So, determined to study both academics and music, she went to the Chicago Normal School where she worked to become a teacher. Later, during her summers off, she attended college for music training. Over time, she earned a master's degree in music.

Her academic and musical interests are clear in the pieces she has written. She set the poems of Paul Laurence Dunbar to music. Some of her other compositions are arrangements of hymns. **(2)** Many of her musical *motifs* sprang from her wide range of life experiences.

Some of Smith's works were composed for children and may have been written specifically for her students. Smith was clearly fond of young people. With that in mind, it's hard not to wonder about how her classroom experiences affected her music. **(3)** Were the *staccato* notes in her "Sinfonietta" inspired by the quick, high-pitched chattering of her students? **(4)** Is the *crescendo* in her "Dream Cycle" a musical representation of the longing and excitement inspired by an approaching summer? It's hard to know what goes on in the mind of a composer, but most composers do draw ideas from real life.

Many also take comfort in their music. **(5)** After a hard day of teaching at school, Smith may have been soothed by the soft notes and calming *cadences* in the pieces she wrote. **(6)** Her three-movement *sonata* is joyful and melodic. **(7)** Smith preferred pleasing tones that were easy to listen to rather than the *dissonance* that is popular with some modern composers.

Even after earning her master's degree in music, Smith remained a student. **(8)** When summer came, she would leave behind the *cacophony* of the schoolyard to study under respected music teachers in the United States and France.

All told, Irene Britton Smith published thirteen compositions, including pieces for orchestras and solo instruments. **(9)** Though she never wrote an opera, the solo in her "Dream Cycle" would have made a good tune for an *aria*. **(10)** And more importantly, if her life were written into a *libretto*, it would provide the text for a powerful tale of dedication to beauty, education, and music.

Each sentence below refers to a numbered sentence in the passage. Write the letter of the choice that gives the sentence a meaning that is closest to the original sentence.

1. The _____ spirituals and choral works that people sang in her church instilled in her a deep love of music.
  a. often-repeated   **b.** beautiful   **c.** deeply felt   **d.** without accompaniment

2. Many of her musical _____ sprang from her wide range of life experiences.
  a. themes   **b.** solos   **c.** disharmony   **d.** rhythms

3. Were the _____ notes in her "Sinfonietta" inspired by the chattering of students?
  a. vocally sung   **b.** harsh, loud   **c.** short, sharp   **d.** rhythmic

4. Does the _____ in "Dream Cycle" represent longing and excitement?
  a. rhythm   **b.** buildup   **c.** slowdown   **d.** theme

_____C_____ **5.** Smith may have been soothed by the calming _____ in the pieces she wrote.
     a. opera texts   **b.** themes   **c.** rhythms   **d.** three-part movements

_____b_____ **6.** Her three-movement _____ is joyful and melodic.
     a. disharmony   **b.** composition   **c.** vocal solo   **d.** disagreeable sound

_____d_____ **7.** Smith preferred pleasing tones that were easy to listen to rather than the _____ that is popular with some modern composers.
     a. buildup   **b.** opera text   **c.** singing   **d.** lack of harmony

_____a_____ **8.** When summer came, she would leave behind the _____ of the schoolyard.
     a. unpleasant noises   **b.** compositions   **c.** solos   **d.** rhythms

_____d_____ **9.** The solo in her "Dream Cycle" would have made a good tune for a(n) _____.
     a. guitar solo   **b.** commercial   **c.** musical theme   **d.** opera solo

_____a_____ **10.** If her life were written into a(n) _____, it would provide the text for a powerful tale of dedication to beauty, education, and music.
     a. autobiography   **b.** three-part piece   **c.** biography   **d.** book of lyrics

Indicate whether the statements below are TRUE or FALSE according to the passage.

_____T_____ **1.** Irene Britton Smith composed in different musical forms.

_____F_____ **2.** Smith composed classical music at a time when many African-American women were doing the same.

_____T_____ **3.** Smith sometimes left the country to study music.

WRITING EXTENDED RESPONSES

Imagine that you are a famous and talented composer or songwriter. If you were to create a piece of music that would become known as a masterpiece, what kind of music would you write? Why would you want to be remembered for that particular piece? Write an expository essay that describes the music you would create and the motivation for your choice. Your essay should be at least three paragraphs long. Use a minimum of three lesson words in your essay and underline them.

WRITE THE DERIVATIVE

Complete the sentence by writing the correct form of the word shown in parentheses. You may not need to change the form that is given.

_____a cappella_____ **1.** I've always thought that "Vocal Chords" was a great name for an _____ singing group. (*a cappella*)

_____cacophonous_____ **2.** It was hard to believe that a group of just three howler monkeys could be so _____. (*cacophony*)

_____staccato_____ **3.** The _____ sound of firecrackers filled the streets during the Chinese New Year celebration. (*staccato*)

cadence 4. _____ is very important to both poets and rappers. *(cadence)*

motif 5. The effect of time on the human body and mind was the novel's main _____. *(motif)*

aria 6. Maria, that _____ you sang took my breath away. *(aria)*

dissonant 7. Was that music purposely _____, or was it simply played by musicians who hadn't rehearsed? *(dissonance)*

libretto 8. The _____ is so moving that it could probably stand on its own, without the music. *(libretto)*

sonata 9. A _____ is a musical form of considerable complexity. *(sonata)*

crescendo 10. At the height of the _____, it felt as though the concert hall itself was actually shaking. *(crescendo)*

FIND THE EXAMPLE

Choose the answer that best describes the action or situation.

a 1. The defining component of *librettos*
    a. words   b. musical notes   c. fancy costumes   d. several movements

d 2. The place where you would most likely hear a *cacophony*
    a. lecture   b. library cubicle   c. hospital room   d. city intersection

a 3. A likely name for a *sonata*
    a. Tears Are Falling   b. DooWop-a-Bop   c. No. 8 for Piano   d. Rage

b 4. That which happens to music's volume or intensity during a *crescendo*
    a. decreases   b. increases   c. no change   d. softens

b 5. An example of a *staccato* sound
    a. complete silence   b. tapping a pot   c. steady wind   d. ocean waves

d 6. Something with a clear *cadence* that you'd hear on a military base
    a. Fifty pushups!   b. Thank you, sir.   c. Peel the carrots!   d. Left-right-left

d 7. A likely example of a literary *motif*
    a. Uncle Joe   b. good nutrition   c. entertainment   d. the futility of anger

a 8. The number of people required to sing an *aria*
        b. four   c. eight   d. sixteen

C 9. Of the following, the LEAST likely to make *dissonant* sounds
    a. rickety old piano   b. kids with kazoos   c. well-tuned guitar   d. rusted foghorn

a 10. Something members of a good *a cappella* group need to have
    a. harmonious voices   b. tuned guitars   c. uniforms   d. piano training

Words from Nature

WORD LIST

arboreal	burgeon	deciduous	fauna	flora
germination	horticultural	lichen	sylvan	verdant

As the Native American leader Chief Seattle said, "Whatever befalls the earth also befalls the sons and daughters of the earth." As human beings, we are part of the interdependent system of nature. Plants, for example help supply the oxygen that we breathe and much of the food that we eat. The words in this lesson deal with some aspects of the natural world.

1. **arboreal** (är-bôr´ē-əl) *adjective* from Latin *arbor*, "tree"
   a. Relating to or resembling a tree
   • When the elm trees in the park began to show signs of disease, the park director consulted an **arboreal** expert to diagnose the problem.
   b. Living in trees
   • Monkeys and gorillas are **arboreal** animals whose lives depend on the health of the forests and jungles.

   arboretum *noun* A place where woody plants are grown and studied
   • Many trees from Asia and Africa are found in the city's public **arboretum.**

2. **burgeon** (bûr´jən) *verb* from Old French *burjon*, "a bud"
   a. To put forth new buds, leaves, or greenery; to sprout; to begin to grow or blossom
   • The unusually warm spring made the cherry trees in Washington, D.C., **burgeon** earlier than usual.
   b. To grow rapidly or flourish
   • There is a **burgeoning** market for real estate in the downtown area.

3. **deciduous** (dĭ-sĭj´ōō-əs) *adjective* from Latin *de-*, "away" + *cadere*, "to fall"
   Shedding or losing leaves at a particular season or stage of growth
   • In autumn, the **deciduous** trees of the northern woodlands turn spectacular colors before losing their leaves.

4. **fauna** (fô´nə) *noun* from Latin, after the goddess of fertility, *Fauna*
   Animals considered as a group, particularly those of one region or period
   • Beth looked forward to studying the **fauna** of Australia, especially the kangaroo and the koala bear.

5. **flora** (flôr´ə) *noun* from Latin, after the goddess of flowers, *Flora*
   Plants considered as a group, particularly those of one region or period
   • Because the area is so dry, much of the **flora** in Arizona consists of succulents, which are plants that can store water in their stems and leaves.

arboreal

An *arbor* is a shady resting place in a garden.

6. germination (jûr´mə-nā´shən) *noun* from Latin *germen*, "seed"
   a. The process by which a plant begins to grow or develop
   • **Germination** takes place when warmth and moisture cause the shell of a seed to break.
   b. The process by which something comes into existence
   • The **germination** of the book's plot stemmed from a dream that the author had.

germinate *verb* The children waited for their seeds to **germinate**.

7. horticultural (hôr´tĭ-kŭl´chər-əl) *adjective* from the Latin *hortus*, "garden" + *cultus*, "tilled"
Relating to tending or growing plants
• The **horticultural** experience that Leon gained while working at the nursery was helpful when he studied landscape design.

horticulture *noun* The study of **horticulture** involves examining the makeup and growth process of plants.

> To *till* is to prepare soil for planting.

8. lichen (lī´kən) *noun* from Greek *leikhein*, "to lick"
A type of vegetation made of fungus and algae growing together and that usually form crustlike or branching growths on rocks or tree limbs and trunks
• Silvery-green **lichen** had grown in a lacy pattern over most of the large, black rocks near the pond.

9. sylvan (sĭl´vən) *adjective* from Latin *silva*, "forest"
Relating to trees or forests and woodlands; wooded
• Mr. Cole's will specified that the **sylvan** acres he left to the town be preserved as conservation land and not developed into housing lots.

10. verdant (vûr´dnt) *adjective* from Latin *viridis*, "green"
Green with vegetation or plants
• We drove through the rolling **verdant** hills of Kentucky's horse country.

ANALOGIES

On the answer line, write the letter of the answer that best completes each analogy. Refer to Lessons 28–30 if you need help with any of the lesson words.

_____ **1.** *Cacophony* is to *dissonant* as _____.
   a. *staccato* is to *smooth*   **c.** *serendipity* is to *lucky*
   b. *flora* is to *fauna*   **d.** *libretto* is to *music*

_____ **2.** *Capricious* is to *predictable* as _____.
   a. *providential* is to *unlucky*   **c.** *dissonant* is to *loud*
   b. *burgeoning* is to *growing*   **d.** *quirky* is to *eccentric*

_____ **3.** *Germinate* is to *sprout* as _____.
   a. *a cappella* is to *accompaniment*   **c.** *amulet* is to *dress*
   b. *motif* is to *theme*   **d.** *sonata* is to *piano*

WRITE THE CORRECT WORD

Write the correct word in the space next to each definition. Use each word only once.

_____ **1.** green with vegetation

_____ **2.** a crustlike growth

fauna **3.** animals of a region

_____ **4.** living in trees

germination **5.** the process by which a plant begins to grow

_____ **6.** losing leaves seasonally

_____ **7.** to grow rapidly

_____ **8.** plants of a region

_____ **9.** wooded

_____ **10.** relating to tending plants

COMPLETE THE SENTENCE

Write the letter for the word that best completes each sentence.

_____ **1.** The flowers and other _____ of a region reflect its climate and geology.
a. germination   **b.** burgeoning   **c.** lichen   **d.** flora

_____ **2.** Many types of _____ animals live in the various layers of a rain forest.
a. arboreal   **b.** deciduous   **c.** germinating   **d.** lichen

_____ **3.** Many of the oldest tree trunks were encrusted with _____ .
a. fauna   **b.** arboretums   **c.** lichen   **d.** horticulture

_____ **4.** Walking among the old trees in the _____ area of the park, we felt a sense of peace.
a. fauna   **b.** sylvan   **c.** germinating   **d.** lichen

_____ **5.** During our hike in the mountains we saw bears, elk, and a variety of other _____ .
a. fauna   **b.** flora   **c.** lichen   **d.** arboretums

_____ **6.** The _____ mountains of Vermont earned that state its name, which means "green mountain" in French.
a. horticultural   **b.** arboreal   **c.** fauna   **d.** verdant

_____ **7.** _____ is the earliest phase in the cycle of a plant's life.
a. Horticulture   **b.** Germination   **c.** Fauna   **d.** Arboretum

_____ **8.** In the summer, the _____ trees outside my window block the view of the ocean, but in the winter, I can see the water clearly.
a. germinating   **b.** flora   **c.** deciduous   **d.** lichen

_____ **9.** Because of the early warm spell, the flowers in our garden are already _____ .
a. deciduous   **b.** sylvan   **c.** burgeoning   **d.** arboreal

_____ **10.** My uncle's _____ skill shows in his beautiful garden.
a. horticultural   **b.** verdant   **c.** sylvan   **d.** germinating

Challenge: The early spring _____ that were _____ throughout the nature preserve delighted the visiting horticulturalists.
_____   **a.** fauna…verdant   **b.** flora…burgeoning   **c.** lichen…arboreal

Nature's Cures

In a way, nature is a giant pharmacy. For thousands of years, humans have used plants as medicines. **(1)** Whether it's a flower plucked from *verdant* grass-covered hills or a seed from a sturdy desert shrub, our plant resources can treat illness.

(2) The reason plants are so useful medically is that the world's *flora* face illnesses themselves. **(3)** Like humans and the *fauna* of every region, plants can catch diseases from germs. From generation to generation plants must protect themselves by genetically creating chemical modifications to fight off these dangers. **(4)** For example, *lichens* produce an acid to ward off germs. Because this acid can also kill a variety of bacteria, we use it in medicinal ointments, as well as soaps and deodorants.

Most medicines, in fact, are derived from plants: Curare tree bark is used in treatments for multiple sclerosis, Madagascar's rosy periwinkle provides a medicine for leukemia, and the foxglove flower is used in heart medicine.

Many of the synthetic chemicals now used in medicines are copies of substances found in plants. For example, willow trees were originally needed to create aspirin. **(5)** But the makers of aspirin no longer rely on *horticultural* skill. Today, aspirin is simply manufactured in a laboratory.

Just one plant can support many uses. **(6)** The roots of the deadly nightshade plant, which grows in shady *sylvan* areas, are used to treat tumors. The leaves produce a substance that treats tongue cancer. This plant is also used to treat asthma, eye ulcers, and whooping cough.

Herbal medicine, which uses actual plants, rather than their chemical components, is an ancient practice that continues today. **(7)** The sale of herbal remedies is currently a *burgeoning* business. Throughout the world, plants are made into teas and pastes to cure ailments as well as to prevent them. **(8)** People buy everything from chamomile tea—to reduce stress—to *germinated* barley grains—to aid digestion.

Animals make use of plants for medicinal purposes as well. In Tanzania, chimpanzees have been observed making faces as they ate nasty-tasting Aspilia leaves. It turns out that Aspilia cures stomach upset and attacks parasites with which the monkeys can be infected.

Scientists say animals only use natural cures when they need them. One proof of this can be observed in the two groups of baboons found in Ethiopia. **(9)** One group is *arboreal,* and the other lives on the ground. Both could eat the fruit of the Balanite tree, which contains a chemical that drives worms from the intestine; but only the baboons that live on the ground, where they can catch worms spread by snails, eat the fruit.

A plethora of undiscovered cures could be growing all around us. Only about 5 percent of the world's plants have been studied for their medicinal use. **(10)** The rain forest in particular, which has far more plants than the *deciduous* forests in cooler climates, is believed to hold many cures.

In southern Africa alone, there are about 24,000 plant species, of which 4,000 are already used in traditional herbal medicine. It is hoped that these plants and many others, as yet untapped, may prove useful to modern medicine.

Each sentence below refers to a numbered sentence in the passage. Write the letter of the choice that gives the sentence a meaning that is closest to the original sentence.

_____ **1.** Whether it's a flower plucked from _____ grass-covered hills or a seed from a sturdy desert shrub, our plant resources can help heal illness.
    a. sprouting   **b.** golden   **c.** green   **d.** shedding

_____ **2.** The reason plants are so useful medicinally is that the world's _____ face illnesses themselves.
    a. animals   **b.** plants   **c.** flowers   **d.** regions

_____ **3.** Like humans and the _____ of every region, plants can catch diseases from germs.
    a. plants   **b.** climate   **c.** trees   **d.** animals

4. For example, _____ produce an acid to ward off germs.
  a. crustlike vegetation   **b.** some laboratories   **c.** some animals   **d.** leaf-shedding trees

5. But the makers of aspirin no longer rely on _____ skill.
  a. plant-growing   **b.** ancient   **c.** old-fashioned   **d.** woodland

6. The roots of the deadly nightshade plant, which grows in shady _____ areas, are used to treat tumors.
  a. desert   **b.** wetland   **c.** wooded   **d.** uninhabited

7. The sale of herbal remedies is currently a _____ business.
  a. tree-related   **b.** plant-tending   **c.** highly prized   **d.** fast-growing

8. People buy everything from chamomile tea—to reduce stress—to _____ barley grains—to aid digestion.
  a. sun-dried   **b.** sprouted   **c.** dehydrated   **d.** treelike

9. One group is _____, and the other lives on the ground.
  a. flourishing   **b.** living in trees   **c.** living underwater   **d.** extinct

10. The rain forest, in particular, which has far more plants than the _____ forests in cooler climates, is believed to hold many cures.
  a. leaf-shedding   **b.** pine   **c.** cactus   **d.** winter-killed

Indicate whether the statements below are TRUE or FALSE according to the passage.

_____ **1.** From the study of plants, scientists have learned how to make many medicines.

_____ **2.** Animals are unable to benefit from the medicinal properties of plants.

_____ **3.** Scientists have already discovered all the medicinal uses that plants have to offer.

FINISH THE THOUGHT

Complete each sentence so that it shows the meaning of the italicized word.

1. In *horticultural* class, students learned _____

2. The *sylvan* surroundings _____

WRITE THE DERIVATIVE

Complete the sentence by writing the correct form of the word shown in parentheses. You may not need to change the form that is given.

_____ **1.** The _____ meadow stretched as far as the eye could see. (*verdant*)

_____ **2.** The annual spring field trip to the local _____ was always popular with the horticultural students. (*arboreal*)

_____ **3.** As we strolled through the _____ preserve, we savored the effect of the sun's rays filtering through the colorful autumn trees. *(sylvan)*

_____ **4.** The hoya, or honey plant, will _____ from stem cuttings. *(germination)*

_____ **5.** Lelia's goal is to become an expert in _____ . *(horticultural)*

_____ **6.** Belinda's musical talent _____ when she was very young. *(burgeon)*

_____ **7.** To amuse himself, Dan refers to _____ as the "fungus among us." *(lichen)*

_____ **8.** _____ trees provide shade for our house during the summer but allow sunshine during the winter. *(deciduous)*

_____ **9.** Aunt Georgina is fascinated by bats and other cave _____ . *(fauna)*

_____ **10.** Generally, the _____ of desert regions is quite different from that seen in other geographic areas. *(flora)*

FIND THE EXAMPLE

Choose the answer that best describes the action or situation.

_____ **1.** Something the leaves of all *deciduous* trees do
    a. kill bacteria   **b.** drop   **c.** multiply   **d.** turn yellow

_____ **2.** Something you'd expect to find in an *arboretum*
    a. art objects   **b.** protected animals   **c.** seed catalogs   **d.** woody plants

_____ **3.** Something that *germinates*
    a. a germ   **b.** a seed   **c.** a disease   **d.** a leaf

_____ **4.** Something a *horticultural* expert might demonstrate
    a. tree pruning   **b.** harvesting oysters   **c.** traditional dances   **d.** cattle raising

_____ **5.** The best way to describe a *burgeoning* talent
    a. well-developed   **b.** long-established   **c.** growing rapidly   **d.** beginning slowly

_____ **6.** The most likely place to find *lichen*
    a. gorillas   **b.** wet roads   **c.** flowers   **d.** tree bark

_____ **7.** A *sylvan* environment
    a. rocky shore   **b.** sandy beach   **c.** city block   **d.** national forest

_____ **8.** Something NOT found in a group of *fauna*
    a. a rose   **b.** a squirrel   **c.** a lizard   **d.** an ant

_____ **9.** Something that is *verdant*
    a. parking lot   **b.** ivy-covered wall   **c.** green truck   **d.** calm sea

_____ **10.** A business most likely to be named "Flora's *flora*"
    a. a restaurant   **b.** a movie theater   **c.** a flower shop   **d.** a supermarket

Prefixes, Roots, and Suffixes

The Prefixes *pan-*, *extra-*, *ultra-*, and *omni-*

The prefixes in this feature deal with aspects of plenty. *Pan-* comes from Greek and *omni-* comes from Latin. Both mean "all." *Extra-*, from Latin, and *ultra-*, from French, both mean "beyond." The table below details their uses.

Element	Prefix Meaning	Word	Word Meaning
pan-	all	*pan*human	referring to all of humanity
extra-	beyond, outside	*extra*galactic	beyond, outside of the galaxy
ultra-	beyond	*ultra*conservative	beyond conservative
omni-	all	*omni*potent	all powerful

Practice

You can combine the use of context clues with your knowledge of these word elements to make intelligent guesses about word meanings. Each of the sentences below contains a word formed with the prefix *pan-*, *extra-*, *ultra-*, or *omni-*. Read each sentence and try to infer what the word in italics means. Then check your definition with the one you find in the dictionary, remembering to choose the definition that best fits in the sentence.

1. Dog's ears are sensitive to *ultrasonic* noises that humans cannot hear.

My definition _____

Dictionary definition _____

2. We should all seek to avoid things that are *extralegal*.

My definition _____

Dictionary definition _____

3. Oxygen is *omnipresent* in Earth's atmosphere.

My definition _____

Dictionary definition _____

4. What types of *extracurricular* activities interest you?

My definition _____

Dictionary definition _____

5. The *ultramicroscope* gave astonishing images.

My definition _____

Dictionary definition _____

6. This *panchromatic* film will show the flowers' colors with great accuracy.

My definition _____

Dictionary definition _____

7. I found it hard to sit in the *ultramodern* chair.

My definition _____

Dictionary definition _____

8. The U.S. Attorney General instituted *extradition* proceedings against the criminal who fled to Colombia.

My definition _____

Dictionary definition _____

9. He was an *omnivorous* reader who read everything he could find.

My definition _____

Dictionary definition _____

10. A shout of "Fire" started *pandemonium* in the theater.

My definition _____

Dictionary definition _____

Review Word Elements

Reviewing word elements helps you to remember them and use them in your reading. Below, write the meanings of the word elements you have studied.

Word	Word Element	Type of Element	Meaning of Word Element
astronaut	*astro-*	prefix	_____
presage	*sag*	root	_____
dissimulate	*sim*	root	_____
gregarious	*greg*	root	_____
geometry	*geo-*	prefix	_____
countervailing	*val*	root	_____
maritime	*mar*	root	_____
inquisitive	*quisit*	root	_____
vanquish	*vinc*	root	_____
interrogate	*rog*	root	_____
hydroelectric	*hydro-*	prefix	_____
terra firma	*terra*	root	_____
cohere	*here*	root	_____
fidelity	*fid*	root	_____
spectacles	*spec*	root	_____
pliant	*pli*	root	_____

LESSON 1	LESSON 1	LESSON 2	LESSON 2	LESSON 3	LESSON 3
annotation	neologism	contingent	perchance	evolve	modulate
appellation	parlance	eventuality	preposterous	immutable	protean
eponym	patois	implausible	proclivity	inveterate	sporadic
linguistics	polyglot	inconceivable	prone	malleable	transmute
malapropism	vulgar	in vain	theoretical	metamorphosis	volatile

annotation (ăn´ō-tā´shen) *n.* An explanatory note

© Great Source

appellation (ăp´ə-lā´shen) *n.* A name or title

© Great Source

eponym (ĕp´ə-nĭm´) *n.* A person whose name is used to make a word

© Great Source

linguistics (lĭng-gwĭs´tĭks) *n.* Study of language

© Great Source

malapropism (măl´ə-prŏp-ĭz´əm) *n.* A humorous confusion of words

© Great Source

neologism (nē-ŏl´ə-jĭz´əm) *n.* A new word

© Great Source

parlance (pär´lens) *n.* A particular manner of speaking

© Great Source

patois (păt´wä´) *n.* A nonstandard dialect

© Great Source

polyglot (pŏl´ē-glŏt) *adj.* Using several languages

© Great Source

vulgar (vŭl´gər) *adj.* Crude or indecent

© Great Source

contingent (kən-tĭn´jent) *adj.* Conditional

© Great Source

eventuality (ĭ-vĕn´chōō-ăl´ĭ-tē) *n.* A possibility

© Great Source

implausible (ĭm-plô´zə-bəl) *adj.* Unlikely

© Great Source

inconceivable (ĭn´kən-sē´və-bəl) *adj.* Impossible to grasp fully

© Great Source

in vain (ĭn vān) *adv.* Without success

© Great Source

perchance (pər-chăns´) *adv.* Perhaps

© Great Source

preposterous (prĭ-pŏs´tər-əs) *adj.* Absurd

© Great Source

proclivity (prō-klĭv´ĭ-tē) *n.* An inclination

© Great Source

prone (prōn) *adj.* Likely to do

© Great Source

theoretical (thē´ə-rĕt´ĭ-kəl) *adj.* Unproven

© Great Source

evolve (ĭ-vŏlv´) *v.* To develop slowly

© Great Source

immutable (ĭ-myōō´tə-bəl) *adj.* Unchangeable

© Great Source

inveterate (ĭn-vĕt´ər-ĭt) *adj.* Established

© Great Source

malleable (măl´ē-ə-bəl) *adj.* Able to be shaped

© Great Source

metamorphosis (mĕt´ə-môr´fə-sĭs) *n.* A transformation

© Great Source

modulate (mŏj´ə-lāt´) *v.* To adjust

© Great Source

protean (prō´tē-ən) *adj.* Readily taking on different forms

© Great Source

sporadic (spə-răd´ĭk) *adj.* Irregular

© Great Source

transmute (trăns-myōot´) *v.* To change form

© Great Source

volatile (vŏl´ə-tl) *adj.* Subject to wide variation

© Great Source

LESSON 4	LESSON 4	LESSON 4	LESSON 4	LESSON 4
abstruse	acumen	ascertain	cerebral	faculty

LESSON 4	LESSON 4	LESSON 4	LESSON 4	LESSON 4
obfuscate	ruminate	stymie	surmise	tenet

LESSON 5	LESSON 5	LESSON 5	LESSON 5	LESSON 5
abeyance	abstemious	circumvent	elude	eschew

LESSON 5	LESSON 5	LESSON 5	LESSON 5	LESSON 5
evasion	malinger	oblique	shirk	shun

LESSON 6	LESSON 6	LESSON 6	LESSON 6	LESSON 6
converge	crux	degradation	initiate	penultimate

LESSON 6	LESSON 6	LESSON 6	LESSON 6	LESSON 6
pivotal	sequel	supersede	tangential	terminate

abstruse (ăb-strōōs´) adj. Hard to understand	obfuscate (ŏb´fə-skāt´) v. Make more difficult	abeyance (ə-bā´əns) n. Suspension	evasion (ĭ-vā´zhən) n. Clever avoidance	converge (kən-vûrj´) v. Come together	pivotal (pĭv´ə-tl) adj. Crucial
© Great Source	© Great Source	© Great Source	© Great Source	© Great Source	© Great Source
acumen (ăk´yə-mən) n. Keen insight	ruminate (rōō´mə-nāt´) v. To think deeply about	abstemious (ăb-stē´mē-əs) adj. Restricted to bare necessities	malinger (mə-lĭng´gər) v. To fake illness to avoid work	crux (krŭks) n. Key point	sequel (sē´kwəl) n. Next in a series
© Great Source	© Great Source	© Great Source	© Great Source	© Great Source	© Great Source
ascertain (ăs´ər-tān´) v. Discover	stymie (stī´mē) v. To frustrate or thwart	circumvent (sûr´kəm-vĕnt´) v. Go around	oblique (ō-blēk´) adj. Not direct	degradation (dĕg´rə-dā´shən) n. A decline	supersede (sōō´pər-sēd´) v. Replace
© Great Source	© Great Source	© Great Source	© Great Source	© Great Source	© Great Source
cerebral (sə-rē´-brəl) adj. Of the brain	surmise (sər-mīz´) v. To guess	elude (ĭ-lōōd´) v. Avoid capture	shirk (shûrk) v. Neglect	initiate (ĭ-nĭsh´ē-āt´) v. To begin	tangential (tăn-jĕn´shəl) adj. Irrelevant
© Great Source	© Great Source	© Great Source	© Great Source	© Great Source	© Great Source
faculty (făk´əl-tē) n. Ability	tenet (tĕn´ĭt) n. Principle, belief	eschew (ĕs-chōō´) v. To avoid, abstain	shun (shŭn) v. To willfully ignore	penultimate (pĭ-nŭl´tə-mĭt) adj. Next to last	terminate (tûr´mə-nāt´) v. End
© Great Source	© Great Source	© Great Source	© Great Source	© Great Source	© Great Source

LESSON 7 aspersions

LESSON 7 compunction

LESSON 7 derision

LESSON 7 disapprobation

LESSON 7 ostracize

LESSON 7 rebuke

LESSON 7 revulsion

LESSON 7 scurrilous

LESSON 7 spurn

LESSON 7 vitriolic

LESSON 8 accountable

LESSON 8 assiduous

LESSON 8 default

LESSON 8 feckless

LESSON 8 incumbent

LESSON 8 liability

LESSON 8 mandatory

LESSON 8 negligence

LESSON 8 onerous

LESSON 8 remiss

LESSON 9 acquiesce

LESSON 9 adamant

LESSON 9 balk

LESSON 9 camaraderie

LESSON 9 cantankerous

LESSON 9 compliance

LESSON 9 presumptuous

LESSON 9 propitiate

LESSON 9 tractable

LESSON 9 volition

aspersions (ə-spûr´zhəns) *n.* Damaging remarks; slanders
© Great Source

compunction (kəm-pŭngk´shən) *n.* Unease due to guilt
© Great Source

derision (dĭ-rĭzh´ən) *n.* Ridicule
© Great Source

disapprobation (dĭs-ăp´rə-bā´shən) *n.* Moral disapproval
© Great Source

ostracize (ŏs´trə-sīz´) *v.* To banish, exclude, or shun
© Great Source

rebuke (rĭ-byook´) *v.* To criticize sharply
© Great Source

revulsion (rĭ-vŭl´shən) *n.* Intense disgust
© Great Source

scurrilous (skûr´ə-ləs) *adj.* Vulgar; abusive
© Great Source

spurn (spûrn) *v.* To reject scornfully
© Great Source

vitriolic (vĭt´rē-ŏl´ĭk) *adj.* Very harsh; bitter
© Great Source

accountable (ə-koun´tə-bəl) *adj.* Responsible
© Great Source

assiduous (ə-sĭj´oo-əs) *adj.* Conscientious
© Great Source

default (dĭ-fôlt´) *n.* The failure to fulfill an obligation
© Great Source

feckless (fĕk´lĭs) *adj.* Ineffective
© Great Source

incumbent (in-kŭm´bənt) *adj.* Holding an office or position
© Great Source

liability (lī´ə-bĭl´ĭ-tē) *n.* A handicap
© Great Source

mandatory (măn´də-tôr´ē) *adj.* Required
© Great Source

negligence (nĕg´lĭ-jəns) *n.* Lack of proper care or attention
© Great Source

onerous (ŏn´ər-əs) *adj.* Difficult to bear
© Great Source

remiss (rĭ-mĭs´) *adj.* Lax or careless
© Great Source

acquiesce (ăk´wē-ĕs´) *v.* To accept or agree
© Great Source

adamant (ăd´ə-mənt) *adj.* Stubborn; unyielding
© Great Source

balk (bôk) *v.* To stop short
© Great Source

camaraderie (kä´mə-rä´də-rē) *n.* Good will; friendliness
© Great Source

cantankerous (kăn-tăng´kər-əs) *adj.* Quarrelsome
© Great Source

compliance (kəm-plī´əns) *n.* Obedience
© Great Source

presumptuous (prĭ-zŭmp´choo-əs) *adj.* Boldly improper
© Great Source

propitiate (prō-pĭsh´ē-āt´) *v.* To soothe or calm
© Great Source

tractable (trăk´tə-bəl) *adj.* Manageable
© Great Source

volition (və-lĭsh´ən) *n.* One's own free will or choosing
© Great Source

- LESSON 10 — acuity
- LESSON 10 — consummate
- LESSON 10 — cunning
- LESSON 10 — deft
- LESSON 10 — endowment
- LESSON 10 — facile
- LESSON 10 — inept
- LESSON 10 — prescient
- LESSON 10 — proficient
- LESSON 10 — prowess
- LESSON 11 — beseech
- LESSON 11 — cajole
- LESSON 11 — elicit
- LESSON 11 — enjoin
- LESSON 11 — exigency
- LESSON 11 — imperious
- LESSON 11 — injunction
- LESSON 11 — mendicant
- LESSON 11 — query
- LESSON 11 — servile
- LESSON 12 — abound
- LESSON 12 — amplitude
- LESSON 12 — augment
- LESSON 12 — behemoth
- LESSON 12 — brevity
- LESSON 12 — diminish
- LESSON 12 — infinitesimal
- LESSON 12 — modicum
- LESSON 12 — prodigious
- LESSON 12 — quotidian

acuity
(ə-kyōō´ĭ-tē) *n.*
Sharpness

© Great Source

consummate
(kŏn´sə-mət) *adj.*
Supremely skilled
or accomplished

© Great Source

cunning
(kŭn´ĭng) *n.*
Cleverness

© Great Source

deft
(dĕft) *adj.*
Quick and skillful

© Great Source

endowment
(ĕn-dou´mənt) *n.*
A natural ability

© Great Source

facile
(făs´əl) *adj.*
Easy

© Great Source

inept
(ĭn-ĕpt´) *adj.*
Incompetent

© Great Source

prescient
(prĕsh´ənt) *adj.*
Having foresight

© Great Source

proficient
(prə-fĭsh´ənt) *adj.*
Thoroughly capable

© Great Source

prowess
(prou´ĭs) *n.*
Superior skill

© Great Source

beseech
(bĭ-sēch´) *v.*
To beg, plead, or implore

© Great Source

cajole
(kə-jōl´) *v.*
To urge with gentle
methods

© Great Source

elicit
(ĭ-lĭs´ĭt) *v.*
To bring out

© Great Source

enjoin
(ĕn-join´) *v.*
To prohibit or forbid

© Great Source

exigency
(ĕk´sə-jən-sē) *n.*
Urgency, or a crisis
situation

© Great Source

imperious
(ĭm-pîr´ē-əs) *adj.*
Domineering; arrogant

© Great Source

injunction
(ĭn-jŭngk´shən) *n.*
A command or order

© Great Source

mendicant
(mĕn´dĭ-kənt) *n.*
A beggar

© Great Source

query
(kwîr´ē) *n.*
A question

© Great Source

servile
(sûr´vəl) *adj.*
Slavish or submissive

© Great Source

abound
(ə-bound´) *v.*
To be plentiful

© Great Source

amplitude
(ăm´plĭ-tōōd´) *n.*
Greatness of size or range

© Great Source

augment
(ôg-mĕnt´) *v.*
To add to; to increase

© Great Source

behemoth
(bĭ-hē´məth) *n.*
A large, powerful thing

© Great Source

brevity
(brĕv´ĭ-tē) *n.*
Shortness of duration

© Great Source

diminish
(dĭ-mĭn´ĭsh) *v.*
To lessen

© Great Source

infinitesimal
(ĭn´fĭn-ĭ-tĕs´ə-məl) *adj.*
Too small to measure

© Great Source

modicum
(mŏd´ĭ-kəm) *n.*
A small amount

© Great Source

prodigious
(prə-dĭj´əs) *adj.*
Extensive or
extraordinary

© Great Source

quotidian
(kwō-tĭd´ē-ən) *adj.*
Everyday; common

© Great Source

LESSON 13	LESSON 13	LESSON 13	LESSON 13	LESSON 13
banal	camouflage	emulate	mimicry	platitude

LESSON 13	LESSON 13	LESSON 13	LESSON 13	LESSON 13
prototype	redundant	rendition	sham	simulation

LESSON 14	LESSON 14	LESSON 14	LESSON 14	LESSON 14
adverse	averse	ingenious	ingenuous	persecute

LESSON 14	LESSON 14	LESSON 14	LESSON 14	LESSON 14
prosecute	quorum	quota	respectfully	respectively

LESSON 15	LESSON 15	LESSON 15	LESSON 15	LESSON 15
abdicate	absolve	catharsis	countermand	impunity

LESSON 15	LESSON 15	LESSON 15	LESSON 15	LESSON 15
recant	recoup	renounce	rescind	waive

banal
(bə-năl´) *adj.*
Commonplace

© Great Source

camouflage
(kăm´ə-fläzh´) *n.*
Concealment
by disguise

© Great Source

emulate
(ĕm´yə-lāt´) *v.*
To imitate

© Great Source

mimicry
(mĭm´ĭ-krē) *n.*
Imitation

© Great Source

platitude
(plăt´ĭ-tōōd´) *n.*
Overused remark

© Great Source

prototype
(prō´tə-tīp´) *n.*
Test model

© Great Source

redundant
(rĭ-dŭn´dənt) *adj.*
More than necessary

© Great Source

rendition
(rĕn-dĭsh´ən) *n.*
An interpretation of
a performance

© Great Source

sham
(shăm) *n.*
A fake

© Great Source

simulation
(sĭm´yə-lā´shən) *n.*
Reproduction of
a situation

© Great Source

adverse
(ăd-vûrs´) *adj.*
Opposing

© Great Source

averse
(ə-vûrs´) *adj.*
Feeling dislike

© Great Source

ingenious
(ĭn-jēn´yəs) *adj.*
Very clever

© Great Source

ingenuous
(ĭn-jĕn´yōō-əs) *adj.*
Openly straightforward

© Great Source

persecute
(pûr´sĭ-kyōōt´) *v.*
To cruelly mistreat

© Great Source

prosecute
(prŏs´ĭ-kyōōt´) *v.*
To bring action against
in court

© Great Source

quorum
(kwôr´əm) *n.*
Number needed to vote

© Great Source

quota
(kwō´tə) *n.*
Amount assigned

© Great Source

respectfully
(rĭ-spĕkt´fə-lē) *adv.*
Politely; with regard

© Great Source

respectively
(rĭ-spek´tĭv-lē) *adv.*
Referring to things
in the order given

© Great Source

abdicate
(ăb´dĭ-kāt´) *v.*
Give up high office

© Great Source

absolve
(əb-zŏlv´) *v.*
Release from obligation

© Great Source

catharsis
(kə-thär´sĭs) *n.*
An emotional release

© Great Source

countermand
(koun´tər-mănd´) *v.*
To cancel

© Great Source

impunity
(ĭm-pyōō´nĭ-tē) *n.*
Exemption from
punishment

© Great Source

recant
(rĭ-kănt´) *v.*
Take back

© Great Source

recoup
(rĭ-kōōp´) *v.*
Regain

© Great Source

renounce
(rĭ-nouns´) *v.*
To formally give up

© Great Source

rescind
(rĭ-sĭnd´) *v.*
Repeal

© Great Source

waive
(wāv) *v.*
Give up voluntarily

© Great Source

LESSON 16 **arbitration**	LESSON 16 **attaché**	LESSON 16 **consul**	LESSON 16 **covenant**	LESSON 16 **discretion**
LESSON 16 **entente**	LESSON 16 **insular**	LESSON 16 **Machiavellian**	LESSON 16 **protocol**	LESSON 16 **status quo**
LESSON 17 **culminate**	LESSON 17 **eclipse**	LESSON 17 **epitome**	LESSON 17 **impeccable**	LESSON 17 **inimitable**
LESSON 17 **optimum**	LESSON 17 **peerless**	LESSON 17 **quintessence**	LESSON 17 **sublime**	LESSON 17 **zenith**
LESSON 18 **affront**	LESSON 18 **altercation**	LESSON 18 **bellicose**	LESSON 18 **breach**	LESSON 18 **contentious**
LESSON 18 **decimate**	LESSON 18 **dissension**	LESSON 18 **rancor**	LESSON 18 **retribution**	LESSON 18 **schism**

Word	Pronunciation / Part of Speech	Definition
arbitration	(är′bĭ-trā′shən) n.	Submitting a dispute to a judge — © Great Source
attaché	(ăt′ə-shā′) n.	Special staff in a diplomatic office — © Great Source
consul	(kŏn′səl) n.	A diplomat who represents his or her government in a foreign country — © Great Source
covenant	(kŭv′ə-nənt) n.	A legal contract — © Great Source
discretion	(dĭ-skrĕsh′ən) n.	Good judgment and self-restraint — © Great Source
entente	(ŏn-tŏnt′) n.	Informal agreement among political powers — © Great Source
insular	(ĭn′sə-lər) adj.	Isolated — © Great Source
Machiavellian	(Măk′ē-ə-vĕl′ē-ən) adj.	Cunning and deceitful — © Great Source
protocol	(prō′tə-kôl′) n.	Ceremonial conduct — © Great Source
status quo	(stăt′əs kwō) n.	Existing state of affairs — © Great Source
culminate	(kŭl′mə-nāt′) v.	To reach completion — © Great Source
eclipse	(ĭ-klĭps′) v.	To exceed or surpass — © Great Source
epitome	(ĭ-pĭt′ə-mē) n.	A representative example — © Great Source
impeccable	(ĭm-pĕk′ə-bəl) adj.	Having no flaws — © Great Source
inimitable	(ĭ-nĭm′ĭ-tə-bəl) adj.	Matchless; unique — © Great Source
optimum	(ŏp′tə-məm) adj.	Best — © Great Source
peerless	(pîr′lĭs) adj.	Incomparable — © Great Source
quintessence	(kwĭn-tĕs′əns) n.	The purest essence — © Great Source
sublime	(sə-blīm′) adj.	Impressive — © Great Source
zenith	(zē′nĭth) n.	The peak — © Great Source
affront	(ə-frŭnt′) n.	An insult — © Great Source
altercation	(ôl′tər-kā′shən) n.	A noisy quarrel — © Great Source
bellicose	(bĕl′ĭ-kōs′) adj.	Eager to fight — © Great Source
breach	(brēch) n.	A violation — © Great Source
contentious	(kən-tĕn′shəs) adj.	Likely to cause disagreement — © Great Source
decimate	(dĕs′ə-māt′) v.	To destroy — © Great Source
dissension	(dĭ-sĕn′shən) n.	Disagreement — © Great Source
rancor	(răng′kər) n.	Bitter resentment — © Great Source
retribution	(rĕt′rə-byoo′shən) n.	Something justly deserved — © Great Source
schism	(skĭz′əm) n.	A split within a group — © Great Source

LESSON 19 **apocryphal**	LESSON 19 **bona fide**	LESSON 19 **candor**	LESSON 19 **cant**	LESSON 19 **charlatan**
LESSON 19 **chicanery**	LESSON 19 **feign**	LESSON 19 **insidious**	LESSON 19 **rectitude**	LESSON 19 **veritable**
LESSON 20 **accrue**	LESSON 20 **arbiter**	LESSON 20 **audit**	LESSON 20 **cartel**	LESSON 20 **collateral**
LESSON 20 **commodity**	LESSON 20 **conglomerate**	LESSON 20 **liquidate**	LESSON 20 **lucrative**	LESSON 20 **security**
LESSON 21 **adulterate**	LESSON 21 **bane**	LESSON 21 **boon**	LESSON 21 **inimical**	LESSON 21 **malevolent**
LESSON 21 **panacea**	LESSON 21 **pernicious**	LESSON 21 **salutary**	LESSON 21 **toxic**	LESSON 21 **vitiate**

apocryphal (ə-pŏk´rə-fəl) adj. Doubtful

© Great Source

bona fide (bō´nə fīd´) adj. Authentic

© Great Source

candor (kăn´dər) n. Frankness

© Great Source

cant (kănt) n. Boring talk filled with platitudes

© Great Source

charlatan (shär´lə-tən) n. An imposter

© Great Source

chicanery (shĭ-kā´nə-rē) n. Trickery

© Great Source

feign (fān) v. To pretend

© Great Source

insidious (ĭn-sĭd´ē-əs) adj. Secretly harmful

© Great Source

rectitude (rĕk´tĭ-tōōd´) n. Righteousness

© Great Source

veritable (vĕr´ĭ-tə-bəl) adj. Real; actual

© Great Source

accrue (ə-krōō´) v. To accumulate

© Great Source

arbiter (är´bĭ-tər) n. The judge in a dispute

© Great Source

audit (ô´dĭt) v. To examine finances

© Great Source

cartel (kär-tĕl´) n. Group of businesses formed to control pricing

© Great Source

collateral (kə-lăt´ər-əl) n. Something pledged as security for a loan

© Great Source

commodity (kə-mŏd´ĭ-tē) n. A product

© Great Source

conglomerate (kən-glŏm´ə-rāt´) n. A corporation made up of a number of companies

© Great Source

liquidate (lĭk´wĭ-dāt´) v. To settle a debt by selling something off

© Great Source

lucrative (lōō´krə-tĭv) adj. Profitable

© Great Source

security (sĭ-kyōōr´ĭ-tē) n. A stock or bond

© Great Source

adulterate (ə-dŭl´tə-rāt´) v. To make impure

© Great Source

bane (bān) n. Cause of harm or annoyance

© Great Source

boon (bōōn) n. A benefit

© Great Source

inimical (ĭ-nĭm´ĭ-kəl) adj. Unfriendly; hostile

© Great Source

malevolent (mə-lĕv´ə-lənt) adj. Showing ill will

© Great Source

panacea (păn´ə-sē´ə) n. A cure-all

© Great Source

pernicious (pər-nĭsh´əs) adj. Very harmful

© Great Source

salutary (săl´yə-tĕr´ē) adj. Helpful or healthful

© Great Source

toxic (tŏk´sĭk) adj. Poisonous

© Great Source

vitiate (vĭsh´ē-āt´) v. To reduce in value, quality, or effect

© Great Source

LESSON 22 auspices	LESSON 22 perspicuous	LESSON 23 complicity	LESSON 23 implicit	LESSON 24 adjudicate	LESSON 24 fiancé
LESSON 22 auspicious	LESSON 22 specious	LESSON 23 deploy	LESSON 23 inexplicable	LESSON 24 affidavit	LESSON 24 fidelity
LESSON 22 circumspect	LESSON 22 spectacle	LESSON 23 explicate	LESSON 23 replica	LESSON 24 confidant	LESSON 24 infidel
LESSON 22 despicable	LESSON 22 specter	LESSON 23 explicit	LESSON 23 supple	LESSON 24 conjure	LESSON 24 jurisprudence
LESSON 22 introspective	LESSON 22 spectrum	LESSON 23 implicate	LESSON 23 supplicant	LESSON 24 fealty	LESSON 24 perjure

auspices
(ô´spǐ-sǐz) n.
Sponsorship, support

© Great Source

perspicuous
(pər-spǐk´yo͞o-əs) adj.
Easy to understand

© Great Source

complicity
(kəm-plǐs´ǐ-tē) n.
Involvement in wrongdoing

© Great Source

implicit
(ǐm-plǐs´ǐt) adj.
Not stated directly

© Great Source

adjudicate
(ə-jo͞o´dǐ-kāt´) v.
To settle a court case

© Great Source

fiancé
(fē´än-sā´) n.
An engaged man

© Great Source

auspicious
(ô-spǐsh´əs) adj.
Favorable

© Great Source

specious
(spē´shəs) adj.
Seeming to be true, but actually false

© Great Source

deploy
(dǐ-ploi´) n.
To put into action

© Great Source

inexplicable
(ǐn-ĕk´splǐ-kə-bəl) adj.
Impossible to explain

© Great Source

affidavit
(ăf´ǐ-dā´vǐt) n.
Written statement made under oath

© Great Source

fidelity
(fǐ-dĕl´ǐ-tē) n.
Total faithfulness

© Great Source

circumspect
(sûr´kəm-spĕkt´) adj.
Cautious, prudent

© Great Source

spectacle
(spĕk´tə-kəl) n.
An impressive display

© Great Source

explicate
(ĕk´splǐ-kāt´) v.
To explain thoroughly

© Great Source

replica
(rĕp´lǐ-kə) n.
A reproduction

© Great Source

confidant
(kŏn´fǐ-dănt´) n.
A trusted person

© Great Source

infidel
(ǐn´fǐ-dəl) n.
Person who doesn't accept a religon

© Great Source

despicable
(dǐ-spǐk´ə-bəl) adj.
Deserving of scorn

© Great Source

specter
(spĕk´tər) n.
A ghost

© Great Source

explicit
(ǐk-splǐs´ǐt) adj.
Clearly expressed

© Great Source

supple
(sŭp´əl) adj.
Easily bent

© Great Source

conjure
(kŏn´jər) v.
To magically produce

© Great Source

jurisprudence
(jo͝or´ǐs-pro͞od´ns) n.
The study of law

© Great Source

introspective
(ǐn´trə-spĕk´tǐv) adj.
Self-examining

© Great Source

spectrum
(spĕk´trəm) n.
A range of qualities

© Great Source

implicate
(ǐm´plǐ-kāt´) v.
To incriminate

© Great Source

supplicant
(sŭp´lǐ-kənt) n.
One who begs or prays

© Great Source

fealty
(fē´əl-tē) n.
Allegiance

© Great Source

perjure
(pûr´jər) v.
To lie under oath

© Great Source

LESSON 25 ambivalence	LESSON 25 invaluable	
LESSON 25 avail	LESSON 26 abrogate	LESSON 26 presage
LESSON 25 countervailing	LESSON 25 valedictorian	
LESSON 25 evaluate	LESSON 26 inquisitive	LESSON 26 requisite
LESSON 25 evince	LESSON 25 vanquish	

LESSON 25	LESSON 25	LESSON 26
ambivalence	invaluable	
avail	abrogate	presage
countervailing	valedictorian	
evaluate	inquisitive	requisite
evince	vanquish	

LESSON 25 ambivalence

LESSON 25 invaluable

LESSON 25 avail

LESSON 25 prevail

LESSON 26 abrogate

LESSON 26 presage

LESSON 25 countervailing

LESSON 25 valedictorian

LESSON 26 conquistador

LESSON 26 adhere

LESSON 25 evaluate

LESSON 25 valiant

LESSON 26 inquisitive

LESSON 26 quest

LESSON 27 aggregate

LESSON 27 ensemble

LESSON 25 evince

LESSON 25 vanquish

LESSON 26 perquisite

LESSON 26 surrogate

LESSON 26 requisite

LESSON 26 sagacity

LESSON 26 interrogate

LESSON 27 cohere

LESSON 27 gregarious

LESSON 27 dissimulate

LESSON 27 inherent

LESSON 27 egregious

LESSON 27 semblance

LESSON 27 facsimile

ambivalence
(ăm-bĭv´ə-ləns) *n.*
Conflicting feelings

© Great Source

avail
(ə-vāl´) *n.*
To be of use to

© Great Source

countervailing
(koun´tər-vāl´ing) *adj.*
Acting against
something

© Great Source

evaluate
(ĭ-văl´yōo-āt´) *v.*
To determine the
value of

© Great Source

evince
(ĭ-vĭns´) *v.*
To clearly show

© Great Source

invaluable
(ĭn-văl´yōo-ə-bəl) *adj.*
Priceless

© Great Source

prevail
(prĭ-vāl´) *v.*
To be greater in strength

© Great Source

valedictorian
(văl´ĭ-dĭk-tôr´ē-ən) *n.*
Student with the
highest ranking

© Great Source

valiant
(văl´yənt) *adj.*
Having bravery

© Great Source

vanquish
(văng´kwĭsh) *v.*
To overcome

© Great Source

abrogate
(ăb´rə-gāt´) *v.*
To cancel or repeal

© Great Source

conquistador
(kŏng-kē´stə-dôr´) *n.*
A Spanish conqueror

© Great Source

inquisitive
(ĭn-kwĭz´ĭ-tĭv) *adj.*
Eager for knowledge

© Great Source

interrogate
(ĭn-tĕr´ə-gāt´) *v.*
To question formally

© Great Source

perquisite
(pûr´kwĭ-zĭt) *n.*
A fringe benefit

© Great Source

presage
(prĕs´ĭj) *n.*
An omen

© Great Source

quest
(kwĕst) *n.*
A search or pursuit

© Great Source

requisite
(rĕk´wĭ-zĭt) *adj.*
Required; essential

© Great Source

sagacity
(sə-găs´ĭ-tē) *n.*
Wisdom

© Great Source

surrogate
(sûr´ə-gĭt) *n.*
A substitute

© Great Source

adhere
(ăd-hîr´) *v.*
To stick to

© Great Source

aggregate
(ăg´rĭ-gĭt) *n.*
A total composed of
different parts

© Great Source

cohere
(kō-hîr´) *v.*
To stick together

© Great Source

dissimulate
(dĭ-sĭm´yə-lāt´) *v.*
To disguise

© Great Source

egregious
(ĭ-grē´jəs) *adj.*
Very bad

© Great Source

ensemble
(ŏn-sŏm´bəl) *n.*
A group that performs
as one

© Great Source

facsimile
(făk-sĭm´ə-lē) *n.*
An exact copy

© Great Source

gregarious
(grĭ-gâr´ē-əs) *adj.*
Seeking the company
of others

© Great Source

inherent
(ĭn-hîr´ənt) *adj.*
Inborn; natural

© Great Source

semblance
(sĕm´bləns) *n.*
An outward appearance

© Great Source

LESSON 28 **alchemy**	LESSON 28 **amulet**	LESSON 28 **capricious**	LESSON 28 **fatalism**	LESSON 28 **propitious**
LESSON 28 **providential**	LESSON 28 **quirk**	LESSON 28 **serendipity**	LESSON 28 **vagary**	LESSON 28 **vicissitude**
LESSON 29 **a cappella**	LESSON 29 **aria**	LESSON 29 **cacophony**	LESSON 29 **cadence**	LESSON 29 **crescendo**
LESSON 29 **dissonance**	LESSON 29 **libretto**	LESSON 29 **motif**	LESSON 29 **sonata**	LESSON 29 **staccato**
LESSON 30 **arboreal**	LESSON 30 **burgeon**	LESSON 30 **deciduous**	LESSON 30 **fauna**	LESSON 30 **flora**
LESSON 30 **germination**	LESSON 30 **horticultural**	LESSON 30 **lichen**	LESSON 30 **sylvan**	LESSON 30 **verdant**

alchemy (ăl´kə-mē) *n.* Ancient chemical art © Great Source	**amulet** (ăm´yə-lĭt) *n.* A good luck charm © Great Source	**capricious** (kə-prĭsh´əs) *adj.* Unpredictable © Great Source	**fatalism** (fāt´l-ĭz´əm) *n.* A belief in destiny © Great Source	**propitious** (prə-pĭsh´əs) *adj.* Advantageous © Great Source
providential (prŏv´ĭ-dĕn´shəl) *adj.* Fortunate © Great Source	**quirk** (kwûrk) *n.* A peculiar behavior © Great Source	**serendipity** (sĕr´ən-dĭp´ĭ-tē) *n.* A lucky accident © Great Source	**vagary** (vā´gə-rē) *n.* An unexpected whim © Great Source	**vicissitude** (vĭ-sĭs´ĭ-tōōd´) *n.* Unexpected change © Great Source
a cappella (ä´kə-pĕl´ə) *adj.* Without instruments © Great Source	**aria** (ä´rē-ə) *n.* A vocal solo, with instruments © Great Source	**cacophony** (kə-kŏf´ə-nē) *n.* An unpleasant and loud mix of sounds © Great Source	**cadence** (kād´ns) *n.* Rhythm or beat © Great Source	**crescendo** (krə-shĕn´dō) *n.* A build-up © Great Source
dissonance (dĭs´ə-nəns) *n.* Disharmony; conflict © Great Source	**libretto** (lĭ-brĕt´ō) *n.* The text of a dramatic musical work © Great Source	**motif** (mō-tēf´) *n.* A theme © Great Source	**sonata** (sə-nä´tə) *n.* Composition with three or four movements © Great Source	**staccato** (stə-kä´tō) *adj.* Short and sharp © Great Source
arboreal (är-bôr´ē-əl) *adj.* Living in trees © Great Source	**burgeon** (bûr´jən) *v.* To grow rapidly © Great Source	**deciduous** (dĭ-sĭj´ōō-əs) *adj.* Losing leaves seasonally © Great Source	**fauna** (fô´nə) *n.* Animals of a region © Great Source	**flora** (flôr´ə) *n.* Plants of a region © Great Source
germination (jûr´mə-nā´shən) *n.* Beginning to grow © Great Source	**horticultural** (hôr´tĭ-kŭl´chər-əl) *adj.* About growing plants © Great Source	**lichen** (lī´kən) *n.* Vegetation made of fungus and algae © Great Source	**sylvan** (sĭl´vən) *adj.* Wooded © Great Source	**verdant** (vûr´dnt) *adj.* Green with plants © Great Source